7/04

RACE FOR THE
PRESIDENCY

RACE FOR THE PRESIDENCY

WINNING THE 2004 NOMINATION

Rhodes Cook

CQ PRESS

A Division of Congressional Quarterly Inc.
Washington, D.C.

CQ Press
1255 22nd Street, N.W., Suite 400
Washington, D.C. 20037

Phone, 202-729-1900
Toll-free, 1-866-4CQ-PRESS (1-866-427-7737)

www.cqpress.com

∞ The paper used in this publication exceeds the requirements of the American National Standard for Information Sciences—Permanence of Paper for Printed Library Materials, ANSI Z39.48-1992.

Cover design: Circle Graphics

Printed and bound in the United States of America

08   07   06   05   04   5   4   3   2   1

Library of Congress Cataloging-in-Publication Data

Cook, Rhodes, 1948–
    Race for the presidency : winning the 2004 nomination / Rhodes Cook.
        p. cm.
    ISBN: 1-56802-900-4 (alk. paper)
1. Presidents—United States—Election—2004. 2. Presidents—United States—Nomination. 3. Primaries—United States.   I. Title.
    JK526.C66 2004
    324.273'15'090511—dc 22   2004000641

CONTENTS

ALPHABETICAL LISTING

PREFACE

Every presidential nominating campaign is a bit different from the one before it, and the 2004 edition has already broken new ground.

For the first time, a dark horse candidate (former Vermont governor Howard Dean) has moved to the front rank of candidates before a single ballot has been cast.

For the first time, more than one major candidate has elected to decline federal matching funds in order to be free of spending limits during the presidential primary season. Democrats Dean and Sen. John Kerry, as well as President George W. Bush, who is running unopposed for renomination on the Republican side, are all opting out of the taxpayer-funded public financing system.

And Democratic candidates must prepare for a larger than ever glut of primaries in the first 10 weeks of 2004 that could very well settle the Democratic nomination before the ides of March.

There is a chance the Democratic race could last longer. Unlike the Republicans, who allow states to award all their delegates to the statewide winner, the Democrats require that delegates be divided among all candidates who win 15 percent of the vote statewide or within a congressional district.

Also, nearly 20 percent of all Democratic delegates are "superdelegates"—prominent party and elected officials such as Democratic governors and members of Congress and the Democratic National Committee (DNC)—who can support whichever candidate they want, regardless of the primary or caucus vote in their state.

And in the early weeks of the 2004 primary season, Democratic candidates will be tested in all parts of the country. Regional appeal could give a candidate a base, but national appeal will be required for one of them to break from the pack.

Still, the trend in recent elections has been for candidates to catch fire early and reel off a string of primary victories that enables him to wrap up party's nomination in short order.

Dean has the inside track to do that this time. His skilled use of the Internet and tough anti-Bush rhetoric, built around opposition to the war in Iraq, have enabled him to raise more money and organize a more passionate cadre of supporters than any of his Democratic rivals in 2003. But there are several other Democrats positioned to make a run for the nomination should Dean stumble.

One thing is certain, though; once the voting begins, it will unfold quickly. The primary season begins unofficially Jan. 13 with a nonbinding, "beauty contest" primary in the District of Columbia. Iowa's precinct caucuses Jan. 19 begin the nationwide process of delegate selection. New Hampshire holds its traditional "first-in-the-nation" primary Jan. 27—an event that, along with the Iowa caucus, is almost certain to winnow the Democratic field.

Unlike previous years—when the first real onslaught of primaries did not occur until March—candidates will barely have time to catch their breath after New Hampshire. Seven states, from Delaware to Arizona, will vote on Feb. 3. Three more, led by Michigan and Washington, will vote over the weekend of Feb. 7–8. On Feb. 10, Tennessee and Virginia hold primaries, followed by Wisconsin on Feb. 17. Three western states—Hawaii, Idaho, and Utah—weigh in on Feb. 24. By the end of the month, Democrats in 19 states will have had the opportunity to cast their primary or caucus vote.

2004 Nominating Season at a Glance

The following primary and caucus calendar for the 2004 presidential nominating process is based on information from the Democratic and Republican national committees as of mid-December 2003, and is subject to minor revisions. The total number of Democratic delegates at the time was 4,317. Republican delegates totaled 2,509.

GOP delegates are elected in primaries and caucuses, and all are accounted for in the chart below. Democrats, though, have a bloc of nearly 800 unpledged delegates (known as "superdelegates") who are reserved seats by virtue of their party or elected positions. They are not included in the Democratic delegate totals. The Democratic total for each state and territory is for pledged delegates, or those who will actually be allocated by the primary or caucus vote. Pledged delegates total 3,520, or 82 percent of all Democratic delegates.

There are three basic options governing voter participation in a primary or caucus:

Closed—Only registered Democrats or Republicans may participate in their party's event.

Semi-open—Generally, registered voters in the party plus unaffiliated (or independent) voters may participate. A pound sign (#) indicates that in certain caucus states the rules are a bit different, and that while the event is not open to independent voters per se, participants may include new voters who register as Democrats at the caucus and/or previously registered voters who change their registration to Democratic.

Open—Any registered voter may participate.

Democrats use a nationwide proportionality rule for allocating their pledged delegates. Any candidate who receives at least 15 percent of the vote statewide or in a district (usually a congressional district) qualifies for a share of the delegates at that level.

Republicans allow considerable variation in the allocation of their delegates, and the state parties use a variety of methods that can range from statewide winner-take-all to proportionality.

A primary is a single-day event. A caucus is usually the first stage of a multitiered process that extends over several weeks or months before the delegates are actually selected.

The chart below is arranged chronologically according to the 2004 Democratic delegate selection calendar. Republican primary or caucus dates are included in a column within the chart. An asterisk (*) indicates that the primary is run by the party and not the state and, as a result, will probably use fewer polling places. The designation "n/a" indicates that no information was available.

All dates are based on information provided by the Democratic and Republican national committees, as of mid-December, and are subject to revision.

Democratic Date	State	Democratic Voter Participation	Republican System and Date	Delegates	
				Dems.	Reps.
EARLY EVENTS					
Jan. 19	Iowa Caucus	Semi-open#	Caucus—Jan. 19	45	32
Jan. 27	New Hampshire Primary	Semi-open	Primary—Jan. 27	22	32
Feb. 3	Arizona Primary	Closed	County Convention—April 3–17	55	52
	Delaware Primary	Closed	State Convention—May 13–14	15	18
	Missouri Primary	Open	Primary—Feb. 3	74	57
	New Mexico Primary*	Closed	Primary—June 1	26	24
	North Dakota Caucus	Open	Caucus—Feb. 3	14	26
	Oklahoma Primary	Closed	Primary—Feb. 3	40	41
	South Carolina Primary*	Open	Caucus—Sept. 23, 2003	45	46
Feb. 6–9	Democrats Abroad Caucus	Open	—	7	—
Feb. 7	Michigan Primary*	Open	County Convention—April 27	128	61
	Washington Caucus	Open	Caucus—March 9	76	41
Feb. 8	Maine Caucus	Semi-open#	Caucus—Jan. 1–March 19	24	21
Feb. 10	Tennessee Primary	Open	Primary—Feb. 10	69	55
	Virginia Primary	Open	Caucus—Feb.–April	82	64
Feb. 14	District of Columbia Caucus	Closed	Caucus—Feb. 10	16	19
	Nevada Caucus	Semi-open#	Caucus—Feb. 10	24	33

Democratic Date	State	Democratic Voter Participation	Republican System and Date	Delegates Dems.	Reps.
EARLY EVENTS *(continued)*					
Feb. 17	Wisconsin Primary	Open	Primary—Feb. 17	72	40
Feb. 24	Hawaii Caucus	Semi-open#	Caucus—Jan. 25–Feb. 7	20	20
	Idaho Caucus	Open	Primary—May 25	18	32
	Utah Primary*	Open	Caucus—March 23	23	36
SUPER TUESDAY					
March 2	California Primary	Semi-open	Primary—March 2	370	173
	Connecticut Primary	Closed	Primary—March 2	49	30
	Georgia Primary	Open	Primary—March 2	86	69
	Maryland Primary	Closed	Primary—March 2	69	39
	Massachusetts Primary	Semi-open	Primary—March 2	93	44
	Minnesota Caucus	Open	Caucus—March 2	72	41
	New York Primary	Closed	Primary—March 2	236	102
	Ohio Primary	Open	Primary—March 2	140	91
	Rhode Island Primary	Semi-open	Primary—March 2	21	21
	Vermont Primary	Open	Primary—March 2	15	18
REST OF THE WAY					
March 8	American Samoa Caucus	Open	Caucus—Feb. 28	3	9
March 9	Florida Primary	Closed	Primary—March 9	177	112
	Louisiana Primary	Closed	Primary—March 9	60	45
	Mississippi Primary	Open	Primary—March 9	33	38
	Texas Primary and Caucus	Open	Primary—March 9	195	138
March 13	Kansas Caucus	Semi-open#	State Committee— between March 1 and June 15	33	39
March 16	Illinois Primary	Open	Primary—March 16	156	73
March 20	Alaska Caucus	Semi-open#	District Convention— prior to April 19	13	29
	Wyoming Caucus	Closed	Caucus—Jan. 9–24	13	28
	Guam Caucus	n/a	Convention—Feb. 21	3	9
April 13	Colorado Caucus	Closed	Caucus—April 13	53	50
April 17	Virgin Islands Caucus	Closed	Caucus—Feb. 28	3	9
April 27	Pennsylvania Primary	Closed	Primary—April 27	151	75
May 4	Indiana Primary	Open	Primary—May 4	67	55
	North Carolina Primary	Semi-open	Primary—May 4	90	67
May 11	Nebraska Primary	Closed	Primary—May 11	24	35
	West Virginia Primary	Closed	Primary—May 11	28	30
May 18	Arkansas Primary	Open	Primary—May 18	36	35
	Kentucky Primary	Closed	Primary—May 18	49	46
	Oregon Primary	Closed	Primary—May 18	46	31
June 1	Alabama Primary	Open	Primary—June 1	54	48
	South Dakota Primary	Closed	Primary—June 1	14	27
June 6	Puerto Rico Caucus	Open	Primary—Feb. 29	51	23
June 8	Montana Primary	Open	State Convention— June 10–12	15	28
	New Jersey Primary	Semi-open	Primary—June 8	107	52

Convention Sites and Sizes: 1960–2004

Democrats in 2004 will be holding their first convention in Boston, and Republicans will be meeting for the first time in New York. The GOP event will also be held later than any previous major-party convention, concluding in September.

Both the Democratic and Republican delegate counts for 2004 are as of mid-December 2003 and are subject to change.

	DEMOCRATS				REPUBLICANS		
Year	Site	Dates	Delegate Votes		Site	Dates	Delegate Votes
1960	Los Angeles	July 11–15	1,521		Chicago	July 25–28	1,331
1964	Atlantic City	Aug. 24–27	2,316		San Francisco	July 13–16	1,308
1968	Chicago	Aug. 26–29	2,622		Miami Beach	Aug. 5–8	1,333
1972	Miami Beach	July 10–13	3,016		Miami Beach	Aug. 21–23	1,348
1976	New York	July 12–15	3,008		Kansas City	Aug. 16–19	2,259
1980	New York	Aug. 11–14	3,331		Detroit	July 14–17	1,994
1984	San Francisco	July 16–19	3,933		Dallas	Aug. 20–23	2,235
1988	Atlanta	July 18–21	4,162		New Orleans	Aug. 15–18	2,277
1992	New York	July 13–16	4,288		Houston	Aug. 17–20	2,210
1996	Chicago	Aug. 26–29	4,289		San Diego	Aug. 12–15	1,990
2000	Los Angeles	Aug. 14–17	4,339		Philadelphia	July 31–Aug. 3	2,066
2004	Boston	July 26–29	4,317		New York	Aug. 30–Sept. 2	2,509

Note: Traditionally, the Republicans have given each delegate a full vote, so the number of GOP delegates equals the number of delegate votes. The Democrats, though, have long allowed some delegates to have a fraction of a vote, so the actual number of Democratic delegates can exceed the total of delegate votes.

Ten more states will vote on March 2, the latest incarnation of "Super Tuesday." California, New York, and Ohio will all be holding primaries that day. And by the end of it, more than 60 percent of the elected Democratic delegates will have been chosen.

Super Tuesday brought down the curtain on both the Democratic and Republican nominating campaigns in 2000, as Al Gore and George W. Bush used sweeping victories that day to drive their rivals from the field. If the 2004 Democratic contest is not settled by then, it should be shortly thereafter.

Four southern states, led by Texas and Florida, vote March 9, followed by Illinois a week later. After that, there will be no presidential primary until April 27, when Pennsylvania votes. But the betting is that the balloting in the Keystone State will be anticlimactic, and by then, both parties will have turned their attention to the November general election.

Methodology

This book does not try to cover all aspects of the nominating process in detail. The roles of the media, campaign financing, and media advertising are left to others to describe. Rather, the focus here is on the rules of the process and the political landscape that they affect.

The introduction seeks to explain the evolution of the presidential nominating process into its present primary-dominated form. Particular emphasis is paid to the years since 1968, an era when voters in each party have replaced party leaders as the true kingmakers.

At the end of the book is related material providing an overview of each Democratic and Republican presidential nominating contest since 1968. With each contest, there is a national map showing the presidential primary winners in each state, a brief text summarizing the campaign, and a box with nationwide primary vote data for the leading candidates.

The heart of this book is the state-by-state material that follows the introduction. The state sections appear in the chronological order in which the Democrats will hold their primary or caucus in 2004, barring an eleventh-hour change in the calendar.

The states are arranged within three time periods. The first covers the early events in January and February, when the field of candidates is traditionally winnowed.

The second period is variously called "Super Tuesday" or "Titanic Tuesday," the huge cross-country vote test for both parties on March 2 that features the bicoastal bookends of California and New York.

The third and last time period covers the primaries and caucuses to be held after Super Tuesday—from the quartet of southern states voting on March 9 through the final day of presidential primaries on June 8.

Each state section begins with an essay that highlights the recent history of the state's presidential primary or caucus. Few references are made to exit polls. Rather, the emphasis is on the actual primary vote, and references to various counties are often used to illustrate a state's political geography and internal voting patterns in the presidential nominating process.

Accompanying the essay is a table that lists the state's presidential primary results since 1968. The turnout for each Democratic and Republican primary is given, along with the vote share for all candidates who received at least 10 percent of their party's primary vote. Each state section also includes a state map that shows its counties and major population centers.

The final element in each state package is a rules box, which provides basic information on the Democratic delegate selection rules for 2004. This material highlights the basic rules that will govern the Democratic campaigns in each state, such as When is the primary or caucus to be held? Who can vote? How does a candidate get on the ballot? How many delegates are at stake? What must a candidate do to win all or a share of the delegates?

Democratic delegates are elected either within congressional districts or at-large (statewide). Democrats also have two other categories of delegates—pledged party leaders and elected officials, and unpledged delegates. The latter group, the so-called superdelegates, are reserved delegate seats by virtue of their position—and are free agents. The other Democratic delegates are elected to reflect the primary or caucus vote.

The Democratic and Republican delegate counts are subject to minor changes. As of early December 2003, there were 4,317 Democratic delegate votes (some states have more delegates than votes), with 2,159 constituting a majority needed to win the party's nomination. Meanwhile, there were 2,508 Republican delegates, with a majority of 1,255 delegates needed to win the GOP nomination.

Basic information on party rules was provided by the Democratic and Republican national committees. Particular thanks are in order to the staff of the Democratic National Committee Rules and Bylaws Committee—especially Phil McNamara, Alicia Kolar Prevost, and Marc Schloss. They furnished detailed state-by-state delegate selection information that is the crux of the rules boxes.

At the Republican National Committee, deputy press secretary David W. James was helpful in providing material that the GOP had available. But with President Bush running unopposed for renomination in 2004, Republican delegate selection information was not available in much detail when this book was being written in late 2003. As a result, it is not a major feature of this edition.

The author also tips his hat to state election boards around the country, which provided data on voter registration on their Web sites and explained voter participation rules for their presidential primaries over the phone. And in states where there are party-run caucuses or primaries, the Democratic state parties were invariably helpful.

Thanks, too, are in order to the staff at CQ Press: acquisitions editor Shana Wagger, who provided the critical green light for this 2004 edition of *Race for the Presidency;* assistant editor Grace Hill, who gracefully handled the flow of copy from start to finish; and production editor Daphne Levitas, who skillfully arranged the material on the pages that follow.

And once again, a special debt of gratitude is owed to Phil Duncan and Ronald D. Elving, former political editors of the *Congressional Quarterly Weekly Report,* who helped shape earlier versions of *Race for the Presidency* that provided the groundwork for this edition.

Rhodes Cook
December 2003

INTRODUCTION

If there is one rule of thumb to describe the presidential nominating process, it is that the constant is change.

The process of nominating presidential candidates is constantly evolving—from congressional caucuses in the early nineteenth century, through the heyday of the national conventions over the next century and a half, to the present, where conventions merely ratify the decisions made earlier by Democratic and Republican primary voters.

That is because the presidential primaries are now where the action is, and they have been since the Democrats' tumultuous convention in Chicago in 1968 encouraged both parties—but the Democrats in particular—to look for ways to open the presidential nominating process to greater grassroots participation.

The principal way to more voter involvement has been through the proliferation of presidential primaries. A product of the Progressive era in the early twentieth century, primaries were few and far between until 1968. But after that, they quickly mushroomed in number—from 15 in 1968, to 36 in 1980, to more than 40 in 2000.

As the number of primaries grew, power in the nominating process quickly shifted from party kingmakers at the national conventions to voters in the primary states. And it has stayed that way.

Long gone are the days when candidates could win their party's nomination without entering the primaries. No Democratic or Republican nominee has done so since Hubert Humphrey in 1968.

And long gone are the days when candidates could be nominated without first proving broad-based popularity among millions of their party's primary voters. Since Democrat George McGovern in 1972, every major-party nominee has been his party's highest vote-getter in the primaries.

In the process, the once climactic conventions have become little more than giant pep rallies, ratifying the choices of Democratic and Republican primary voters made months earlier.

Front-Loaded Process

In recent years, the nominations have been settled earlier and earlier, as more and more states have moved their primaries forward to dates near the beginning of the election year in a bid to heighten their influence (a process that is known as "front-loading").

In 1968, only one presidential primary (New Hampshire's) was held before the end of March. In 1980, 10 states held primaries that early. By 1988, the number surpassed 20, and by 2000, well over half the country had voted by the end of March.

The result in recent years has been an increasingly truncated nominating process that has followed a clear pattern. Early votes in Iowa and New Hampshire have winnowed the field to a handful of candidates. Then, after a short period of unpredictability, one candidate has scored a knockout in the glut of March primaries, with his victory ratified by a string of votes at the end of the nominating process.

That is what happened in 1992. The first five Democratic primaries that year produced four different winners. But Bill Clinton broke from the pack with a sweep of the early March primaries in his native South and ended up winning all but two of the primaries that followed.

The story was similar on the Republican side in 2000. George W. Bush struggled through a series of primary contests

Primary Wins Bring Convention Success

No candidate since Hubert Humphrey in 1968 has won the nomination of a major party without first entering its presidential primaries. And no candidate since George McGovern in 1972 has won the Democratic or Republican nomination without being the top vote-getter in his party's primaries; Humphrey won more votes in the Democratic primaries that year.

The chart below compares each nominee's share of his party's primary vote with the share of the delegate votes he won on the first ballot at his party's convention; not since 1952 has a convention taken more than one ballot to settle a presidential nomination. An asterisk (*) indicates an incumbent president. The presidential roll call has become almost an afterthought at recent conventions. Democrat Al Gore's percentage of the convention vote in 2000 is based on an unofficial total.

	DEMOCRATS			REPUBLICANS		
Election Year	Nominee	% of Primary Vote	% of Convention Vote	Nominee	% of Primary Vote	% of Convention Vote
1968	Hubert Humphrey	2	67	Richard Nixon	38	52
1972	George McGovern	25	57	Richard Nixon*	92	99.9
1976	Jimmy Carter	39	74	Gerald Ford*	53	53
1980	Jimmy Carter*	51	64	Ronald Reagan	61	97
1984	Walter Mondale	38	56	Ronald Reagan*	99	99.9
1988	Michael Dukakis	43	69	George Bush	68	100
1992	Bill Clinton	52	79	George Bush*	72	99
1996	Bill Clinton*	89	99.7	Bob Dole	59	97
2000	Al Gore	76	100	George W. Bush	63	100

scattered across the opening weeks of the nominating process, losing almost as many as he won.

But once the calendar flipped to March and the primaries began to occur in large groupings, Bush's advantages of widespread party support, a large campaign chest, and high name familiarity kicked in. Bush lost a handful of New England primaries in early March to his principal rival, John McCain. But Bush won everywhere else and drove McCain from the race by the ides of March.

Neither party has had an elongated tug-of-war since 1984, when Walter Mondale and Gary Hart battled for the Democratic nomination into the final week of the primary season. And neither party has had a nominating contest that was even vaguely competitive by the time of its national convention since the 1976 Republican race between President Gerald R. Ford and Ronald Reagan.

Starting Points

Even though much of the primary calendar has changed dramatically over the past few decades, the accepted starting points have remained Iowa and New Hampshire (even though other states have occasionally voted before them).

Both states have made their early events into cottage industries, but the candidates and the media have helped make them so. More than ever, Iowa and New Hampshire are about the only places left where candidates have some control over their destinies. They can woo voters one-on-one, whether in bowling alleys, coffee shops, or the frequent gatherings in neighborhood living rooms.

For if there is one thing that has become certain in recent years, once the New Hampshire primary is over, there is a frenetic burst of tarmac-to-tarmac campaigning heavily dependent on media advertising.

Occasionally, candidates have tried to skip Iowa or New Hampshire, or both, and launch their campaigns on terrain more to their choosing. Democrat George Wallace did that in 1976. So, to a degree, did Democrat Al Gore in 1988. And Republican McCain skipped Iowa before winning New Hampshire. But McCain is a rarity in making such a selective strategy pay off.

With one exception, every presidential nominee since 1976 has won either Iowa or New Hampshire and finished no lower than third in the other. The exception was Clinton in 1992, who did not seriously contest Iowa in deference to the home-state appeal of Sen. Tom Harkin and finished second in New Hampshire behind former Massachusetts senator Paul Tsongas.

The two states illustrate the two different types of delegate selection processes that states have to choose from. Iowa is a caucus. New Hampshire is a primary. Primaries require voters only to cast a ballot, an exercise that usually takes just a few minutes. The deliberative nature of a neighborhood caucus, though, often requires the commitment of an afternoon or evening.

A Small Slice of the Electorate

Voter turnout is usually much higher in a primary than a caucus, but even in primaries the turnout is much lower than in a general election. In New Hampshire, for instance, where interest in the presidential primary is probably greater than in any other state, slightly less than 400,000 voters turned out in February 2000 for the presidential primary, whereas nearly 570,000 cast ballots in the general election that fall.

The disparity is much greater in many other states. Even though both parties held competitive nominating contests in 2000, barely 31 million votes were cast in the parties' presidential primaries—roughly 17 million on the Republican side and 14 million on the Democratic. Activity in the handful of states that held caucuses involved several hundred thousand more voters. And better than 2 million voters (mainly in California and Washington) cast ballots outside the Democratic and Republican primaries.

By comparison, more than 105 million voters turned out for the November general election that year, roughly three times the number that took part in the nominating process.

Rules governing voter participation play a role in the comparatively low turnouts for the nominating process. Every primary is not as open as a general election, where any registered voter can participate. A number of states limit partici-

pation to registered Democratic and Republican voters. Some others allow independents to participate but list them on the voting rolls afterward as members of the party for which they cast their primary ballot.

Still, the vast majority of registered voters across the country can participate in a presidential primary or caucus if they want. The fact that more do not has generated the conventional wisdom that the nominating process is dominated by ideological activists—liberals on the Democratic side, conservatives on the Republican.

That is debatable in the primaries in which the winners in recent years have been from the mainstreams of both parties. An ideological bent is more evident in the low-turnout world of the caucuses, where a small cadre of dedicated voters can dominate the outcome.

When religious broadcaster Pat Robertson tried for the Republican presidential nomination in 1988, for instance, he won first-round caucus voting in three states and finished second in three others, including Iowa. But Robertson did not come close that year to winning a presidential primary.

And the Last Shall Be First

The importance of states in the fall presidential election is closely related to population. The major battlegrounds are nearly always the eight to ten largest states.

But the connection between size and clout is more tenuous in the presidential nominating process. Lead-off spots on the calendar and the weight of political tradition have ensured Iowa and New Hampshire an importance that far outweighs any of the larger, vote-rich states that hold their primaries later. Of the roughly 31 million votes that were cast in the Democratic and Republican presidential primaries in 2000, approximately 60 percent were cast in the nation's ten most populous states and only 2 percent in Iowa and New Hampshire.

Following is a comparison of voter turnout in the nominating contest in 2000 in each of the ten largest states with that in Iowa and New Hampshire. Each state's primary (or in the case of Iowa, precinct caucus) date in 2000 is given, as well as the proportion of the nationwide primary vote that the state's turnout represented.

The Republican primary in 2000 in New York was for the selection of delegates only; turnout there is an estimate and was not included in the national total. In parentheses is each state's national ranking according to the 2000 census. Iowa, for instance, is the thirtieth most populous state in the country; New Hampshire is forty-first.

State	2000 Date	Democratic-Republican Turnout	Percentage of Nationwide Primary Vote
Iowa (30)	Jan. 24	148,233	0.5
New Hampshire (41)	Feb. 1	392,845	1.3
Michigan (8)	Feb. 22	1,321,620	4.2
California (1)	March 7	5,502,035	17.6
Georgia (10)	March 7	927,619	3.0
New York (3)	March 7	1,694,463	5.4
Ohio (7)	March 7	2,376,040	7.6
Florida (4)	March 14	1,251,498	4.0
Texas (2)	March 14	1,913,647	6.1
Illinois (5)	March 21	1,546,588	5.0
Pennsylvania (6)	April 4	1,359,799	4.4
New Jersey (9)	June 6	619,082	2.0
Nationwide Primary Vote		31,201,862	

Presidential Primary Turnouts Since 1968

Since the inception of presidential primaries in 1912 through 1968, there were never more than twenty primaries in one year. But since then, the number of presidential primaries has grown steadily to the point that in 1996 there were more than forty.

The most votes cast in the presidential primaries came in 1988 when more than 35 million were cast. Nearly 23 million voters turned out for the Democratic presidential primaries in 1988, the most in any election before or since. The Republican high was in 2000, when more than 17 million ballots were cast in the GOP presidential primaries.

Through much of the first half of the twentieth century, starting with the contest between former president Theodore Roosevelt and President William Howard Taft in 1912, more votes were cast in Republican than Democratic presidential primaries. But that was not the case in the last half of the century. Republicans had a higher turnout only twice—in 1952, when Dwight D. Eisenhower and Robert Taft had a vigorous contest for the GOP nomination—and in 1996, when President Bill Clinton ran virtually unopposed for the Democratic nomination. In 2000, more ballots were cast again in the Republican primaries.

Year	Number of States Holding Primaries	Democratic Vote	Republican Vote	Total Vote
1968	14 and D.C.	7,535,069	4,473,551	12,008,620
1972	20 and D.C.	15,993,965	6,188,281	22,182,246
1976	26 and D.C.	16,052,652	10,374,125	26,426,777
1980	35 and D.C.	18,747,825	12,690,451	31,438,276
1984	29 and D.C.	18,009,192	6,575,651	24,584,843
1988	36 and D.C.	22,961,936	12,165,115	35,127,051
1992	38 and D.C.	20,239,385	12,696,547	32,935,932
1996	41 and D.C.	10,947,364	13,991,649	24,939,013
2000	42 and D.C.	14,045,745	17,156,117	31,201,862

Note: The number of primary states is those in which at least one of the major parties held a primary that allowed a direct vote for presidential candidates or in which there was an aggregated statewide vote for delegates. The vote tally, though, does not include the 2000 New York Republican primaries in 1996 and 2000 for the election of delegates only.

Primary Clues

It has been a matter of debate within the political community whether the current primary-dominated nominating process is better than the old system, in which party leaders controlled the selection process.

But it is a fact that the increased number of primaries helps provide valuable clues about the vote-getting potential of candidates in the general election. Nominees who have exhibited broad-based appeal among the diverse array of primary voters in the winter and spring have gone on to be quite competitive in the fall, whereas those nominees who have struggled through the primaries showing limited appeal among one or two of their party's major constituency groups have usually been buried under landslides in November.

A less reliable indicator of what will happen in the fall is the number of votes cast in each party's primaries. In every year from 1956 through 1992, more ballots were cast in Democratic than Republican primaries, in part due to the simple fact that through much of this period, Democrats outnumbered Republicans. But it also reflected the fact that the Democratic primaries drew more voter interest because they often exhibited more conflict between competing constituencies within the party. That kind of political drama and angst was good for primary turnout but not for the party's chances in the fall election, as Republicans won most of the presidential contests in this period.

One Election: Two Systems

The quadrennial process of electing a president has two distinct parts—the nominating process and the general election. The latter is straightforward: a one-day nationwide vote on the first Tuesday after the first Monday in November between the Democratic and Republican nominees and any independent and third-party candidates who have met the various state ballot requirements. All registered voters may participate in the general election, and the winner is the candidate who wins a majority of the state electoral votes.

By contrast, the presidential nominating process can seem like Alice in Wonderland. Primaries and caucuses are scattered across the calendar from January to June, culminating with party conventions in the summer. A nomination is won by a candidate attaining a majority of delegates, an honor that is formally bestowed at the conventions but for years has informally occurred months earlier during the primary season.

Size is less important in determining a state's importance in the nominating process than its tradition and place on the calendar (early is best), hence the quadrennial starring roles for Iowa and New Hampshire and the bit parts frequently handed out to California and New York.

States have different ground rules in the nominating process. Some have caucuses; many more have primaries. Most primaries allocate a state's delegates, but in some it is a nonbinding "beauty contest." And rules on voter participation can vary from state to state.

The parties themselves also have different playing fields. Democrats require states to distribute delegates among the candidates in proportion to their vote, statewide and in congressional districts, with 15 percent required to win a share. Republicans allow a variety of allocation systems, including winner-take-all, where the top vote-getter in a state is awarded all the delegates.

Democrats reserve nearly 20 percent of their delegate seats for high-level party and elected officials (such as Democratic governors, members of Congress, and members of the party's national committee), who are free agents and do not have to declare a presidential preference.

Then there is the business of campaign financing. In the wake of the Watergate scandal, a system of public financing was instituted in 1976. Participation is optional for candidates in the nominating process. Those who opt to take part must raise much of their money in small chunks and have it matched by federal funds up to a certain amount in exchange for acceptance of spending limits. Over the years, most candidates have participated in the system, although a few conspicuously have not and spent as much as they wanted.

An Evolutionary Process

But if there is a basic difference between the nominating process and the general election, it is that the latter is generally static in form whereas the former is constantly changing.

During the early years of the Republic, presidential nominations were decided by party caucuses in Congress (derided by their critics as "King Caucus"). At the dawn of the Jacksonian era in the 1830s, though, the nominating role shifted to national conventions, a broader-based venue at which party leaders from around the country held sway.

In the early twentieth century, presidential primaries appeared on the scene, adding a new element of grassroots democracy and voter input. But for the next half century, the primaries were relatively few in number and played a limited advisory role. Nominations continued to be decided in the party conventions.

Yet after World War II, as the society became more mobile and media oriented, and once-powerful party organizations began to lose their clout, more presidential aspirants saw the primaries as a way to generate popular support that might overcome the resistance of party leaders. Both Dwight D. Eisenhower in 1952 and John F. Kennedy in 1960 scored a string of primary victories that demonstrated their vote-getting appeal and made their nominations possible.

The Electorate: Primaries and General

It is often said that Republican primary voters are more conservative and that Democratic primary voters are more liberal than the electorate as a whole.

If true, it is due to the basic fact that only a fraction of those who participate in the November general election participate in the presidential nominating process. As the number of primaries has grown since 1968 and voter participation in the nominating process has increased, the difference has been reduced, although the total vote in the presidential primaries has never surpassed 40 percent of the turnout for the general election.

Following is a comparison of the votes in presidential primaries with those in general elections since 1968. The number of primaries includes those in which at least one of the major parties featured a vote for presidential candidates or in which there was an aggregated statewide vote for delegates. The total number includes the District of Columbia.

The total primary vote includes both Democratic and Republican primaries. Not included are the voter turnouts for primaries held outside the two major parties; for primaries for delegates only, such as that held by New York Republicans in 1996 and 2000; or for nonprimary states in which caucuses were held. The latter usually do not total more than several hundred thousand votes for both parties combined in an election year.

| Year | Presidential Primaries | Voter Turnout | | Primary Vote as Percentage of General Election Vote |
		Primaries	General Election	
1968	15	12,008,620	73,211,875	16.4
1972	21	22,182,246	77,718,554	28.5
1976	27	26,426,777	81,555,889	32.4
1980	36	31,438,276	86,515,221	36.3
1984	30	24,584,843	92,652,842	26.5
1988	37	35,127,051	91,594,809	38.4
1992	39	32,935,932	104,425,014	31.5
1996	42	24,939,013	96,277,872	25.9
2000	43	31,201,862	105,396,627	29.6

Presidential Primaries: A Brief History

1912: The first presidential primaries are held in thirteen states. Most votes are cast in the Republican contests, nine of them won by former president Theodore Roosevelt. But President William Howard Taft retains control of the party machinery and wins renomination at the GOP convention. In his annual message the following year, President Woodrow Wilson includes a call for the overhaul of the nominating process so primaries across the country would determine each party's presidential nominee.

1916: The number of presidential primaries grows to twenty, before declining once the Progressive era is over. It the largest number of primaries until the 1970s.

1924: Democrats nominate John W. Davis on the one-hundred-third ballot to culminate the longest convention ever held. In what was normal for the period, Davis had not competed in any of the presidential primaries.

1944: Wendell Willkie, the GOP's dark horse nominee in 1940, tries to mount a comeback in 1944 in the Republican presidential primaries. Willkie's distant fourth-place finish in Wisconsin, though, dashes his presidential ambitions.

1948: New York governor Thomas E. Dewey and former Minnesota governor Harold E. Stassen go head-to-head in the Oregon GOP primary, the high point of which is a coast-to-coast radio debate on the question of whether the Communist Party should be outlawed in the United States. Dewey wins the primary over Stassen by barely 10,000 votes and goes on to win the Republican nomination.

1952: Former general Dwight D. Eisenhower uses the Republican presidential primaries to demonstrate his broad vote-getting appeal to party leaders. Eisenhower wins the newly important, first-in-the-nation New Hampshire primary over then Ohio senator Robert A. Taft and goes on to win the GOP nomination. Senator Estes Kefauver of Tennessee also follows the primary route on the Democratic side. But Illinois governor Adlai E. Stevenson wins the Democratic nomination on the third ballot, the last time that any major party convention takes more than a single roll call to decide its presidential nomination.

1960: Sen. John F. Kennedy of Massachusetts enters the Democratic primaries to show his electability. Kennedy scores a pivotal primary victory in heavily Protestant West Virginia that demonstrates his Catholicism is not a disqualifying liability.

1968: Vice President Hubert H. Humphrey becomes the last presidential candidate to win a major party nomination without entering the presidential primaries. Humphrey is nominated at a tumultuous Democratic convention in Chicago, where delegates approve a review of the party's nominating rules that would ensure a more open process in the future.

1972: Democratic rules reforms encourage more grassroots participation in the presidential nominating process, with a growth in primaries one result. Sen. George McGovern of South Dakota, who headed the party's rules commission for a time, mounts a long-shot, anti–Vietnam War candidacy that wins the Democratic nomination. McGovern, though, is the last nominee of either party not to win at least a plurality of his party's primary vote.

1976: The presidential nominating process continues to evolve quickly. For the first time, a majority of states hold presidential primaries. For the first time, public money is made available to candidates through a system of matching federal funds. And for the first time, Democrats ban statewide winner-take-all primaries, used for years in California. (Republicans continue to allow winner-take-all contests.)

1980: After winning some attention but no victories, Rep. John B. Anderson of Illinois quits the Republican primaries, bolts the party, and runs as an independent presidential candidate in the fall campaign. He follows in the footsteps of Theodore Roosevelt, who, after losing the Republican nomination in 1912, left the GOP to run on the Progressive Party ticket.

1984: Democrats create a large new category of delegates for party and elected officials that prove to be a key component in former vice president Walter F. Mondale's successful bid for the Democratic nomination. The new category comes to be known as "superdelegates."

1988: Super Tuesday is at its zenith. All the Southern states except South Carolina hold primaries on the second Tuesday in March. Vice President George H. W. Bush sweeps the Republican voting and essentially wraps up the GOP nomination. The Democratic results are more muddled. Rev. Jesse Jackson, senator Al Gore of Tennessee, and the eventual nominee, Massachusetts governor Michael S. Dukakis, all win primaries in the South.

1996: For the first time, the number of states holding presidential primaries breaks forty, more than two-thirds of which are held before the end of March.

2000: Republican George W. Bush becomes the first presidential candidate to decline public financing and go on to win his party's nomination. Bush spends roughly $100 million, a record up to that time.

The conventions continued to reign supreme through the 1960s, though 1968 proved to be a watershed year in the evolution of the nominating process. Sens. Eugene McCarthy of Minnesota and Robert F. Kennedy of New York used the handful of Democratic primaries that spring to protest the war in Vietnam, together taking more than two-thirds of the primary vote and driving President Lyndon B. Johnson from the race.

History might have been different if Kennedy had not been gunned down after his victory in the California primary in June. But without Kennedy on the scene, the party's embattled leadership was able to maintain tenuous control of the convention that August in Chicago, nominating Vice President Humphrey, who had not competed in any primary state.

But Humphrey's nomination came at a price. For the first time in several generations, the legitimacy of the convention itself was thrown into question. And as an outgrowth, a series of Democratic rules review commissions began to overhaul the presidential nominating process to encourage much greater grass-roots participation.

Change Comes Rapidly

An immediate result of the Democratic reform of the nominating process was a dramatic increase in presidential primaries that enhanced the chances of long-shot outsiders, such as George McGovern and Jimmy Carter, who captured the Democratic nomination in 1972 and 1976, respectively.

In the 1970s, the primary season started slowly, giving little-known candidates the time to raise money and momentum after doing well in the early rounds. Most of the primaries then were held in May and June.

But the layout of the nominating process has been less favorable to dark horses since then. In the 1980s, Democrats reinserted party and elected officials into the process, creating a new category of automatic delegate seats for them that have come to be known as "superdelegates."

And states began to move forward on the calendar in a bid to increase their influence. Democrats sought to put a brake on the calendar sprawl toward New Year's Day by instituting the "window," which prohibited any of the party's primaries or caucuses from being held before early March, with the exception of Iowa, New Hampshire, and for a time, Maine.

With the creation of that early March firewall, many states parked their primary in March—gradually at first, but then in tidal wave proportions in 1988, with the creation of a full-scale primary vote across the South on the second Tuesday in March that came to be known as "Super Tuesday."

The event did not have the effect that its Democratic sponsors had hoped for, in terms of steering the nomination toward a centrist son of the South, such as then-senator Al Gore of Tennessee. And in the 1990s, the early March Southern primary lost some of its members.

But the concept of early regional primaries took hold elsewhere. In 1996, all of New England except New Hampshire voted on the first Tuesday in March. Six Southern states, led by Texas and Florida, voted on the second Tuesday. Four states in the industrial Midwest—Illinois, Michigan, Ohio, and Wisconsin—voted on the third Tuesday in March. And California anchored a three-state Western primary on the fourth Tuesday.

There continued to be regional groupings in March 2000. One involved a collection of Mountain West states. Another involved the same half dozen states in the South that voted on the same day in 1996. But the dominant event in 2000 came on the first Tuesday in March and was a "national sampler" of sorts—an array of roughly a dozen primaries and caucuses scattered across the country—anchored by New York on one coast and California on the other.

The upshot in recent years has been both a shorter and earlier nominating season in which only well-financed and well-known candidates have been able to effectively compete.

But it is a process that increasingly has drawn the ire of leaders in both parties. And for once, the Republicans appeared as concerned as the Democrats.

When they were regularly winning the White House in the 1970s and 1980s, the GOP showed little interest in tinkering with the nominating process. But once they began to lose presidential elections in the 1990s, many Republicans began to decry the "front-loaded" primary calendar that produced nominees within a few weeks of voting.

At their convention in San Diego in 1996, Republicans approved a rules change designed to help spread out the calendar by offering states bonus delegates the later they held their primary or caucus. It did not get many takers, though, in 2000 and was rescinded.

Neither party these days is agitating for wholesale reform of the nominating process. The most significant change in 2004 is that the Democrats have moved forward their window a month to match the Republicans, allowing states to hold their primaries or caucuses in February immediately after Iowa and New Hampshire. The move underscores the fact that even when the parties opt not to make major changes, the process is still different every four years, because when it comes to the presidential nominating process, the constant is change.

Growth of Presidential Primaries . . .

The Primaries: A Front-Loaded Process

Over the years, there have been more and more states holding primaries earlier and earlier in the presidential election year. The result is that a nominating system that once featured primaries sprinkled across the spring is now front-loaded with the bulk of the primaries held during the winter months of February and March.

Following is a list of primaries held in each month of every nominating season from 1968 through 2000. Primaries included are those in the fifty states and the District of Columbia in which at least one of the parties permitted a direct vote for presidential candidates or in which there was an aggregated statewide vote for delegates.

Month	1968	1972	1976	1980	1984	1988	1992	1996	2000
February	0	0	1	1	1	2	2	5	7
March	1	3	5	9	8	20	15	24	20
April	3	3	2	4	3	3	5	1	2
May	7	11	13	13	11	7	10	8	9
June	4	4	6	9	7	5	7	4	5
TOTAL	15	21	27	36	30	37	39	42	43

1968

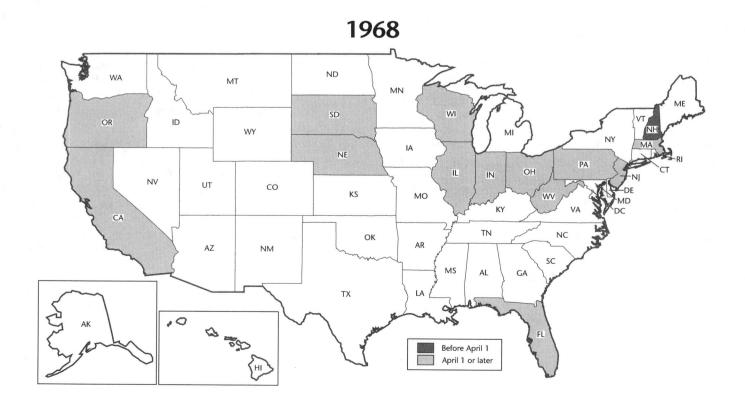

Before April 1
April 1 or later

. . . More and More, Earlier and Earlier

1980

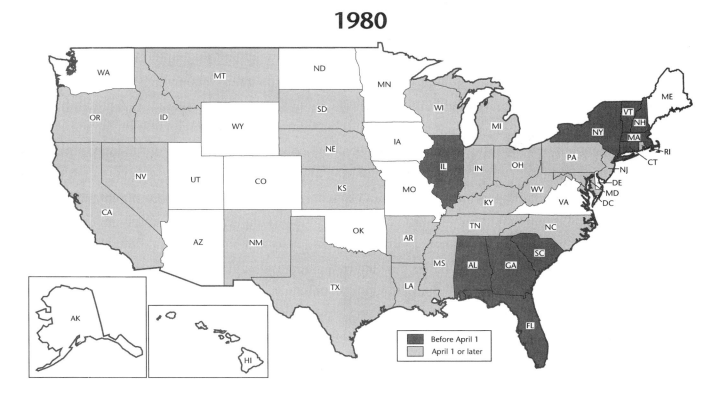

2000

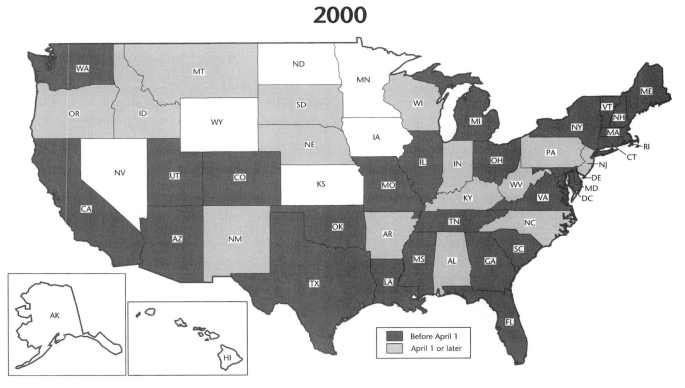

EARLY EVENTS

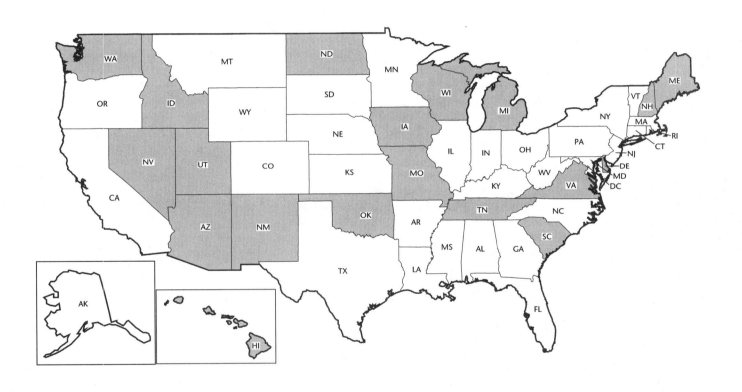

IOWA

January 19

For all its importance, Iowa is a relative newcomer to the national spotlight. It stepped into the nation's political consciousness on a snowy January night in 1972, when George McGovern ran unexpectedly close to Edmund Muskie in the Democratic precinct caucus voting. While the results drew only a smidgen of attention in the next day's newspapers, it was enough to lend credibility to McGovern's dark-horse candidacy.

McGovern spent only a day and a half campaigning in Iowa before he made his breakthrough in 1972. Now it is routine for virtually every candidate to spend at least several weeks in the state, and for little-known dark-horse contenders to devote even more time than that.

Candidates who have tried to win Iowa by making only an occasional stop in the state do so at their peril. Ronald Reagan essentially bypassed the state in 1980 and lost the caucuses to George Bush, and then had to work overtime in New Hampshire to regain his position as the Republican front-runner.

Yet the thinking of Reagan's strategists was understandable. Front-runners, by and large, have little to gain in Iowa. At best, they survive.

That ability to flummox the experts has helped make the Iowa caucuses one of the most successful political inventions of recent times. And results are often not measured by who won and who lost, but who exceeded expectations and who did

Recent Iowa Caucus Results

Iowa held its only presidential primary in 1916. Since 1972, its precinct caucuses have been a notable part of the political scene.

Year	Estimated Turnout	DEMOCRATS Candidates	%	Turnout	REPUBLICANS Candidates	%
2000 (Jan. 24)	61,000	AL GORE	63	87,233	GEORGE W. BUSH	41
		Bill Bradley	35		Steve Forbes	30
					Alan Keyes	14
1996 (Feb. 12)	50,000	BILL CLINTON*	100	96,451	BOB DOLE	26
					Pat Buchanan	23
					Lamar Alexander	18
					Steve Forbes	10
1992 (Feb. 10)	30,000	TOM HARKIN	76	—	NO CAUCUS VOTE	
		Uncommitted	12			
1988 (Feb. 8)	126,000	RICHARD GEPHARDT	31	108,838	BOB DOLE	37
		Paul Simon	27		Pat Robertson	25
		Michael Dukakis	22		George Bush	19
					Jack Kemp	11
1984 (Feb. 20)	75,000	WALTER MONDALE	49	—	NO CAUCUS VOTE	
		Gary Hart	16			
		George McGovern	10			
1980 (Jan. 21)	100,000	JIMMY CARTER*	59	106,051	GEORGE BUSH	32
		Edward Kennedy	31		Ronald Reagan	30
					Howard Baker	15
1976 (Jan. 19)	38,500	UNCOMMITTED	39	20,000	GERALD FORD*	45
		Jimmy Carter	29		Ronald Reagan	43
		Birch Bayh	11			
1972 (Jan. 24)	20,000	UNCOMMITTED	36	—	NO CAUCUS VOTE	
		Edmund Muskie	36			
		George McGovern	23			

Note: Democratic turnouts are estimates. Republican results are from the straw vote held in conjunction with the precinct caucuses. Percentages for Democratic candidates are based on a weighted measurement compiled by the Iowa Democratic Party. The 1976 GOP results are based on returns from a sampling of precincts. All candidates are listed that drew at least 10 percent of their party's vote. The names of winning candidates are capitalized. An asterisk (*) indicates an incumbent president.

not. Sometimes, it has been the runner-up who enjoyed the big "Iowa bounce" and landed at the center of the national imagination.

McGovern was the first beneficiary of this momentum in 1972. Four years later, Iowa helped create the phenomenon of Jimmy Carter. Perhaps the quintessential Iowa bounce, though, was the one that surprised even its beneficiary, Gary Hart.

Walter Mondale came down from Minnesota to claim about half the 1984 Democratic caucus vote. But Hart got half the momentum with just 16 percent of the vote because he exceeded the modest expectations of the media (and because John Glenn and Alan Cranston fell miserably short by the same standard). A week later, Hart won New Hampshire.

From 1988 through 1996, Iowa was more successful at winnowing the field than serving as a harbinger of things to come. In 1988, the eventual nominees—Michael Dukakis and George Bush—both placed third in Iowa, while the two Iowa winners—Richard Gephardt and Bob Dole—were both out of the race by the end of March.

In 1992, Iowa Democrats rallied around their home-state senator, Tom Harkin, who was unable to gain traction elsewhere and also quit the race in March.

In 1996, Pat Buchanan got the Iowa bounce with a close second-place finish to Dole, but was unable to make the momentum extend beyond victory in New Hampshire.

Dole's winning vote share in Iowa fell by more than 10 percentage points from eight years earlier to 26 percent. Meanwhile, Buchanan nearly matched the 25 percent share that runner-up Pat Robertson had garnered in 1988.

But Buchanan's showing was not simply a reprise of Robertson's. Robertson carried 14 Iowa counties, mostly in the industrialized eastern half of the state and many in Democratic areas where the Republican caucuses offered a vacuum to be filled.

Buchanan carried 24 counties, mostly in rural southwest Iowa, where concern about the encroachment of big agricultural interests melded with social-issue conservatism. (Exit polling in recent elections has shown that religious conservatives cast about one-third of the statewide GOP caucus vote.)

Still, Dole was able to make his victory go further in 1996 than he had eight years earlier, when his failures in the rest of the country led to joking references to him as "the president of Iowa."

In 2000, both parties held competitive contests in the Hawkeye State for the first time since 1988. But unlike a dozen years earlier, the eventual nominees in 2000 won Iowa handily—George W. Bush on the Republican side, Al Gore on the Democratic.

What made the caucus results interesting was how their principal opponents dealt with Iowa. Republican John McCain

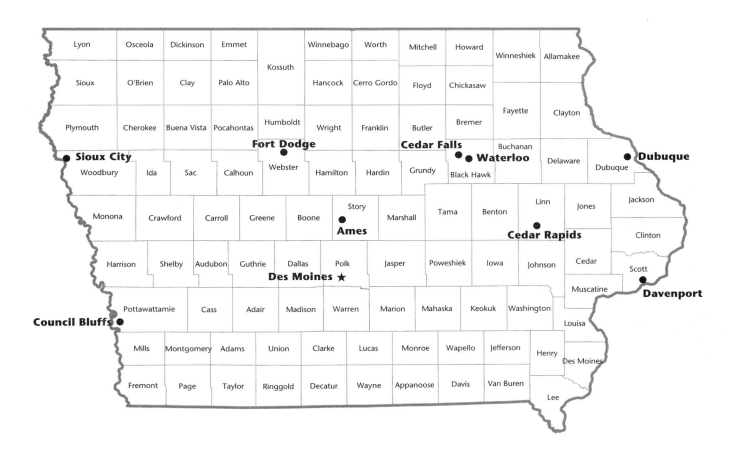

14

skipped the caucuses in favor of a more intensive effort in New Hampshire, which he won. Meanwhile, Democrat Bill Bradley battled Gore head-to-head in Iowa, losing time, money and momentum with a nearly 2-to-1 loss to the vice president that undoubtedly contributed to Bradley's narrow defeat in New Hampshire.

Bradley did carry Johnson County (Iowa City), a liberal, academically oriented enclave that includes the University of Iowa. But with the active support of organized labor and teachers, Gore won virtually everywhere else in the state.

The result underscored the accepted fact that low-turnout caucuses reward candidates with superior organization. And by Iowa standards, turnout was particularly low in 2000. While nearly a quarter million voters participated in the state's Democratic and Republican caucuses in 1988, the combined turnout for the two parties in 2000 was less than 150,000.

The Iowa Rules

Iowa elects its delegates through a four-tier caucus process, with national convention delegates selected in the final stages. But it is the first stage—the precinct caucuses—that the political world cares about.

Democratic caucuses the night of Jan. 19 offer the first big test of voter sentiment in 2004. Democrats will caucus in the state's 1,997 precincts, with the Democratic vote traditionally tallied in terms of projected delegates to the state convention. For their part, Iowa Republicans often hold a straw vote in conjunction with their precinct caucuses. But with President George W. Bush running unopposed for renomination, no straw vote is scheduled this time.

Participation in both the Democratic and Republican caucuses is open to any of the party's registered voters, plus any voter who wishes to register as a member of the Democratic or Republican parties on caucus night, including those who will be 18 years old after the caucuses but before the November general election. As of October 2003, there were roughly 570,000 registered Democrats in Iowa, 620,000 Republicans, and 780,000 voters who were not registered in either party. (Totals include both active and inactive voters.)

DEMOCRATS

THE CALENDAR

Precinct Caucuses (meeting time)	Jan. 19 (6:30 p.m.)
County Conventions	March 13
Congressional District Conventions	April 24
State Convention	June 12

THE DELEGATES

Number (% of national total)	56 (1.3%)
Distribution:	
By congressional district	29 (5 or 6 per district)
At-Large	10
Pledged PEOs	6
Superdelegates	11
Method of Allocation	Proportional—15% of vote needed to win a share of statewide or district delegates.

NEW HAMPSHIRE

January 27

Like the New York Yankees, the New Hampshire presidential primary has never been willing to settle for anything less than first.

A state, of course, has means beyond a baseball team: New Hampshire has decreed that its primary be held before that of any other state as a matter of law. Despite all the frowning and frustration in other states, New Hampshire has attracted candidates to its first-in-the-nation presidential primary since it became a major part of the political landscape in 1952.

The primary has lost a bit of its luster over the last dozen years. In 1992 Bill Clinton became the first candidate since 1952 to be elected president without first winning the New

Hampshire primary; he was second in the state's Democratic voting. In 1996 Pat Buchanan won the Republican balloting in New Hampshire but no other primary that followed. And in 2000, John McCain upset the eventual Republican nominee George W. Bush, throwing into question for the third straight election the whole idea that momentum accrues to a Granite State winner.

Yet New Hampshire has remained a rite of passage for anyone who seriously covets the White House, and for long shots it is a place where hope springs eternal. In a state whose motto is "Live Free or Die," voters have never been reluctant to deliver a blow against the politically high and mighty.

Recent New Hampshire Primary Results

New Hampshire held its first presidential primary in 1916.

	DEMOCRATS			REPUBLICANS		
Year	Turnout	Candidates	%	Turnout	Candidates	%
2000 (Feb. 1)	154,639	AL GORE Bill Bradley	50 46	238,206	JOHN McCAIN George W. Bush Steve Forbes	49 30 13
1996 (Feb. 20)	91,562	BILL CLINTON*	84	208,938	PAT BUCHANAN Bob Dole Lamar Alexander Steve Forbes	27 26 23 12
1992 (Feb. 18)	167,819	PAUL TSONGAS Bill Clinton Bob Kerrey Tom Harkin	33 25 11 10	174,165	GEORGE BUSH* Pat Buchanan	53 37
1988 (Feb. 16)	123,512	MICHAEL DUKAKIS Richard Gephardt Paul Simon	36 20 17	157,644	GEORGE BUSH Bob Dole Jack Kemp Pierre du Pont	38 28 13 10
1984 (Feb. 28)	101,131	GARY HART Walter Mondale John Glenn	37 28 12	75,570	RONALD REAGAN*	86
1980 (Feb. 26)	111,930	JIMMY CARTER* Edward Kennedy	47 37	147,157	RONALD REAGAN George Bush Howard Baker	50 23 13
1976 (Feb. 24)	82,381	JIMMY CARTER Morris Udall Birch Bayh Fred Harris	28 23 15 11	111,674	GERALD FORD* Ronald Reagan	49 48
1972 (March 7)	88,854	EDMUND MUSKIE George McGovern	46 37	117,208	RICHARD NIXON* Paul McCloskey	68 20
1968 (March 12)	55,464	LYNDON JOHNSON*# Eugene McCarthy	50 42	103,938	RICHARD NIXON Nelson Rockefeller#	78 11

Note: All candidates are listed that drew at least 10 percent of their party's primary vote. The names of winning candidates are capitalized. An asterisk (*) indicates an incumbent president. A pound sign (#) indicates a write-in candidate.

Two presidents—Harry Truman and Lyndon Johnson—decided not to seek reelection after poor showings in New Hampshire. Truman was upset in the 1952 Democratic primary by Sen. Estes Kefauver of Tennessee. A write-in campaign for Johnson in the 1968 Democratic balloting could muster only 49.6 percent of the vote against the lightly regarded anti–Vietnam War candidacy of Eugene McCarthy.

Since then, Presidents Gerald Ford (in 1976), Jimmy Carter (in 1980), and George Bush (in 1992) have also been chastened by New Hampshire primary voters. They won, but with less than 55 percent of the vote, and all three lost the general election that followed.

New Hampshire is a great leveler. It is small enough that any candidate with time, energy and a knack for grassroots organization has a good chance of winning. As Kefauver and McCarthy came to national prominence in New Hampshire, so did George McGovern in 1972, Gary Hart in 1984, and McCain in 2000.

McGovern did not beat the Democratic front-runner, Sen. Edmund Muskie of Maine, but he ran so far above expectations that Muskie's campaign lost respect and soon slid into political oblivion. Hart defeated Walter Mondale in the 1984 Democratic contest, sending the erstwhile front-runner into a tailspin from which he barely recovered. McCain's upset of

Bush in 2000 enabled the Arizona senator to battle the well-funded Bush on even terms throughout the first month of primaries—a window of opportunity that closed, though, with the nationwide array of contests in early March that Bush was prepared to contest.

For all its traditionalism, New Hampshire lacks strong party structures and the politically potent interest groups that all but rule in other states. But the state's primary places great pressure on dark-horse hopefuls. For those who do not make a breakthrough in Iowa, a caucus state, New Hampshire can be their last chance. It certainly is the final opportunity for candidates to extensively woo voters personally before the whirl of subsequent primaries forces surviving candidates to focus on media advertising campaigns.

New Hampshire's Republican electorate has a conservative hue, but in presidential primaries it has not always supported the champion of the GOP right. Robert Taft lost to Dwight Eisenhower in 1952; Barry Goldwater ran far behind the 1964 write-in winner, Henry Cabot Lodge; and in 1976 Ronald Reagan lost narrowly to President Ford.

Voices on the right are amplified by the unabashedly conservative Manchester *Union Leader,* which plays a role in shaping political debate within the state. In 1992 and 1996, the *Union Leader* backed the insurgent candidacy of Pat Buchanan, who staggered President Bush by taking 37 percent of the vote in the 1992 GOP primary and won the event over a crowded Republican field four years later.

For conservative candidates from Taft to Buchanan, the city of Manchester has been a most reliable source of votes. The state's largest urban center, it was the only New Hampshire city to back Taft in 1952 and Goldwater in the 1964 GOP contest. It also went overwhelmingly for Reagan in both 1976 and 1980, as well as Buchanan in 1996.

That year, Buchanan also won old mill towns around the state, much of the conservative mountainous North Country, communities near Manchester that were loyal readers of the *Union Leader,* and communities where Ross Perot ran particularly well as an independent presidential candidate in 1992.

Generally, the strongholds of moderate Republicanism mirror the hotbeds of liberal Democrats—the seacoast area of southeast New Hampshire, the major academic communities of Hanover (Dartmouth College) and Durham (University of New Hampshire), and the state capital of Concord and its environs. Bob Dole won many of these communities in the 1996 GOP primary. So did McCain in 2000, in a victory that was stunning for its completeness.

Traversing the state in his campaign bus, the "Straight Talk Express," and holding scores of town meetings along the way, McCain masterfully tapped into the grassroots nature of New Hampshire politics. On primary day, he swamped Bush in all 10 counties and won communities of all stripes. McCain's statewide margin of victory was nearly 20 percentage points.

On the Democratic side, Al Gore's 4-point victory over Bill Bradley in 2000 was about as decisive as a close victory could be. Gore easily won New Hampshire's two largest cities, Manchester and Nashua, swept most of the old mill towns, and carried many of the smaller cities across the state. Altogether, the vice president won eight of New Hampshire's 10 counties, losing only two small ones (Carroll and Grafton) to Bradley.

Bradley found a toehold in upscale suburbs and academic communities. But his chance for an upset victory was blunted by McCain's greater success at winning independent voters, which in New Hampshire can participate in either party's primary.

Gore's narrow victory in 2000 was the latest in a long line of successes by Southern Democrats in the Granite State. The Democratic primary was won by Georgia's Carter in 1976 and 1980, Arkansas' Clinton in 1996, and Tennessee's Gore in 2000.

But possibly the most critical showing by any Democratic candidate in New Hampshire did not result in a victory. A month or so before the 1992 New Hampshire primary, it looked like Clinton was well positioned to win. But in short order, he suffered two big blows: a tabloid tale of womanizing and hints of draft evasion during the Vietnam War. Yet by finishing a clear second in New Hampshire, Clinton survived, and he could leave New Hampshire boasting that he was the "Comeback Kid."

The New Hampshire Rules

Candidates have never been drawn to New Hampshire by its delegate reward. It has roughly 1 percent of each party's national total, which in recent elections has been divided among candidates to proportionally represent the primary vote. Rather, candidates come to New Hampshire because it has earned a reputation as a giant focus group—ready and willing to evaluate the candidates and recommend one or two in each party to the states that follow.

New Hampshire has jealously guarded its first-in-the-nation presidential primary status, to the point that in 2004 the event will be on Jan. 27, the earliest date in the state's history.

The primary is open to registered members of each party, plus undeclared voters, who automatically become members of the party in which they cast their primary ballot (although they can change back as they leave the polling place). As of November 2002, there were roughly 250,000 registered Republicans in New Hampshire, 175,000 Democrats, and 260,000 undeclared.

DEMOCRATS

THE CALENDAR	
Primary Date (polling hours)	Jan. 27 (open by 11 a.m., cannot close before 7 p.m.)
Filing Deadline	Nov. 21, 2003
Filing Procedure	Candidates must pay a $1,000 filing fee to the secretary of state; no petitions are required.
THE DELEGATES	
Number (% of national total)	27 (0.6%)
Distribution:	
By congressional district	14 (7 per district)
At-Large	5
Pledged PEOs	3
Superdelegates	5
Method of Allocation	Proportional—15% of vote needed to win a share of statewide or district delegates.

ARIZONA

February 3

Every dozen years since 1964, Arizona has fielded a presidential candidate—Republican Barry Goldwater in 1964, Democrat Morris Udall in 1976, Democrat Bruce Babbitt in 1988, and Republican John McCain in 2000.

What Arizona did not have until 1996 was a presidential primary. And that it has one at all is due in no small part to McCain, who lobbied hard for the creation of the February event. Travelling in Asia when the legislation was being debated, he reportedly made a call from Hanoi to a wavering state legislator.

That first primary did not go as McCain had hoped. As national chairman of Texas senator Phil Gramm's presidential campaign, McCain saw his candidate drop out of the race before Arizona even voted. But as a candidate himself in 2000, McCain won the next primary easily.

From its outset, the presidential primary proved a success—attracting candidates to Arizona and voters to the polls.

Steve Forbes mounted a lavish media campaign in 1996 that accented his flat tax proposal and outsider image. Pat Buchanan and Bob Dole seemed at times to engage in a battle of photo opportunities. Dole was photographed visiting Goldwater, his most famous Arizona supporter. Buchanan cultivated a frontier image, culminating with a visit to the OK Corral in Tombstone where he dressed in cowboy garb.

Buchanan came into Arizona fresh from an upset victory over Dole in New Hampshire. And the state's decision to save money by opening barely one-quarter of the usual polling places seemed to favor Buchanan and his energetic cadre of supporters.

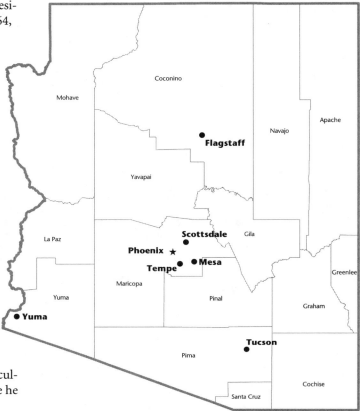

Yet the turnout was larger than expected. More Republican ballots were cast in Maricopa County (Phoenix) alone (roughly 215,000) than had been cast the previous week in the entire state of New Hampshire.

Recent Arizona Primary Results

Arizona held its first presidential primary in 1996, which was used then by the Republicans only.

	DEMOCRATS			REPUBLICANS		
Year	Turnout	Candidates	%	Turnout	Candidates	%
2000 (Feb. 22 Reps.; March 11 Dems.)	86,762	AL GORE	78	322,669	JOHN McCAIN	60
		Bill Bradley	19		George W. Bush	36
1996 (Feb. 27)	—	NO PRIMARY		347,482	STEVE FORBES	33
					Bob Dole	30
					Pat Buchanan	28

Note: All candidates are listed that drew at least 10 percent of their party's primary vote. The names of winning candidates are capitalized.

Maricopa was one of only two counties that Forbes won statewide, but he carried it decisively enough to win the state by more than 10,000 votes over Dole.

Buchanan finished a close third by winning much of rural Arizona, including the two major Native American counties, Apache and Navajo. But his tough stance on immigration did not serve him well in voting along the Mexican border. Dole carried three of the four counties that border Mexico, including populous Pima (Tucson).

According to exit polling, Dole had the edge among Arizona's large contingent of voters age 60 and older (which cast more than four out of every ten GOP primary ballots). Buchanan showed a narrow lead among middle-aged voters. But neither could overcome the consistency of Forbes, who took about one-third of the Arizona primary ballots among all age groups and both sexes. Yet for Forbes, it was his second and last victory of the 1996 primary season.

Arizona Democrats expressed interest in joining the Republicans on their February primary date. But with national Democratic rules prior to 2004 preventing states from establishing primaries so early, they had to content themselves with a small, party-run preference vote at a limited number of polling places around the state.

Turnout for the Democratic event was comparatively light. The contest in 2000 drew less than 90,000 voters—slightly more than 25 percent of the turnout for the Republican presidential primary that year.

Arizona Democrats, though, were innovative about how they conducted their primary in 2000, using it as a laboratory to experiment with Internet voting. Concerns were raised that the "digital divide" might work to the disadvantage of the state's large minority population of Hispanics, Indians and blacks. But several dozen Internet voting sites were established in communities with limited Internet access, as were some additional polling places. Ultimately, nearly half the Democratic primary ballots in 2000 were cast on the Internet, nearly 40 percent by mail, and the rest by traditional paper ballots at polling places.

The Arizona Rules

Arizona Republicans will not have a presidential primary in 2004, giving the state's Democrats their moment in the sun.

Only registered Democrats can vote in the Democratic primary and registered Republicans in the GOP primary (when there is one). As of October 2003, there were roughly 920,000 registered Republican voters in Arizona and 790,000 Democrats.

DEMOCRATS

THE CALENDAR	
Primary Date (polling hours)	Feb. 3 (6 a.m.–7 p.m.)
Filing Deadline	Dec. 24
Filing Procedure	Candidates must file a letter of intent with the state party, including a pledge to support the Democratic platform.
THE DELEGATES	
Number (% of national total)	64 (1.5%)
Distribution:	
By congressional district	36 (from 3 to 7 per district)
At-Large	12
Pledged PEOs	7
Superdelegates	9
Method of Allocation	Proportional—15% of vote needed in primary to win a share of statewide or district delegates.

DELAWARE

February 3

Delaware never held a presidential primary before 1996. But when it did, it aimed high, setting a date just four days after New Hampshire's first-in-the-nation primary.

That created conflict for Delaware on two fronts—with the national Democratic Party, which forbids states from voting before Iowa and New Hampshire—and with the Granite State itself, which has a state statute requiring a seven-day hiatus between its primary and any that follow.

New Hampshire's displeasure with Delaware's chutzpah had its effect. In deference to the Granite State and its political importance, most of the Republican candidates scaled back their Delaware campaigning. One who did not was Steve Forbes, who campaigned around the state by bus and ran his usual media blitz.

Forbes, though, did not have a clear track to victory. His main rivals were on the Delaware ballot.

And Bob Dole had the backing of several big-name Delaware Republicans, including Sen. William V. Roth Jr., who endorsed Dole three days before the primary. But Dole did not come to the state to receive the endorsement. He accepted it by phone while traveling on his campaign plane.

Meanwhile, Forbes's assiduous personal attention to the state probably provided him with the margin of victory, as he defeated Dole by barely 5 percentage points.

Four years later, Delaware Republicans held their primary one week after New Hampshire. George W. Bush participated in the event and won, scoring a low-profile, but badly needed, victory just a week after he had been routed by John McCain in New Hampshire. McCain did not campaign in Delaware, though, enabling Bush to register his first win of the 2000 primary season by a comfortable margin.

In terms of political geography, Delaware is divided into two parts by the Chesapeake and Delaware Canal, which slices across the northern quarter of the state. The portion north of the canal comprises the heart of populous New Castle County, with Wilmington and its suburbs. It is part of the busy Northeast Corridor. Below the canal, the state is rural and lightly settled; its values, attitude, and voting behavior are similar to those of the border South.

Bush ran best in the southern portion of Delaware in the 2000 Republican primary, a precursor of his critical victory in South Carolina less than two weeks later. But elections in Delaware tend to be won and lost in New Castle County, which cast a clear majority of the vote in both the Democratic and Republican presidential primaries in 2000.

Recent Delaware Primary Results

Delaware held its first presidential primary in 1996.

Year	DEMOCRATS			REPUBLICANS		
	Turnout	Candidates	%	Turnout	Candidates	%
2000 (Feb. 5 Dems.; Feb. 8 Reps.)	11,141	AL GORE	57	30,060	GEORGE W. BUSH	51
		Bill Bradley	40		John McCain	25
					Steve Forbes	20
1996 (Feb. 24)	10,740	BILL CLINTON*	90	32,773	STEVE FORBES	33
					Bob Dole	27
					Pat Buchanan	19

Note: All candidates are listed that drew at least 10 percent of their party's primary vote. The names of winning candidates are capitalized. An asterisk (*) indicates an incumbent president.

The Delaware Rules

Delaware scheduled its first two presidential primaries in 1996 and 2000 within New Hampshire's self-defined seven-day territorial limit, feeling the wrath of the Granite State both times. In 2004, Delaware will join a cadre of states voting one week after New Hampshire, anchoring the Northeastern flank of the day's primary balloting.

Only registered Democrats and Republicans may participate in their party's primary. As of November 2003, there were almost 225,000 registered Democrats in Delaware and nearly 175,000 Republicans. With President Bush unopposed for renomination, no Republican primary is scheduled in 2004.

DEMOCRATS

THE CALENDAR	
Primary Date (polling hours)	Feb. 3 (7 a.m.–8 p.m.)
Filing Deadline	Jan. 1
Filing Procedure	Democratic candidates can qualify for the Democratic primary ballot by submitting petitions signed by 500 registered Democrats or being eligible for matching federal funds. In either case, candidates must pay a $2,000 filing fee, which goes to the Democratic state party.

THE DELEGATES	
Number (% of national total)	23 (0.5%)
Distribution:	
By congressional district	10
At-Large	3
Pledged PEOs	2
Superdelegates	8
Method of Allocation	Proportional—15% of vote needed to win a share of statewide or district delegates.

MISSOURI

February 3

Situated at the juncture of the industrial Frost Belt, the agrarian Midwest and the rural South, Missouri likes to present itself as one of the nation's foremost political bellwethers. In all but two presidential elections since 1900, it has voted for the winning candidate.

But Missouri has not had much chance to prove its perspicacity in presidential primaries. The first—in 1988—was skewed toward the home-state candidacy of Rep. Richard Gephardt.

The primary itself had been created largely to aid Gephardt, as Democratic officials thought such an event would do their native son more good than the traditional caucuses the state had held previously.

None of the other Democratic presidential hopefuls seriously challenged Gephardt in Missouri. He rolled up nearly 60 percent of the vote, easily his best showing of the primary season.

There was some embarrassment for Gephardt, though, in the returns. He narrowly lost his home base, the city of St. Louis, to Jesse Jackson. Jackson won handily in the heavily black precincts in the northern part of the city. Gephardt, though, did swamp Jackson in that southern portion of St. Louis that was part of his congressional district. Meanwhile, Al Gore had trouble finding a toehold anywhere in Missouri and drew only 3 percent of the vote statewide.

The tables were turned, though, in 2000, as Gore swamped Missouri native Bill Bradley in the state's second Democratic presidential primary. Bradley carried only two counties,

Recent Missouri Primary Results

Missouri held its first presidential primary in 1988.

Year	DEMOCRATS			REPUBLICANS		
	Turnout	Candidates	%	Turnout	Candidates	%
2000 (March 7)	265,489	AL GORE	65	475,363	GEORGE W. BUSH	58
		Bill Bradley	34		John McCain	35
1996	—	NO PRIMARY		—	NO PRIMARY	
1992	—	NO PRIMARY		—	NO PRIMARY	
1988 (March 8)	527,805	RICHARD GEPHARDT	58	400,300	GEORGE BUSH	42
		Jesse Jackson	20		Bob Dole	41
		Michael Dukakis	12		Pat Robertson	11

Note: All candidates are listed that drew at least 10 percent of their party's primary vote. The names of winning candidates are capitalized.

one of which—Jefferson—included his birthplace of Crystal City. Thus far, the only competitive primary for president in Missouri was on the Republican side in 1988. Bob Dole, who did not win any Super Tuesday primary that year, came closest to victory in Missouri. For much of the night it appeared that he might defeat George Bush in the Show Me State, and in the end he lost by less than 5,000 votes out of 400,000 cast.

Dole's basic asset was the proximity of western Missouri to his home state of Kansas. Dole swept most of western Missouri, including the Kansas City area. Bush won most of the eastern half, including St. Louis and its suburbs.

In its caucus days, Democrats in Harry Truman's home state showed a clear preference for traditional "New Deal" Democrats, such as Hubert Humphrey, Henry Jackson, and Walter Mondale. Bill Clinton won Missouri's first-round caucuses in 1992, although the turnout of about 25,000 was less than 5 percent of the number that participated in the Democratic primary four years earlier.

Meanwhile, if Missouri Republicans needed an excuse to reinstitute the presidential primary, their 1996 caucus process gave them one. Tapping into strong anti-abortion sentiment in suburban St. Louis County, Pat Buchanan won the first-round caucuses over Dole by 8 percentage points, with 9 percent going to Alan Keyes. But to the chagrin of the Buchanan legions, Keyes's supporters aligned with the Dole forces at the state convention to give Dole a majority of the Missouri delegates.

The Republican primary in 2000 produced a victory for George W. Bush by a much more comfortable margin than his father registered in 1988. John McCain triumphed in Missouri's two largest cities, Kansas City and St. Louis. But there are not many Republican votes in either. Bush carried the rest of the state easily.

The Missouri Rules

Missouri will be holding only its third presidential primary in history on Feb. 3. But like the first two, the Show Me State will be able to boost one of its own. In 1988, it was Democratic Rep. Richard Gephardt. In 2000, it was Bill Bradley, a native of Crystal City (south of St. Louis) who formally launched his bid for the Democratic presidential nomination there in September 1999. In 2004, Gephardt is making his second bid for the Democratic presidential nomination.

Missouri does not have party registration, so any of its nearly 3.7 million registered voters (as of August 2002) may participate in either the Democratic or Republican primary.

DEMOCRATS

THE CALENDAR	
Primary Date (polling hours)	Feb. 3 (6 a.m.–7 p.m.)
Filing Deadline	Nov. 18, 2003
Filing Procedure	Candidates must submit to the secretary of state verification of having paid their state party a $1,000 filing fee or, if indigent, submit petitions signed by at least 1,000 registered voters in each congressional district.
THE DELEGATES	
Number (% of national total)	87 (2.0%)
Distribution:	
By congressional district	48 (4 to 7 per district)
At-Large	16
Pledged PEOs	10
Superdelegates	13
Method of Allocation	Proportional—15% of vote needed to win a share of statewide or district delegates.

NEW MEXICO

February 3

New Mexico is different than other states in the Mountain West in the degree to which minorities affect its demographics. The state is more than 40 percent Hispanic and almost 10 percent Native American, so that anyone who wants to win comfortably, especially in the Democratic primary, must be able to bridge the gap between non-Hispanic whites and minorities.

Clinton was able to do so in 1992, carrying every county, from those of Hispanic northern New Mexico to conservative, overwhelmingly non-Hispanic "Little Texas" in the southeast part of the state. New Mexico was the only Western state where he captured a majority of the primary vote.

Michael Dukakis also ran well in both parts of New Mexico in the 1988 Democratic primary. Jesse Jackson carried McKinley County (Gallup), the lone Native American-majority county in New Mexico, but Jackson's limited appeal to the Hispanic vote was apparent in his failure to win any of the Hispanic-majority counties. Jackson came fairly close in a few, such as Taos County, which has a large artists' colony and a more liberal bent. But in others, he was beaten soundly by Dukakis, whose ability to speak fluent Spanish was widely publicized.

Recent New Mexico Primary Results

New Mexico held its first presidential primary in 1972.

Year	DEMOCRATS			REPUBLICANS		
	Turnout	Candidates	%	Turnout	Candidates	%
2000 (June 6)	132,280	AL GORE	75	75,230	GEORGE W. BUSH	83
		Bill Bradley	21		John McCain	10
1996 (June 4)	121,362	BILL CLINTON*	90	70,464	BOB DOLE	76
1992 (June 2)	181,443	BILL CLINTON	53	86,967	GEORGE BUSH*	64
		Uncommitted	19		Uncommitted	27
		Jerry Brown	17			
1988 (June 7)	188,610	MICHAEL DUKAKIS	61	88,744	GEORGE BUSH	78
		Jesse Jackson	28		Bob Dole	10
1984 (June 5)	187,403	GARY HART	47	42,994	RONALD REAGAN*	95
		Walter Mondale	36			
		Jesse Jackson	12			
1980 (June 3)	159,364	EDWARD KENNEDY	46	59,546	RONALD REAGAN	64
		Jimmy Carter*	42		John Anderson	12
1976	—	NO PRIMARY		—	NO PRIMARY	
1972 (June 6)	153,293	GEORGE McGOVERN	33	55,469	RICHARD NIXON*	88
		George Wallace	29			
		Hubert Humphrey	26			

Note: All candidates are listed that drew at least 10 percent of their party's primary vote. The names of winning candidates are capitalized. An asterisk (*) indicates an incumbent president.

But in some of the earlier Democratic primaries, there were racial fault lines. In the state's first presidential primary in 1972, "Little Texas" went for George Wallace, enabling him to finish within 5 percentage points of statewide winner George McGovern. In 1980, the region voted virtually en masse for President Jimmy Carter, as he nearly offset the large lead that Edward Kennedy built up in Bernalillo County (Albuquerque), Santa Fe and heavily Catholic Hispanic counties to the north.

New Mexico Republicans have not had much luck with their presidential primary. It was created just in time to elect the only delegate to vote against the renomination of President Richard Nixon. (The delegate went to GOP Rep. Paul McCloskey of California, who mounted a quixotic antiwar challenge to Nixon in the 1972 primaries.)

The primary was abandoned in 1976, just in time to miss the party's hottest nominating battle of the last quarter century. Since its revival in 1980, the state has seen a succession of GOP contests that were decided long before New Mexico voted in June.

When New Mexico Republicans have put together their delegation through the caucus process, it has tended to mirror the conservatism of their GOP counterparts in other Rocky Mountain states. The delegation voted as a bloc for Barry Goldwater in 1964 and Ronald Reagan in 1976.

The New Mexico Rules

New Mexico has traditionally held its presidential primary in June. But in order to be a part of the early action, the state's Democrats have scheduled a party-run primary on Feb. 3. At least several dozen polling places are expected to be established for the day's event.

Only registered Democrats may vote in the primary. As of December 2003, New Mexico had roughly 480,000 registered Democrats and 300,000 Republicans.

DEMOCRATS

THE CALENDAR
Primary Date (polling hours) — Feb. 3 (noon–7 p.m.)
Filing Deadline — Dec. 15, 2003
Filing Procedure — Candidates file a statement of candidacy with the Democratic state chair and pay a $2,500 filing fee.

THE DELEGATES
Number (% of national total) — 37 (0.9%)
Distribution:
By congressional district — 17 (5 or 6 per district)
At-Large — 6
Pledged PEOs — 3
Superdelegates — 11
Method of Allocation — Proportional—15% of vote needed to win a share of statewide or district delegates.

NORTH DAKOTA

February 3

North Dakota has a long populist tradition characterized by a suspicion of concentrated business interests—such as railroads, banks and grain companies. When the new innovation of the presidential primary blossomed across the country in 1912, it was North Dakota that was first in line to vote.

But the idea of a late-winter primary on the frigid upper Plains did not last long, and by the mid-1930s North Dakota had switched to a caucus process to select its delegates. The presidential primary was resurrected in the 1980s. But again it failed to take root, as candidates relegated it to the ranks of states whose scant prize was appraised as less precious than the time needed to win it.

George Bush's lone opponent in the Republican primary in 1988 was Mary Jane Rachner, a retired teacher from Minnesota who sought to buy billboard space to read: "Stamp Out Homosexuality." Bush won with 94 percent of the vote. The primary ballot in 1992 included Lyndon LaRouche and two comedians. Bush won the GOP primary again; Ross Perot won the Democratic primary on write-ins.

From 1984 through 1992, North Dakota held its presidential primary in June after all the other states had balloted. In 1996, it moved to the front end of the calendar, joining South Dakota on a date in late February. Bob Dole carried both Dakotas to win his first primaries of the year. With his farm-state roots, Dole garnered more votes in North Dakota's Republican primary than runner-up Steve Forbes and third-place finisher Pat Buchanan combined.

Buchanan had the benefit of momentum from his victory the previous week in New Hampshire. But he failed to connect in North Dakota. On one hand, he had to deal with the "ghost" of Phil Gramm in bidding for votes on the right side of the Republican spectrum. By the time of the North Dakota primary, Gramm was out of the race. But with North Dakota allowing votes to be cast by mail beginning in January (when Gramm was still an active candidate), the Texas senator drew nearly 10 percent.

Nor was Buchanan, a native of Washington, D.C., helped by his urban roots. "Buchanan is a city kid," read an editorial in North Dakota's largest newspaper, the *Forum* of Fargo. "If he knows the difference between production agriculture and 'Green Acres,' he's yet to articulate it."

The early primary date in 1996, though, was unable to make the event a rousing hit at the ballot box. Turnout on the Republican side was barely half the number that voted in the GOP primary in 1924, which was won by President Calvin Coolidge. Barely 1,500 North Dakotans voted in the Democratic primary in 1996, which President Bill Clinton skipped. The primary was abandoned by both parties in 2000.

Recent North Dakota Primary Results

North Dakota held its first presidential primary in 1912, but none were held between 1932 and 1984 or again in 2000.

Year	DEMOCRATS			REPUBLICANS		
	Turnout	Candidates	%	Turnout	Candidates	%
2000	—	NO PRIMARY		—	NO PRIMARY	
1996 (Feb. 27)	1,584	ROLAND RIEMERS	41	63,734	BOB DOLE	42
		Lyndon LaRouche	35		Steve Forbes	20
		Vernon Clemenson	24		Pat Buchanan	18
1992 (June 9)	32,786	ROSS PEROT#	29	47,808	GEORGE BUSH*	83
		Lyndon LaRouche	21			
		Charles Woods	20			
		Tom Shiekman	15			
		Bill Clinton#	15			
1988 (June 14)	3,405	MICHAEL DUKAKIS#	85	39,434	GEORGE BUSH	94
		Jesse Jackson#	15			
1984 (June 12)	33,555	GARY HART	85	44,109	RONALD REAGAN*	100
		Lyndon LaRouche	12			

Note: All candidates are listed that drew at least 10 percent of their party's primary vote. The names of winning candidates are capitalized. An asterisk (*) indicates an incumbent president. A pound sign (#) indicates candidate received votes as a write-in.

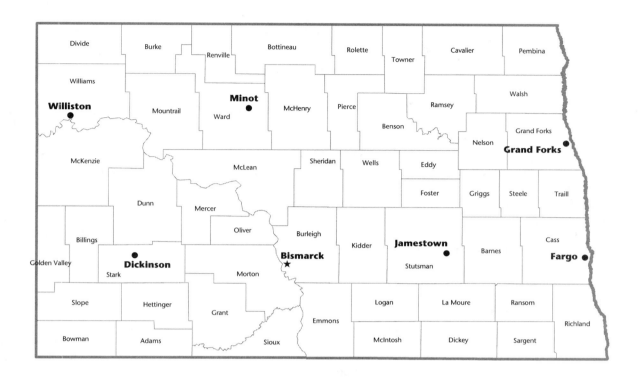

The North Dakota Rules

In recent years, North Dakota has experimented with holding their presidential primary at the end of the nominating process (June) and near the beginning (late February). But in 2000, it did not hold a primary at all and none is scheduled in 2004.

This time, North Dakota Democrats are using what has been termed a caucus process. But it is anchored by what is in essence a party-run primary on Feb. 3, with roughly 100 polling places planned across the state. All candidates who wanted to be on the ballot had merely to notify the state Democratic Party by Oct. 1. Those that draw at least 15 percent on Feb. 3 are to have their vote reflected as closely as possible in the selection of national convention delegates.

North Dakota has no formal system of voter registration, so anyone of voting age (roughly 475,000 in 2002) may participate in the Democratic caucuses, although participants must sign a statement indicating they are a Democrat.

DEMOCRATS

THE CALENDAR
- Precinct Caucus (polling hours)   Feb. 3 (2–7 p.m.)
- Legislative District Conventions   Feb. 17–March 12
- State Convention   April 4

THE DELEGATES
- Number (% of national total)   22 (0.5%)
- Distribution:
    - By congressional district   9
    - At-Large   3
    - Pledged PEOs   2
    - Superdelegates   8
- Method of Allocation   Proportional—15% of vote on Feb. 3 needed to win a share of the delegates.

OKLAHOMA

February 3

Oklahoma's first presidential primary was in 1988, as the Sooner State helped anchor the western flank of that year's huge, Southern-oriented primary dubbed Super Tuesday. No primary since then, though, has been as compelling as the first one. And in an effort to regain some of the primary's initial luster, it has been moved forward in 2004 to early February.

In 1988, Oklahoma Republicans staged one of the closest and most evenly contested votes of the truncated GOP primary season. George Bush beat Bob Dole, as he did in every primary on Super Tuesday. But in Oklahoma, as almost nowhere else, the outcome was in doubt until the next day.

It was a border war—Bush from Texas, Dole from Kansas. And in the end, Bush won Oklahoma by barely 5,000 votes out of more than 200,000 cast, with his winning 37 percent vote share by far his lowest in the vast array of primaries held on Super Tuesday that year.

Dole swept much of the Republican-oriented farm and ranch country in the northern part of the state that abuts Kansas. But Bush capitalized on the urban orientation of the Oklahoma GOP to narrowly prevail. More than half the vote was cast in Oklahoma (Oklahoma City), Tulsa and Cleveland (Norman) counties, and Bush won all three.

Evangelist Pat Robertson ran a strong third in Oklahoma with 21 percent of the vote, his best showing in any 1988 primary. Robertson ran particularly well in the rural counties of southern Oklahoma, carrying nine and finishing second in roughly a dozen more.

Oklahoma's Republican presidential primaries in the 1990s were less competitive. Bush won big in 1992; so did Dole in 1996. Pat Buchanan was a distant runner-up both times, carrying none of Oklahoma's 77 counties in 1992, and only one (McCurtain) in 1996. George W. Bush was also a convincing winner in 2000 as Oklahoma voted after his road to the nomination was already clear.

Oklahoma's Democratic primary has given a boost to the ambitions of candidates from Dixie—Al Gore in 1988, Bill Clinton in the 1990s, and Gore again in 2000. Gore exploited his Southern roots in 1988, his relatively conservative image, and his support from an array of big-name Oklahoma Democrats, featuring Sen. David L. Boren.

Gore rolled up his highest percentages that year in the rural counties of south-central Oklahoma, including historically Democratic "Little Dixie." But like Bush in the Republican primary voting, Gore also carried Oklahoma's major population centers. The only three counties not carried by Gore were won by Richard Gephardt, the most populous being Ottawa in the northeast corner of the state adjacent to Gephardt's native Missouri.

Clinton easily won Oklahoma's Democratic primary in the 1990s. His 70 percent share was one of his highest of the 1992 primary season, but his 76 percent share in 1996 was his lowest of the year. That fall, Republicans carried Oklahoma's electoral votes for the eighth straight election—a streak that was extended to nine in 2000.

Recent Oklahoma Primary Results

Oklahoma held its first presidential primary in 1988.

| Year | DEMOCRATS | | | REPUBLICANS | | |
	Turnout	Candidates	%	Turnout	Candidates	%
2000 (March 14)	134,850	AL GORE	69	124,809	GEORGE W. BUSH	79
		Bill Bradley	25		John McCain	10
1996 (March 12)	366,604	BILL CLINTON*	76	264,542	BOB DOLE	59
		Lyndon LaRouche	13		Pat Buchanan	22
		Elvena Lloyd-Duffie	11		Steve Forbes	14
1992 (March 10)	416,129	BILL CLINTON	70	217,721	GEORGE BUSH*	70
		Jerry Brown	17		Pat Buchanan	27
1988 (March 8)	392,727	AL GORE	41	208,938	GEORGE BUSH	37
		Richard Gephardt	21		Bob Dole	35
		Michael Dukakis	17		Pat Robertson	21
		Jesse Jackson	13			

Note: All candidates are listed that drew at least 10 percent of their party's primary vote. The names of winning candidates are capitalized. An asterisk (*) indicates an incumbent president.

The Oklahoma Rules

Oklahoma is one of the most Republican states in the country in voting for federal office. But with its presidential primary, this time on Feb. 3, Oklahoma could play a critical role in settling the 2004 Democratic nominating contest. Oklahoma holds a closed primary, with only registered Democrats allowed to vote in the Democratic primary and registered Republicans in the GOP primary. In January 2003, there were 1.1 million registered Democrats in Oklahoma and nearly 760,000 Republicans.

DEMOCRATS

THE CALENDAR
Primary Date (polling hours)   Feb. 3 (7 a.m.–7 p.m.)
Filing Deadline   Dec. 1, 2003
Filing Procedure   Candidates must pay a $2,500 filing fee to the state board of elections or submit petitions signed by 1% or 1,000 registered Democratic voters in each congressional district, whichever is lower.

THE DELEGATES
Number (% of national total)   47 (1.1%)
  Distribution:
  By congressional district   26 (5 or 6 per district)
  At-Large   9
  Pledged PEOs   5
  Superdelegates   7
Method of Allocation   Proportional—15% of vote needed to win a share of statewide or district delegates.

SOUTH CAROLINA

February 3

After years of watching the quadrennial trek of Republican presidential candidates to South Carolina, the state's Democrats are responding in 2004 with an early primary of their own. But they will be hard-pressed to be as successful as their GOP counterparts, who have made their primary a major event in Republican presidential politics.

During the 1980s and 1990s, South Carolina was the gateway to the South for Republican candidates—a New Hampshire below the Mason-Dixon line. But in 2000, it was more than that. South Carolina was the place where George W. Bush stopped John McCain and put his badly dented candidacy back on track toward the Republican nomination.

Bush campaigned in South Carolina with a gusto he had not shown in New Hampshire, where he lost badly to McCain. Attempting to mute McCain's reform image, the Texas governor campaigned across the Palmetto State as a "reformer with results." But his prime focus was on South Carolina's large conservative Republican base, which he successfully courted with a hard-hitting campaign.

Bush won the primary by nearly a dozen percentage points. But he built up roughly twice that margin in Greenville County, the leading source of GOP primary votes in the state and

the home of Bob Jones University, where Bush made a well-publicized appearance before the primary. Meanwhile, McCain carried only eight of South Carolina's 46 counties, four of them along the Atlantic coast where there is a large number of veterans and newcomers from other parts of the country.

The state's presidential primary is a legacy of Lee Atwater. A native South Carolinian, Atwater worked the state for Reagan and Bush and encouraged holding the primary at least a few days before Super Tuesday to dominate the news leading up to the Dixie event.

It has proved an effective party-building tool for South Carolina Republicans. Before its creation, turnout for statewide GOP primaries rarely exceeded the 35,000 voters that turned out for the party's gubernatorial contest in 1974, when the featured candidate was retired general William C. Westmoreland.

But the party's first presidential primary in 1980 drew nearly 150,000 voters. The second in 1988 attracted almost 200,000, and turnout for the GOP presidential primary in 2000 surpassed 570,000. In the process, the South Carolina GOP has expanded beyond white-collar professionals and well-heeled retirees to include Christian conservatives and converts from the Democratic Party.

Recent South Carolina Primary Results

South Carolina Republicans held their first presidential primary in 1980; South Carolina Democrats in 1992.

Year	DEMOCRATS			REPUBLICANS		
	Turnout	Candidates	%	Turnout	Candidates	%
2000 (Feb. 19)	—	NO PRIMARY		573,101	GEORGE W. BUSH	53
					John McCain	42
1996 (March 2)	—	NO PRIMARY		276,741	BOB DOLE	45
					Pat Buchanan	29
					Steve Forbes	13
					Lamar Alexander	10
1992 (March 7)	116,414	BILL CLINTON	63	148,840	GEORGE BUSH*	67
		Paul Tsongas	18		Pat Buchanan	26
1988 (March 5)	—	NO PRIMARY		195,292	GEORGE BUSH	49
					Bob Dole	21
					Pat Robertson	19
					Jack Kemp	11
1984	—	NO PRIMARY		—	NO PRIMARY	
1980 (March 8)	—	NO PRIMARY		145,501	RONALD REAGAN	55
					John Connally	30
					George Bush	15

Note: All candidates are listed that drew at least 10 percent of their party's primary vote. The names of winning candidates are capitalized. An asterisk (*) indicates an incumbent president.

While the state's presidential primary has often been crucial, it has never been particularly close. In 1980, Reagan beat runner-up Connally by a margin of nearly 2-to-1. Connally carried only a handful of counties, including Beaufort (with the coastal resort of Hilton Head).

Bush made a belated effort in the 1980 primary but finished a distant third. His leading backer in the state, former Nixon White House aide Harry Dent, sought to win votes for Bush by promoting him as "a good ol' Southern boy from Texas."

As a sitting vice president, Bush did better in 1988, sweeping every county in the state and winning almost as many votes as his rivals combined. Robertson had hoped to tap the state's large cadre of fundamentalist voters. According to exit polls, one-third of the Republican primary voters in South Carolina were born-again Christians. But Bush did nearly as well among these voters as Robertson.

In 1996, it was Dole who harnessed the momentum from victory in South Carolina, with a decisive triumph that covered all but three small counties in the northwest part of the state. Dole had lost three of the first five presidential primaries before the South Carolina primary in early March. After South Carolina, he was not to lose again.

As for the Democrats, they held their one and only presidential primary in 1992. It was a little-noticed event, won easily by the region's native son, Bill Clinton, that attracted barely 100,000 voters.

The South Carolina Rules

South Carolina Republicans have made themselves the New Hampshire of the South with their early primary. In 2004, Palmetto State Democrats will try to follow suit.

Their Feb. 3 event is to be run by the state Democratic party, which plans to establish up to 2,000 polling places around the state. Yet while the Republican primary was a predominantly white event, the Democratic contest this time could test the party's presidential candidates among a primary electorate that is nearly one-half black.

South Carolina does not have party registration, so any of the state's 2.1 million registered voters (as of October 2003) can participate in the Democratic primary if they sign a statement indicating they are a Democrat.

DEMOCRATS

THE CALENDAR

Primary Date (polling hours)	Feb. 3 (7 a.m.–7 p.m.)
Filing Deadline	Jan. 2
Filing Procedure	Candidates must pay a filing fee of $2,500 to the state party or submit petitions signed by at least 3,000 registered voters.

THE DELEGATES

Number (% of national total)	55 (1.3%)
Distribution:	
By congressional district	29 (from 4 to 6 per district)
At-Large	10
Pledged PEOs	6
Superdelegates	10
Method of Allocation	Proportional—15% of vote needed to win a share of the statewide or district delegates.

MICHIGAN

February 7

Leaders of both the Democratic and Republican parties in Michigan have never fully embraced the state's presidential primary, in large part because its open nature has produced an unpredictable environment and unwelcome results—at least for them.

In 1972, a flood of independents and Republicans entered the Democratic primary to vote for then Alabama governor George Wallace, who won easily despite the opposition of Democratic leaders.

In 2000, a flood of independents and Democrats entered the Republican primary to vote for John McCain, who won easily in spite of GOP Gov. John Engler's energetic support for George W. Bush.

For McCain, victory in Michigan was the last big hurrah of his upstart 2000 presidential campaign. He swept roughly 70 of Michigan's 83 counties, including Wayne (Detroit) and the major suburban counties of Macomb and Oakland. Bush was basically left with only the state's Republican strongholds, such as Ottawa (Holland) and Kent (Grand Rapids) counties, the latter the longtime congressional base of Gerald Ford.

Voter turnout for the Republican contest in 2000 exceeded one and one-quarter million, a record for a GOP presidential

primary in Michigan. Meanwhile, participation in the 1972 Democratic primary had approached 1.6 million, a record turnout on the Democratic side.

But often, party officials in Michigan have opted to do without the presidential primary, choosing to have tighter control over the process at the expense of light turnouts and sometimes controversy. In 1980, the Democratic statewide caucuses attracted only 16,000 voters. Strict rules on caucus participation that reduced turnout in 1980 were relaxed in 1984 so voters did not have to go through a pre-enrollment process. Still, the Democratic turnout barely reached 130,000.

Labor support for Walter Mondale provided him with a big win in the 1984 caucuses. But critics complained that the administration of the event was stacked in Mondale's favor. It was estimated that roughly 10 percent of the voting places were union halls. And separate ballot boxes were set up for each of the candidates, publicly discouraging any union member from casting their vote for anyone but Mondale.

In 1988, it was the Republicans who were the center of controversy. In a bid to be first on the calendar, the GOP held caucuses that were called the "Beirut of American politics." The caucuses revealed the organizational muscle of George Bush's

Recent Michigan Primary Results

Michigan held its first presidential primary in 1916, although no primary was held between 1928 and 1972.

	DEMOCRATS				REPUBLICANS		
Year	Turnout	Candidates	%	Turnout	Candidates	%
2000 (Feb. 22)	44,850	UNCOMMITTED	71	1,276,770	JOHN McCAIN	51
		Lyndon LaRouche	29		George W. Bush	43
1996 (March 19)	142,750	UNCOMMITTED	87	524,161	BOB DOLE	51
					Pat Buchanan	34
1992 (March 17)	585,972	BILL CLINTON	51	449,133	GEORGE BUSH*	67
		Jerry Brown	26		Pat Buchanan	25
		Paul Tsongas	17			
1988	—	NO PRIMARY		—	NO PRIMARY	
1984	—	NO PRIMARY		—	NO PRIMARY	
1980 (May 20)	78,424	UNCOMMITTED	46	595,176	GEORGE BUSH	57
		Jerry Brown	29		Ronald Reagan	32
		Lyndon LaRouche	13			
1976 (May 18)	708,666	JIMMY CARTER	43	1,062,814	GERALD FORD*	65
		Morris Udall	43		Ronald Reagan	34
1972 (May 16)	1,588,073	GEORGE WALLACE	51	336,743	RICHARD NIXON*	96
		George McGovern	27			
		Hubert Humphrey	16			

Note: All candidates are listed that drew at least 10 percent of their party's primary vote. The names of winning candidates are capitalized. An asterisk (*) indicates an incumbent president.

campaign and the potency of Pat Robertson's "invisible army." But the convoluted and often rancorous nature of the process led many party leaders to favor the primary format in 1992, a move that Democratic leaders were ready to join.

Pat Buchanan targeted Michigan and its large blue-collar constituency in both 1992 and 1996. His first time out Buchanan was thrown on the defensive, as the Bush campaign pounded away at the nationalistic-sounding Buchanan for driving a Mercedes-Benz and for referring to two Cadillacs he had bought as "lemons." It helped Bush win the Michigan primary for the second time. He had won the previous Republican primary in 1980 over Ronald Reagan and beat Buchanan even more convincingly in 1992.

Jerry Brown made his own effort on the Democratic side to harness the economic discontent of the working class. He regaled union members in his white turtleneck and a blue UAW (United Auto Workers) windbreaker. He managed to win the support of several union locals, and he even drew kind words from filmmaker Michael Moore, who chronicled the decline of Flint in the documentary *Roger and Me*.

But Brown was more successful attracting publicity than votes in the 1992 primary. Going from union hall to union hall, he stirred the passions of the assembled members, but he failed to expand his base beyond them. Clinton beat Brown by a margin of nearly 2-to-1.

Brown was gone by 1996, but Buchanan was back on the GOP side and ran better in Michigan than he had the first

time. Bob Dole easily won the primary vote statewide, but Buchanan's 34 percent vote share was the highest he would receive in the 1996 primaries.

The Michigan Rules

Michigan's on-again, off-again relationship with its presidential primary is off again in 2004, although Democrats will hold an event Feb. 7 that is termed a caucus but is in reality a party-run primary. Michigan Democrats are planning to set up roughly 600 polling places around the state, and also will allow voting by mail or on the Internet.

There is no party registration in Michigan. Any of the state's roughly 6.8 million registered voters (as of November 2002), as well as those who will turn 18 years old before the November general election, can participate in the Democratic voting if they sign a statement indicating they are a Democrat.

DEMOCRATS

THE CALENDAR
Primary Date (polling hours) — Feb. 7 (10 a.m.–4 p.m.)
Filing Deadline — Jan. 2
Filing Procedure — Democratic candidates must file a statement of candidacy with the state party to qualify for the caucus voting.

THE DELEGATES
Number (% of national total) — 152 (3.5%)
Distribution:
By congressional district — 83 (from 4 to 8 per district)
At-Large — 28
Pledged PEOs — 17
Superdelegates — 24
Method of Allocation — Proportional—15% of vote needed in the presidential caucus to win a share of statewide or district delegates.

WASHINGTON

February 7

Washington held a unique presidential primary in 2000, which included a Republican vote that George W. Bush won easily, a Democratic vote that Al Gore won handily, and a generic contest for other voters which featured all the candidates on one ballot. John McCain emerged the top vote-getter in that popularity contest.

The only real casualty of the late February votefest was Democrat Bill Bradley, who spent nearly a week of valuable campaign time in Washington in a bid to jumpstart his lagging candidacy. He failed, taking less than one-third of the Democratic primary ballots and carrying just one county (San Juan), which is basically a cluster of islands northeast of the Olympic Peninsula.

If a bit confusing in operation—only the Republican primary was for the selection of delegates—the whole affair was a hit at the ballot box, attracting more than 1.3 million Washington voters. But it will not be repeated in 2004, as the primary is being replaced by a caucus process for delegate selection.

As it is, the state's flirtation with a presidential primary has been brief, but the event has often been noteworthy. Before the first primary in May 1992, the Ross Perot phenomenon was plainly visible in the polls. In Washington, Perot's clout began to be felt at the ballot box, as he drew nearly 20 percent of the vote in both the Democratic and Republican primaries on

the basis of write-in votes. In both primaries, he carried San Juan County, a cluster of islands near the Canadian border. The strong vote for Perot overshadowed primary victories by President George Bush and Bill Clinton.

In 1996, the Washington primary went more to form. Dole was the easy winner on the Republican side; Clinton was virtually unopposed on the Democratic. But two-thirds of the

Recent Washington Primary Results

Washington held its first presidential primary in 1992.

	DEMOCRATS			REPUBLICANS		
Year	Turnout	Candidates	%	Turnout	Candidates	%
2000 (Feb. 29)	297,001	AL GORE	68	491,148	GEORGE W. BUSH	58
		Bill Bradley	31		John McCain	39
1996 (March 26)	98,946	BILL CLINTON*	99	120,684	BOB DOLE	63
					Pat Buchanan	21
1992 (May 19)	147,981	BILL CLINTON	42	129,655	GEORGE BUSH*	67
		Jerry Brown	23		Ross Perot#	20
		Ross Perot#	19		Pat Buchanan	10
		Paul Tsongas	13			

Note: All candidates are listed that drew at least 10 percent of their party's primary vote. The names of winning candidates are capitalized. An asterisk (*) indicates an incumbent president. A pound sign (#) indicates a write-in candidate. In 1996, there was also an unaffiliated ballot that listed candidates from both parties. A total of 444,619 votes were cast in this all-party primary, led by Democrat Bill Clinton with 51 percent and Republican Bob Dole with 28 percent.

A similar unaffiliated ballot was cast in 2000 by 521,218 voters, with Republican John McCain the favorite of 40 percent. Fellow Republican George W. Bush drew 23 percent of the unaffiliated votes, followed by Democrat Al Gore with 21 percent.

primary voters cast a third ballot that listed both Democratic and Republican candidates. The results of this unique balloting had nothing to do with the delegate-selection process but did prove prescient. Clinton won the all-party primary with 51 percent of the vote. In the general election, his winning share in Washington was 50 percent.

Conservative Republicans have long enjoyed the upper hand in the state's GOP caucus process. Barry Goldwater swept nearly all the Washington delegates in his successful 1964 insurgency. So did Ronald Reagan in his 1976 challenge to President Gerald Ford.

But neither was as traumatic as Pat Robertson's dominance in 1988, providing George Bush with his lone defeat in a day of one-sided primary victories. Robertson's success was based in part on his ability to organize many precincts that had been neglected by party regulars in the past. He took about 40 percent of the vote in a statewide straw vote held in conjunction with the March caucuses, and his supporters filled most of the delegation, even though Robertson's candidacy had collapsed nationally long before it was chosen.

The Washington Rules

Washington continues to be an early stop on the presidential nominating trail, but it has temporarily suspended the primary that has been held since 1992.

Any of the state's 3.2 million registered voters (the total as of November 2002) may participate in the Democratic precinct caucuses if they sign a statement indicating they are a Democrat.

DEMOCRATS

THE CALENDAR	
Precinct Caucuses	Feb. 7
County Conventions	April 24
Legislative District Caucuses	May 1
Congressional District Caucuses	May 29
State Convention	June 6
THE DELEGATES	
Number (% of national total)	95 (2.2%)
Distribution:	
By congressional district	49 (from 4 to 7 per district)
At-Large	17
Pledged PEOs	10
Superdelegates	19
Method of Allocation	Proportional—15% of vote needed at all stages of the caucus process.

MAINE

February 8

The Bush family is identified with Kennebunkport in particular and Maine in general. The family ties, as well as the political networking that went with it, no doubt helped George W. Bush win the state's Republican presidential primary in 2000—the only one in New England that he took from John McCain.

That "against the grain" quality underscored Maine's recent image as a place where political contrariness and individualism flourish. In the presidential elections of 1992 and 1996, Maine gave Ross Perot a higher percentage of the vote than any other state. In 1994 and 1998, Maine was the only state to elect an independent governor (Angus King). And in the Democratic caucuses in 1992, Maine gave Jerry Brown his first victory of the year, a narrow 1 percentage point victory over the New Hampshire primary winner and regional favorite son, Paul Tsongas.

Brown's victory broke a trend evident throughout the 1980s—that the winner in New Hampshire would also win the Maine vote several days later. In 1980, the double winner was President Jimmy Carter, whose New Hampshire and Maine victories put an early chill on Edward Kennedy in his New England backyard. In 1984, Gary Hart's stunning breakthrough win in New Hampshire yanked him from down-in-the-weeds status in Maine to a victorious 50-percent share of the caucus vote. In 1988, Michael Dukakis swept out of New Hampshire to win Maine's caucuses handily 12 days later.

Meanwhile, on the Republican side, Maine was long the personal preserve of George Bush. From his youth, he had vacationed at his family's seaside compound in Kennebunkport, establishing a personal relationship with Maine voters that helped launch him onto the presidential stage with an upset victory in a party-sponsored straw poll in late

Maine Primary Results

Maine held its first presidential primary in 1996.

	DEMOCRATS				REPUBLICANS	
Year	Turnout	Candidates	%	Turnout	Candidates	%
2000 (March 7)	64,279	AL GORE	54	96,624	GEORGE W. BUSH	51
		Bill Bradley	41		John McCain	44
1996 (March 5)	27,027	BILL CLINTON*	88	67,280	BOB DOLE	46
					Pat Buchanan	24
					Steve Forbes	15

Note: All candidates are listed who drew at least 10 percent of their party's primary vote. The names of winning candidates are capitalized. An asterisk (*) indicates an incumbent president.

1979. The following spring he swept virtually all of Maine's delegates, even as his first bid for the White House was crumbling nationally.

Maine was also in Bush's corner when he successfully pursued the GOP presidential nomination in 1988 and 1992. Dole won the state's first Republican presidential primary in 1996, although he drew a majority of the vote in only two counties. One of them, though, was Cumberland (Portland), the state's most populous. The primary runner-up, Pat Buchanan, could dent the 30 percent-mark in only two counties, the largest of which was historically blue-collar and heavily Democratic Androscoggin (Lewiston).

In 2000, both the Democratic and Republican primaries were comparatively close. The winners, Al Gore and George W. Bush, respectively, each carried 12 of Maine's 16 counties.

Three of the four counties that Bush lost to McCain, as well as all four counties that Gore lost to Bill Bradley, were along the Atlantic coast, where voters are apt to be more liberal and environmentally conscious than in the interior of the state. Bradley carried both the most populous county in the state (Cumberland) and the largest city (Portland). He also won the college town of Orono (home of the University of Maine) by one vote over Gore.

The Maine Rules

Maine's brief flirtation with a presidential primary has at least temporarily ended, even though the turnout on both the Democratic and Republican sides in 2000 was higher than the first time the primary was held in 1996. Participation in the Democratic caucuses is limited to registered Democrats, including new or unenrolled voters who register as Democrats on caucus day. As of November 2002, there were nearly 360,000 unenrolled voters in Maine, compared to nearly 300,000 Democrats and 280,000 Republicans.

DEMOCRATS

THE CALENDAR	
Municipal caucuses	Feb. 8
State convention	May 22–23
THE DELEGATES	
Number (% of national total)	35 (0.8%)
Distribution:	
By congressional district	16 (8 per district)
At-Large	5
Pledged PEOs	3
Superdelegates	11
Method of Allocation	Proportional—15% of vote needed to win a share of statewide or district delegates.

TENNESSEE

February 10

Tennessee has fielded a number of presidential candidates over the last half century—Republicans Howard Baker and Lamar Alexander on one side, Democrats Estes Kefauver and Al Gore on the other. But Gore was the only one to make it to Tennessee's presidential primary as an active candidate, both in 1988 and 2000.

The state did not have a primary when Kefauver ran for president in the 1950s, and Baker (in 1980) and Alexander (in 1996) both had withdrawn from the race before the Volunteer State voted.

But Gore showed what Tennessee would do for a popular native son, taking 72 percent of the 1988 Democratic primary vote—a higher percentage than any of the other major contenders won in their home states that year.

Despite Gore's dominance, Jesse Jackson was able to establish a toehold in southwest Tennessee. Jackson carried three counties, including vote-rich Shelby (Memphis), which has a population nearly 50 percent black. But Jackson had done better than that in the 1984 primary, when he ran against Walter Mondale and Gary Hart. In that earlier race, Jackson was also able to win populous Davidson (Nashville) and Ham-

ilton (Chattanooga) counties. Running against Gore, Jackson was trampled everywhere outside the Memphis area.

One reason was that Gore's presence on the 1988 ballot nearly doubled the Democratic primary turnout. Fewer than 325,000 voted in 1984, while more than 575,000 did so in 1988. It was a record high for a Democratic or Republican presidential primary in Tennessee.

With the active support of then-Gov. Ned McWherter, a skilled political operator with strong links to the rural courthouse crowd, Gore outpolled Jackson by a margin of at least 10-to-1 in many counties. In a few rural ones around Gore's home base of Carthage in Middle Tennessee, the margins approached 100-to-1.

Bill Clinton swept Tennessee's Democratic primary in 1992 with two-thirds of the vote. He boasted endorsements from much of the state party leadership, but not Gore, who was never especially close to Clinton before being tapped as his running mate in July 1992. As Arkansas governor, Clinton had made no secret of his preference for Dukakis over Gore in the 1988 primaries.

The classic Republican presidential primary in Tennessee took place in 1976 between President Gerald Ford and Ronald

Recent Tennessee Primary Results

Tennessee held its first presidential primary in 1972.

Year	DEMOCRATS			REPUBLICANS		
	Turnout	Candidates	%	Turnout	Candidates	%
2000 (March 14)	215,203	AL GORE	92	250,791	GEORGE W. BUSH	77
					John McCain	15
1996 (March 12)	137,797	BILL CLINTON*	89	289,386	BOB DOLE	51
		Uncommitted	11		Pat Buchanan	25
					Lamar Alexander	11
1992 (March 10)	318,482	BILL CLINTON	67	245,653	GEORGE BUSH*	73
		Paul Tsongas	19		Pat Buchanan	22
1988 (March 8)	576,314	AL GORE	72	254,252	GEORGE BUSH	60
		Jesse Jackson	21		Bob Dole	22
					Pat Robertson	13
1984 (May 1)	322,063	WALTER MONDALE	41	82,921	RONALD REAGAN*	91
		Gary Hart	29			
		Jesse Jackson	25			
1980 (May 6)	294,680	JIMMY CARTER*	75	195,210	RONALD REAGAN	74
		Edward Kennedy	18		George Bush	18
1976 (May 25)	334,078	JIMMY CARTER	78	242,535	GERALD FORD*	50
		George Wallace	11		Ronald Reagan	49
1972 (May 4)	492,721	GEORGE WALLACE	68	114,489	RICHARD NIXON*	96
		Hubert Humphrey	16			

Note: All candidates are listed that drew at least 10 percent of their party's primary vote. The names of winning candidates are capitalized. An asterisk (*) indicates an incumbent president.

Reagan, which pitted the two major power centers of Tennessee Republicanism against each other. Reagan swept the western half of the state, anchored by the burgeoning conservative suburbs around Memphis. Ford swept nearly all of the eastern half of the state, anchored by mountain counties that had been a bastion of racially moderate Republicanism since the Civil War. Nearly a quarter-million votes were cast and Ford won by less than 2,000.

GOP contests since then have been much more one-sided. Reagan beat George Bush in all of Tennessee's 95 counties in 1980. Bush came back to win all 95 in 1988. Bush's dominance was a bit surprising in that former senator William Brock, originally from the Chattanooga area, was the national chairman of Bob Dole's campaign.

Bush easily won the Tennessee primary again in 1992, even though Pat Buchanan sought to identify with the local economy by campaigning in a Saturn, a Tennessee-built car. Buchanan did not peak in Tennessee until his second try, when he took 25 percent of the GOP primary vote. But that was still less than half of the winning share in 1996 for Dole, who also ran better in Tennessee on his second try.

The Tennessee Rules

For the first time since 1992, Tennessee will not have one of its own on the state's presidential primary ballot. Former governor Lamar Alexander was on the Republican ballot in 1996, although he had withdrawn from the race before Tennessee's Super Tuesday primary. In 2000, Vice President Al Gore headlined the Democratic ballot.

Tennessee does not have party registration, so that any of the state's more than 3.4 million registered voters (as of June 2003) can vote in either the Democratic or Republican primary.

DEMOCRATS

THE CALENDAR	
Primary Date (polling hours)	Feb. 10 (open a minimum of 10 hours; close by 8 p.m. EST)
Filing Deadline	Jan. 6
Filing Procedure	By Jan. 6, the secretary of state compiles the names of nationally recognized candidates to be placed on the primary ballot. Other candidates must file petitions signed by 2,500 registered voters.

THE DELEGATES	
Number (% of national total)	85 (2.0%)
Distribution:	
By congressional district	45 (from 4 to 6 per district)
At-Large	15
Pledged PEOs	9
Superdelegates	16
Method of Allocation	Proportional—15% of vote needed to win a share of statewide or district delegates.

VIRGINIA

February 10

Primaries are not a regular part of the political scene in Virginia. They have only been employed twice at the presidential level—in 1988 by both parties and in 2000 by the Republicans alone.

That last GOP contest arguably gave George W. Bush his second most important victory of the Republican primary season, ranking just behind his critical triumph 10 days earlier in South Carolina. For Bush's victory in Virginia, along with his win the same day in Washington, blunted the momentum that John McCain had gained the previous week with primary successes in Michigan and Arizona.

Virginia's primary was open like the one in Michigan—allowing independents and Democrats to participate in the GOP balloting. But Virginia was never considered very friendly terrain for McCain. As in many other states, the party establishment—led by GOP Gov. James S. Gilmore III—was lined up behind Bush. And McCain made himself an object of controversy by attacking two Virginia-based pillars of the Christian Right, televangelists Pat Robertson and Jerry Falwell, as "agents of intolerance."

With the sparks flying, voter turnout for the primary surpassed 660,000—more than the combined number that participated in the Democratic and Republican primaries in 1988.

Bush prevailed by a margin of nearly 10 percentage points, as McCain was successful only on the fringes of the state. The former Naval Academy graduate carried Norfolk and Virginia Beach, with their strong navy presence, and the suburbs of Northern Virginia closest to Washington, D.C., including

Fairfax County, the most populous jurisdiction in the state. But Bush dominated primary balloting in the rest of the state.

That Virginia has held a presidential primary at all is in large part a tribute to Democratic Sen. Charles S. Robb. He was instrumental in the creation of the Democratic Leadership Council in the 1980s as a counterweight to party liberals, and he pushed the Southern regional primary in 1988 (commonly known as Super Tuesday) as a means toward nominating a Southern-oriented candidate for president. The event, though, proved to be a disappointment for its sponsors, both in Virginia and across the region.

Michael Dukakis and Jesse Jackson both won chunks of the South away from Al Gore, the favorite of many Democratic leaders across the region. And in Virginia, Jackson was an easy winner.

The Democratic vote, though, did highlight the demographic diversity of the state. Dukakis won the northern Virginia suburbs outside Washington, D.C. (the southern fringe of the megalopolis that extends from Boston to Washington). Gore won the rural white counties west of the Blue Ridge Mountains, rolling up his best numbers in Virginia's mountainous western panhandle, which borders Gore's home state of Tennessee. Jackson won almost everywhere else, from the old plantation country of the Piedmont to the bustling cities of the Tidewater, where a heavy military presence mingles with a large black population.

Jackson carried some of the prime symbols of the old Confederacy in 1988, including Richmond, which has a black majority, and Lexington, a small college town in the Shenan-

Recent Virginia Primary Results

Virginia held its first presidential primary in 1988.

| Year | DEMOCRATS | | | REPUBLICANS | | |
	Turnout	Candidates	%	Turnout	Candidates	%
2000 (Feb. 29)	—	NO PRIMARY		664,093	GEORGE W. BUSH	53
					John McCain	44
1996	—	NO PRIMARY		—	NO PRIMARY	
1992	—	NO PRIMARY		—	NO PRIMARY	
1988 (March 8)	364,899	JESSE JACKSON	45	234,142	GEORGE BUSH	53
		Al Gore	22		Bob Dole	26
		Michael Dukakis	22		Pat Robertson	14

Note: All candidates are listed who drew at least 10 percent of their party's primary vote. The names of winning candidates are capitalized.

doah Valley that is the burial place of Robert E. Lee. Virginia handed Jackson the highest vote share he received in any primary in 1988, even though it had the smallest black population of any primary state that he carried.

On the Republican side, the 1988 presidential primary spurred limited interest because it was a "beauty contest" that bound no delegates. George Bush dominated both the primary and the later caucuses that actually chose the delegates.

Probably the chief casualty of Bush's easy win was Pat Robertson. The son of a Virginia senator,

Robertson had based his nationwide television ministry in Virginia Beach. But Bush swept all of the state's 95 counties and 41 independent cities; Robertson could run no better than third, even in Virginia Beach. In the separate caucuses, Robertson controlled only the one held in Virginia Beach.

The Virginia Rules

Virginia held a presidential primary near the front of the calendar for the Republicans in 2000 and will do so again for the Democrats in 2004.

Virginia does not have party registration, so any of the state's roughly 4.2 million registered voters (as of November 2003) can participate in the Democratic primary.

DEMOCRATS

THE CALENDAR
Primary Date (polling hours)   Feb. 10 (6 a.m.–7 p.m.)
Filing Deadline   Dec. 12, 2003
Filing Procedure   Candidates must submit petitions to the state board of elections signed by at least 10,000 registered voters, with at least 400 from each congressional district. The petitions are sent on to the Democratic state party to be certified by Dec. 17.

THE DELEGATES
Number (% of national total)   96 (2.2%)
Distribution:
By congressional district   53 (4 to 6 per district)
At-Large   18
Pledged PEOs   11
Superdelegates   14
Method of Allocation   Proportional—15% of vote needed to win a share of statewide or district delegates.

DISTRICT OF COLUMBIA

February 14

The District of Columbia is heavily black and even more heavily Democratic. Yet while District Democrats have held a presidential primary since the 1950s, voter interest did not reach its apex until 1984, when Jesse Jackson made his first run for the Democratic presidential nomination.

Jackson's initial run for the White House that year helped boost turnout above the 100,000 mark, with Jackson the choice of two-thirds of the voters. Although participation declined in 1988, he fared even better with those who turned out—winning with 80 percent.

In both 1984 and 1988, Jackson won all but affluent northwest Washington. Bill Clinton swept all the city's wards in the 1992 primary, but barely 60,000 Democrats voted.

To gain a modicum of attention for the city in 2004, District officials moved the primary forward from its traditional May date to Jan. 13—six days before the Iowa caucuses. But the early event had not been sanctioned by the national

Recent District of Columbia Primary Results

The District of Columbia held its first presidential primary in 1952.

Year	DEMOCRATS			REPUBLICANS		
	Turnout	Candidates	%	Turnout	Candidates	%
2000 (May 2)	19,417	AL GORE	96	2,433	GEORGE W. BUSH John McCain	73 24
1996 (May 7)	20,959	BILL CLINTON*	98	2,987	BOB DOLE Uncommitted	76 13
1992 (May 5)	61,904	BILL CLINTON Paul Tsongas	74 10	5,235	GEORGE BUSH* Pat Buchanan	81 19
1988 (May 3)	86,052	JESSE JACKSON Michael Dukakis	80 18	6,720	GEORGE BUSH	88
1984 (May 1)	102,731	JESSE JACKSON Walter Mondale	67 26	5,692	RONALD REAGAN*	100
1980 (May 6)	64,150	EDWARD KENNEDY Jimmy Carter*	62 37	7,529	GEORGE BUSH John Anderson	66 27
1976 (May 4)	33,291	JIMMY CARTER Walter Fauntroy Morris Udall Walter Washington	32 30 21 16	—	NO PRIMARY	
1972 (May 2)	29,560	WALTER FAUNTROY Uncommitted	72 28	—	NO PRIMARY	
1968 (May 7)	92,114	ROBERT KENNEDY Hubert Humphrey	62 35	13,430	NIXON-ROCKEFELLER	90

Note: All candidates are listed that drew at least 10 percent of their party's primary vote. The names of winning candidates are capitalized. An asterisk (*) indicates an incumbent president. The remainder of the vote in the 1968 Democratic primary was cast for an independent Humphrey slate. The 1968 Republican primary was won by a joint slate pledged to Richard Nixon and Nelson Rockefeller; they divided the delegates.

Democratic Party. As a result, the Democratic primary this time will be nonbinding, while delegate selection will reflect the results of a separate caucus process that begins in mid-February.

Since 1968, victories in the District's Democratic presidential primary have tended to come in pairs. Jackson won twice. So did Clinton. Together, the Kennedy brothers also won a pair—Robert in 1968, Edward in 1980; each with 62 percent of the District's primary vote.

By and large, District Republicans are a very small and moderate lot. George Bush won the city's GOP primary in 1980, 1988 and 1992. Bob Dole won handily in 1996.

With few exceptions, conservative GOP candidates have either fared poorly or have not even tried to win delegates from the District. Ronald Reagan bypassed the Republican primary in both 1976 and 1980. And in spite of his roots in the Washington area, Pat Buchanan could not crack 20 percent in either of his runs for the GOP presidential nomination in the 1990s.

Meanwhile, John McCain drew nearly 25 percent of the vote in the District's Republican primary in 2000, even though he had quit the race nearly two months earlier.

The District of Columbia Rules

Whatever attention the heavily Democratic District of Columbia receives in the 2004 election is likely to be limited to the party's nonbinding presidential primary to be held Jan. 13—six days before the Iowa caucuses. Polls are to be open in the District from 7 a.m. to 8 p.m. Democratic delegates, however, will be chosen to reflect the result of a separate caucus process that begins Feb. 14.

Participation in both the primary and caucus voting is limited to registered Democratic voters. As of October 2003, there were roughly 260,000 registered Democrats in the District of Columbia and 25,000 Republicans. For delegate-selection purposes, Democrats divide the city into two districts.

DEMOCRATS

THE CALENDAR	
Ward Caucuses	Feb. 14
District Caucuses	March 6
"State" Committee Meeting	April 29
Filing Deadline	Jan. 13
Filing Procedure	To participate in the caucuses, candidates must submit petitions signed by at least 2,000 registered Democrats (at least 1,000 in each district) to the D.C. Democratic Party or pay a $1,500 filing fee.
THE DELEGATES	
Number (% of national total)	38 (0.9%)
Distribution:	
By district	10 (5 per district)
At-Large	4
Pledged PEOs	2
Superdelegates	22
Method of Allocation	Proportional—15% of vote needed at all levels of the caucus process.

NEVADA

February 14

The mention of Nevada often conjures up images of garish gambling palaces, quickie marriages and speedy divorces. And when it comes to presidential nominating politics, there is an open climate as well.

Nevada has been willing to bet its chips on candidates that face long odds at the national level, or to vote "no" on all the candidates when dissatisfied with the choices. It has even turned thumbs down on its presidential primary, holding ones in 1976 and 1980, then taking an hiatus until 1996, before abandoning the primary again in 2000 and 2004.

Nevada's freewheeling behavior was evident from the start. In 1976, its primary voters opted for two Californians, Jerry Brown and Ronald Reagan, neither of whom was to win his party's nomination that year. Faced with a choice in 1980 between Jimmy Carter and Edward Kennedy, one-third of Nevada primary voters cast ballots for the line marked "None of These Candidates."

In 1988, Nevada Democrats gave a first-round caucus victory to Al Gore, one of only two caucus states that Gore was to win on his first try for the White House. (Wyoming was the other.) Gore had help from his Senate colleague, Harry Reid, and won the state by combining support in Reid's home base of Clark County (Las Vegas) with a strong showing in many of the more conservative, lightly populated "Cow Counties" to the north.

But the real action that year was on the Republican side, where well-organized and procedure-savvy supporters of Pat Robertson not only took over the caucus process but stayed to

Recent Nevada Primary Results

Nevada held its first presidential primary in 1976, but has held only one since 1980.

Year	DEMOCRATS			REPUBLICANS		
	Turnout	Candidates	%	Turnout	Candidates	%
2000	—	NO PRIMARY		—	NO PRIMARY	
1996 (March 26)	—	NO PRIMARY		140,637	BOB DOLE	52
					Steve Forbes	19
					Pat Buchanan	15
1992	—	NO PRIMARY		—	NO PRIMARY	
1988	—	NO PRIMARY		—	NO PRIMARY	
1984	—	NO PRIMARY		—	NO PRIMARY	
1980 (May 27)	66,948	JIMMY CARTER*	38	47,395	RONALD REAGAN	83
		"None"	34		"None"	10
		Edward Kennedy	29			
1976 (May 25)	75,242	JERRY BROWN	53	47,749	RONALD REAGAN	66
		Jimmy Carter	23		Gerald Ford*	29

Note: All candidates are listed that drew at least 10 percent of their party's primary vote. The names of winning candidates are capitalized. An asterisk (*) indicates an incumbent president.

45

contend for control of the state GOP apparatus. In the end, Robertson's followers won a majority of the Nevada delegation.

In 1992, Nevada Democrats were back in Brown's corner, giving him a first-round caucus victory over Bill Clinton. While campaigning in Nevada, Brown took an unusual step to cultivate labor support, grabbing a picket sign and joining striking culinary workers outside a Las Vegas hotel. The Culinary Union, a major factor in a state dependent on the tourist industry, returned the favor with a caucus-eve endorsement of Brown.

In 1996, the presidential primary was back, but only for the Republicans, and only with balloting by mail. Bob Dole won the late March event easily, a vote that also served to underscore the booming population growth of the state in general and the Republican Party in particular. Roughly 140,000 GOP primary ballots were cast, nearly double the number in any previous presidential primary in Nevada, Democrat or Republican. Slightly more than half the ballots were cast in Clark County and one-quarter in Washoe County (Reno).

The Nevada Rules

Nevada's on-again, off-again relationship with its presidential primary is off-again in 2004.

Democrats will be electing delegates through a caucus process that begins in mid-February and culminates with the selection of delegates at the state convention in April.

Participation in the Democratic caucuses is limited to registered Democrats, although voters may register as Democrats at the caucuses. As of October 2003, there were roughly 375,000 Republicans and 365,000 Democrats in Nevada.

DEMOCRATS

THE CALENDAR	
Precinct Caucuses	Feb. 14
County Conventions	March 13
State Convention	April 17
THE DELEGATES	
Number (% of national total)	32 (0.7%)
Distribution:	
By congressional district	16 (4 to 6 per district)
At-Large	5
Pledged PEOs	3
Superdelegates	8
Method of Allocation	Proportional—15% of vote at state convention needed to win a share of statewide or district delegates.

46

WISCONSIN

February 17

If Virginia can claim to be the "mother of presidents," then Wisconsin could boast that it is the "mother of presidential primaries." It was from the progressive agenda of Wisconsin's legendary Robert M. La Follette that presidential primaries got a major boost, and Wisconsin initiated one of the first in 1912.

For more than a half-century afterwards, the Badger State was a necessary stop for candidates traveling the primary route to their party's nomination. But the recent proliferation of primaries, especially early ones, has robbed Wisconsin's contest of much of its luster.

In 1968, Wisconsin voted second after New Hampshire. But in 2000, more than two dozen states held primaries in between the two. Reflecting the old saying "if you can't beat them, join them," Wisconsin has moved its traditional early spring primary forward in 2004 to mid-February.

In the realm of presidential primaries, few states have as rich a heritage as Wisconsin or as distinctive a voting process—the state's long-standing open primary rules make it effortless to vote in either party's primary.

Wisconsin has gained an image as an outpost of Midwestern liberalism. But that is based largely on just two Democratic primaries—Eugene McCarthy's victory in 1968 and George McGovern's in 1972. Both were fueled by opposition to the Vietnam War.

The list is longer of liberal contenders who needed a breakthrough win in Wisconsin and failed to get it. Democrats Morris Udall in 1976, Jerry Brown in 1980, and Jesse Jackson in 1988, as well as Republican John Anderson in 1980, all made Wisconsin either the cornerstone of their campaigns or viewed it as a major target of opportunity. Yet all four lost the Wisconsin primary.

Recent Wisconsin Primary Results

Wisconsin held its first presidential primary in 1912.

	DEMOCRATS				REPUBLICANS		
Year	Turnout	Candidates	%	Turnout	Candidates	%
2000 (April 4)	371,196	AL GORE	89	495,769	GEORGE W. BUSH	69
					John McCain	18
1996 (March 19)	356,168	BILL CLINTON*	98	576,575	BOB DOLE	52
					Pat Buchanan	34
1992 (April 7)	772,596	BILL CLINTON	37	482,248	GEORGE BUSH*	76
		Jerry Brown	34		Pat Buchanan	16
		Paul Tsongas	22			
1988 (April 5)	1,014,782	MICHAEL DUKAKIS	48	359,294	GEORGE BUSH	82
		Jesse Jackson	28			
		Al Gore	17			
1984 (April 3)	635,768	GARY HART	44	294,813	RONALD REAGAN*	95
		Walter Mondale	41			
1980 (April 1)	629,619	JIMMY CARTER*	56	907,853	RONALD REAGAN	40
		Edward Kennedy	30		George Bush	30
		Jerry Brown	12		John Anderson	27
1976 (April 6)	740,528	JIMMY CARTER	37	591,812	GERALD FORD*	55
		Morris Udall	36		Ronald Reagan	44
		George Wallace	12			
1972 (April 4)	1,128,584	GEORGE McGOVERN	30	286,444	RICHARD NIXON*	97
		George Wallace	22			
		Hubert Humphrey	21			
		Edmund Muskie	10			
1968 (April 2)	733,002	EUGENE McCARTHY	56	489,853	RICHARD NIXON	80
		Lyndon Johnson*	35		Ronald Reagan	10

Note: All candidates are listed that drew at least 10 percent of their party's primary vote. The names of winning candidates are capitalized. An asterisk (*) indicates an incumbent president.

It would be closer to the mark to say that Wisconsin has a soft spot for outsiders. George Wallace bolted onto the national scene in 1964 by taking one-third of the Democratic primary vote in Wisconsin after campaigning against the pending civil rights bill. Jimmy Carter's dark-horse candidacy also was pushed along by a Wisconsin victory in 1976 (over Udall). Gary Hart edged Walter Mondale in the 1984 Democratic primary (a nonbinding primary that year by national party fiat). And Brown nearly beat Bill Clinton in the state in 1992.

Brown had focused on Wisconsin early, knowing its terrain and proclivities well from his 1980 run. He carried a swath of counties on the eastern side of the state, from Racine through the Milwaukee suburbs north to Brown County (Green Bay). But Brown was hurt badly by his inability to win decisively in Dane County (Madison), home to the University of Wisconsin and a legion of liberal activists. McCarthy, McGovern, and Udall had all carried Dane County by more than 20,000 votes; Brown won it by barely 2,000.

That enabled Clinton to win with a coalition of city and countryside. He carried Milwaukee County, source of nearly one-quarter of the Democratic primary vote, and swept the vast majority of counties in rural Wisconsin.

Clinton's winning 37 percent share of the primary vote was more than double the total that his fellow Southerner, Al Gore, had drawn in Wisconsin four years earlier. Looking for a post-Super Tuesday toehold in the Frost Belt, Gore came to Wisconsin calling for higher dairy price supports. But he finished third statewide, although he did leapfrog Jesse Jackson for second place in a number of rural counties.

Wisconsin's Democratic primary is usually where the action has been over the years. Only three times since 1956—in 1980, 1996, and 2000—have more votes been cast on the Republican side of the ballot. The reason in 1996 was obvious; there was no contest in the Democratic primary. Pat Buchanan took advantage of the situation to win his second-highest vote share of the primary season (33.8 percent—just one-tenth of a percentage point behind his showing the same day in Michigan). But Buchanan could carry only one small county in Wisconsin and was unable to crack 40 percent of the vote in any of the more populous ones.

The more compelling Republican primary was in 1980. Stakes were high for John Anderson, who had lost the primary in his home state of Illinois two weeks earlier. But Ronald Reagan won the Wisconsin vote comfortably, giving Anderson a final nudge out of the GOP race and reducing George Bush's already slim prospects for that year's GOP nomination.

Bush ran virtually even with Reagan in the Milwaukee area and in prosperous Republican farm country in the south-central part of Wisconsin. But Reagan won almost everywhere else, including most of the smaller industrial centers. Anderson carried only three counties, all containing a branch of the University of Wisconsin.

The Wisconsin Rules

Once again Wisconsin will hold one of the earliest presidential primaries in the election year. But it will vote in mid-February this time, rather than its traditional date in early April.

Wisconsin does not have a system of statewide voter registration, and any voter can cast a ballot in either the Democratic or Republican primary.

DEMOCRATS

THE CALENDAR

Primary Date (polling hours)	Feb. 17; (polls must open by 9 a.m., close at 8 p.m.)
Filing Deadline	Jan. 6
Filing Procedure	By Dec. 9, a committee of party leaders will certify the names of Democratic candidates to be placed on the ballot. Other candidates must submit petitions signed by 1,000 voters in each congressional district to the state board of elections.

THE DELEGATES

Number (% of national total)	87 (2.0%)
Distribution:	
By congressional district	47 (5 to 8 per district)
At-Large	16
Pledged PEOs	9
Superdelegates	15
Method of Allocation	Proportional—15% of vote needed to win a share of statewide or district delegates.

HAWAII

February 24

If it were simply a matter of the candidates' personal preference, Hawaii most likely would be glutted with presidential aspirants canvassing its beaches for the state's late-winter caucuses. But the small size of the delegate harvest and the absence of a presidential primary to attract some media attention has kept Hawaii a distant sideshow in the presidential nominating process.

Hawaii Republicans sought to make a splash in 1988 by scheduling their precinct caucuses in late January—before even Iowa had spoken. And for much of 1987, Bob Dole looked like the best bet to win the early event. He was the choice of the moderate element dominant within the Hawaii GOP.

But in the month preceding the caucuses, the party was inundated with new registrants, most wanting to vote for evangelist Pat Robertson. The number of card-carrying Republicans swelled from barely 11,000 to more than 18,000. State GOP officials were stunned by the unexpected influx. First, they postponed the caucuses indefinitely. Then, with Robertson denouncing "banana republic" politics, the vote was rescheduled for a week after the original date.

When the caucuses were finally held in early February, an estimated 4,000 to 5,000 Republicans showed up and voted overwhelmingly for Robertson delegates to the June state convention. His candidacy had collapsed by the time the state convention was held, but his supporters pushed through a platform that emphasized the conservative "family values" that he had espoused in his campaign.

Robertson's control of the state GOP, though, proved temporary. Party regulars regained the upper hand in 1992 and the state party issued no platform at all.

For most of the state's history, Hawaii—with its rainbow-hued electorate—has not harbored any affection for ideological activism on either end of the political spectrum. Hawaii Republicans gave President Gerald Ford all but one of their delegates in 1976 and were slow to embrace Ronald Reagan in 1980. Even as opposition to Reagan was crumbling nationally in the spring of 1980, the state party selected a predominantly uncommitted delegation to send to the national convention in Detroit.

Democratic caucus voters in Hawaii have traditionally followed the wishes of their party leadership. Typical was the situation in 1988. The multiracial nature of Hawaii's political landscape seemed tailor-made for Jesse Jackson. But less than a week before the early March caucuses, then-Gov. John Waihee III endorsed his gubernatorial colleague, Michael Dukakis. A stream of endorsements for Dukakis followed from lesser Democratic elected officials on the islands. And when the caucuses were held, Dukakis won easily with 55 percent of the nearly 5,000 votes cast.

Four years later the result was similar. Waihee threw his support to another gubernatorial colleague, Bill Clinton, who also won a majority of the Democratic caucus vote.

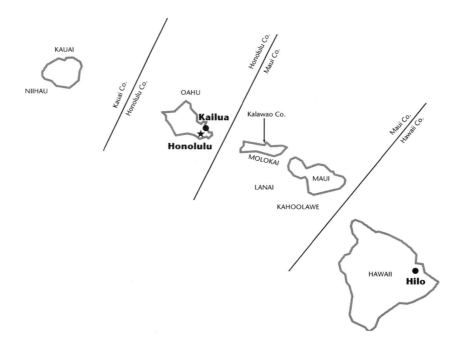

The Hawaii Rules

Hawaii Democrats allocate delegates on the basis of a presidential preference vote taken at the Feb. 24 precinct caucuses.

There is no formal system of party registration in Hawaii. "Card-carrying" Democrats—which numbered about 21,000 in November 2003—may participate in the party's precinct caucuses, as well as any of Hawaii's 675,000 registered voters (as of November 2002) who are willing to sign a statement at the caucuses indicating they are a Democrat.

DEMOCRATS

THE CALENDAR	
Precinct Caucuses	Feb. 24 (7 p.m.)
State Convention	May 30
Filing Deadline	Jan. 28
Filing Procedure	Candidates must pay a qualifying fee of $1,500 to the state Democratic Party or declare themselves indigent and submit petitions signed by 100 members of the state Democratic Party in order to compete in the caucuses.

THE DELEGATES	
Number (% of national total)	29 (0.7%)
Distribution:	
By congressional district	13 (6 in 1st District, 7 in 2nd)
At-Large	4
Pledged PEOs	3
Superdelegates	9
Method of Allocation	Proportional—15% of vote needed in presidential preference vote taken at the precinct caucuses in order to win a share of statewide or district delegates.

IDAHO

February 24

Idaho has held a presidential primary for the last quarter century, but never has it been competitive. None of the Democratic or Republican contests have been decided by less than 20 percentage points.

That is largely because Idaho votes late in the primary season, well after the field has been winnowed. But Idaho voters are far from a rubber stamp. Nearly 40 percent of those who participated in the 1992 and 1996 Republican primaries withheld their votes from the presumptive nominees, George Bush and Bob Dole, respectively.

Meanwhile, Bill Clinton won Idaho's Democratic primary in 1992 with less than a majority of the vote, and actually lost resort-oriented Blaine County (Sun Valley) to a line designated "None of the Names Shown."

Idaho Democrats in recent years have held both a primary and a caucus. The caucus process that begins now in late February is to select delegates, while Democrats use the May primary as a "beauty contest" to reflect broader popular sentiment.

The low-turnout caucuses tend to be influenced by liberal elements within the Democratic Party. In 1992, for instance, Clinton ran a distant fourth in the caucus vote of roughly 3,000 Democrats. The winner was Sen. Tom Harkin of Iowa, who ran as an unapologetic New Deal liberal. In 2000, when the turnout

Recent Idaho Primary Results

Idaho held its first presidential primary in 1976.

		DEMOCRATS			REPUBLICANS	
Year	Turnout	Candidates	%	Turnout	Candidates	%
2000 (May 23)	35,688	AL GORE	76	158,446	GEORGE W. BUSH	73
		"None"	16		Alan Keyes	19
1996 (May 28)	40,228	BILL CLINTON*	88	118,715	BOB DOLE	62
		"None"	12		Pat Buchanan	22
					"None"	10
1992 (May 26)	55,124	BILL CLINTON	49	115,502	GEORGE BUSH*	63
		"None"	29		"None"	23
		Jerry Brown	17		Pat Buchanan	13
1988 (May 24)	51,370	MICHAEL DUKAKIS	73	68,275	GEORGE BUSH	81
		Jesse Jackson	16		"None"	10
1984 (May 22)	54,722	GARY HART	58	105,687	RONALD REAGAN*	92
		Walter Mondale	30			
1980 (May 27)	50,482	JIMMY CARTER*	62	134,879	RONALD REAGAN	83
		Edward Kennedy	22			
		"None"	12			
1976 (May 25)	74,405	FRANK CHURCH	79	89,793	RONALD REAGAN	74
		Jimmy Carter	12		Gerald Ford*	25

Note: All candidates are listed that drew at least 10 percent of their party's primary vote. The names of winning candidates are capitalized. An asterisk (*) indicates an incumbent president.

was half as large, Bill Bradley took one-third of the state convention delegates elected in the first round of caucus voting—his best showing in any caucus state outside Iowa. In the process, Bradley carried several rural Idaho counties, among them liberal Blaine County, which includes the resort town of Sun Valley.

Idaho Republicans have stuck with the primary as their principal method of delegate selection. The backbone of GOP strength is the farm and ranch country of southeast Idaho, a heavily Mormon area that ranks among the most conservative in the country. In his 1976 primary victory over President Gerald Ford, Ronald Reagan carried a number of counties in the region with more than 80 percent of the vote.

Moderate Republicans are more apt to be found in the Boise area. In the 1980 GOP primary, John Anderson drew nearly one out of every five ballots in Ada County (Boise), even though he had already bolted the party to mount his independent presidential campaign. Reagan, though, still won handily in the Boise area, as he did statewide.

The Idaho Rules

Idaho is a small part of the huge February vote, holding Democratic caucuses on Feb. 24 that begin the state party's delegate-selection process.

Idaho does not have party registration. As of March 2003, the state had slightly more than 610,000 registered voters who can participate in either party's delegate-selection process, although participants in the Democratic county caucuses must sign a statement indicating they are a Democrat.

DEMOCRATS

THE CALENDAR	
County Caucuses	Feb. 24
State Convention	June 19
THE DELEGATES	
Number (% of national total)	23 (0.5%)
Distribution:	
By congressional district	12 (6 per district)
At-Large	4
Pledged PEOs	2
Superdelegates	5
Method of Allocation	Proportional—15% of vote needed at all levels of the process.

UTAH

February 24

Utah's first presidential primary in 2000 was something of a dud. The competitive stage of the nominating campaign was over in both parties when the primary was held in March. And Utah voters could not even cast a complimentary vote for the state's senior senator, Orrin G. Hatch, who had quit the Republican race several weeks earlier.

As it was, probably the most noteworthy element of the GOP primary was Alan Keyes' solid second-place finish. He won 30 percent of the vote in Utah County (Provo), where he personally campaigned, and took 21 percent of the vote statewide—Keyes' best showing in any contest in the 2000 primary season.

Utah has not funded a presidential primary for 2004. But Democrats will be back with a party-run primary of their own. The question is whether the event will draw much voter interest. Barely 15,000 voters cast ballots in the Democratic primary in 2000, and the party is hardly a growth stock these days in the Beehive State.

Democrats have not elected a governor in Utah since 1980, a

Recent Utah Primary Results

Utah held its first presidential primary in 2000.

		DEMOCRATS			REPUBLICANS	
Year	Turnout	Candidates	%	Turnout	Candidates	%
2000	15,687	AL GORE	80	91,053	GEORGE W. BUSH	63
(March 10)		Bill Bradley	20		Alan Keyes	21
					John McCain	14

Note: All candidates are listed that drew at least 10 percent of their party's primary vote. The names of winning candidates are capitalized.

U.S. senator since 1970, or carried the state in a presidential election since 1964. In five of the last seven presidential elections, Utah has given the Republican presidential nominee a higher share of the vote than any other state. (It was third in 2000 behind Wyoming and Idaho).

Despite its large membership, the Utah Republican Party has often been of one mind when selecting a presidential nominee. In the party's great moderate-conservative nominating contests of the last half century, Utah consistently cast its vote for the conservative—from Robert A. Taft in 1952 to Barry Goldwater in 1964 to Ronald Reagan in 1976.

Utah's smaller cadre of Democrats have been more eclectic in their tastes. In 1984, the party's caucus attendees favored Gary Hart of neighboring Colorado. But in 1988 and 1992,

Utah Democrats went for two Massachusetts natives, Michael Dukakis and Paul Tsongas, respectively. In 1992, Tsongas swept the populous four-county "Front Range" and took 33 percent of the 31,638 caucus votes cast statewide to defeat Jerry Brown (28 percent) and Bill Clinton (18 percent) in the early March balloting.

Yet over the years, Utah has rarely been more than a blip on the radar screen during the nominating season. In 1988, Utah's GOP caucuses were conducted so late in the process that the party ended up holding a straw vote to gauge preferences for vice president rather than for president. In 1996, Utah Republicans did not bother to hold a straw vote at all, either for president or vice president.

The Utah Rules

Utah will be one of three Western states to vote on Feb. 24, the lone Democratic action anywhere in the country between Feb. 17 and March 2. Democrats in Hawaii and Idaho Feb. 24 will hold caucuses; Utah Democrats will have a party-run primary.

Participation in the presidential primary is open to any of Utah's roughly 1.1 million registered voters (as of April 2003), plus any other U.S. citizen living in the state who will be 18 years old at the time of the November 2004 general election. Democratic primary voting will take place at roughly 110 libraries around the state. Voters have the option of casting their ballot on the Internet, either from their home or at a polling place.

DEMOCRATS

THE CALENDAR

Primary Date (polling hours) — Feb. 24 (noon–8 p.m.)
Filing Deadline — Jan. 8
Filing Procedure — Candidates must pay a $2,500 filing fee to the state Democratic Party or submit petitions signed by at least 4,500 registered Democratic voters statewide, with at least 1,500 from each of the three congressional districts. (As of late 2003, there were roughly 50,000 registered Democrats in Utah.)

THE DELEGATES

Number (% of national total) — 29 (0.7%)
Distribution:
By congressional district — 15 (15 per district)
At-large — 5
Pledged PEOs — 3
Superdelegates — 6
Method of Allocation — Proportional—15% of vote needed to win a share of statewide or district delegates.

SUPER TUESDAY

California	56	Minnesota	68
Connecticut	59	New York	70
Georgia	61	Ohio	73
Maryland	64	Rhode Island	76
Massachusetts	66	Vermont	78

CALIFORNIA

March 2

Hubert Humphrey once called California "the Super Bowl of the primaries." But during the last quarter century, the nation's most populous state has been anything but that. The proliferation of primaries that increased the clout of Iowa and New Hampshire at the beginning of the calendar reduced California's significance at the end.

A generation ago, California's late-inning position often lent drama to the proceedings in one party or the other. The state's 1964 primary was critical for the Republicans; the 1968 and 1972 events offered high drama for Democrats.

But for more than two decades after that, the California primary receded to the status of epilogue. In 1976, it was a mere formality, thanks to the home-state candidacies of then-governor Jerry Brown and former governor Ronald Reagan. In the presidential contests since then, California has voted long after the nominees in both parties were all but certain, or in the case of 2000, when its early March vote helped wrap up the nominations for Republican George W. Bush and Democrat Al Gore.

Over the years, the California primary has been hospitable to political outsiders willing to take on their national party establishment. Two of the Kennedy brothers—Robert and Edward—won the Democratic primary; so did George McGovern and Gary Hart. Barry Goldwater won the 1964 Republican primary, a pivotal triumph for him and for conservative insurgents attempting to take over the party.

California voters have also been willing to support the presidential ambitions of their governors, giving Democrat Brown and Republican Reagan one-sided primary victories (Brown in 1976; Reagan each time he was on the primary ballot since 1968). In national terms, both Brown and Rea-

Recent California Primary Results

California held its first presidential primary in 1912.

	DEMOCRATS				REPUBLICANS		
Year	Turnout	Candidates	%	Turnout	Candidates	%
2000 (March 7)	2,654,114	AL GORE Bill Bradley	81 18	2,847,921	GEORGE W. BUSH John McCain	61 35
1996 (March 26)	2,523,062	BILL CLINTON*	93	2,452,312	BOB DOLE Pat Buchanan	66 18
1992 (June 2)	2,863,609	BILL CLINTON Jerry Brown	47 40	2,156,464	GEORGE BUSH* Pat Buchanan	74 26
1988 (June 7)	3,138,734	MICHAEL DUKAKIS Jesse Jackson	61 35	2,240,387	GEORGE BUSH Bob Dole	83 13
1984 (June 5)	2,970,903	GARY HART Walter Mondale Jesse Jackson	39 35 18	1,874,975	RONALD REAGAN*	100
1980 (June 3)	3,363,969	EDWARD KENNEDY Jimmy Carter* Unpledged	45 38 11	2,564,072	RONALD REAGAN John Anderson	80 14
1976 (June 8)	3,409,701	JERRY BROWN Jimmy Carter	59 20	2,450,511	RONALD REAGAN Gerald Ford*	65 35
1972 (June 6)	3,564,518	GEORGE McGOVERN Hubert Humphrey	44 39	2,283,922	RICHARD NIXON*	90
1968 (June 4)	3,181,753	ROBERT KENNEDY Eugene McCarthy No Preference	46 42 12	1,525,091	RONALD REAGAN	100

Note: All candidates are listed that drew at least 10 percent of their party's primary vote. The names of winning candidates are capitalized. An asterisk (*) indicates an incumbent president. There was no direct vote for candidates in the 1984 Democratic primary; results are based on the vote for delegates. In 2000, there was also an unaffiliated ballot that listed candidates from all parties. A total of 2,082,124 votes were cast in this all-party primary, led by Republican John McCain with 38 percent, Democrat Al Gore with 22 percent, and Republican George W. Bush with 21 percent.

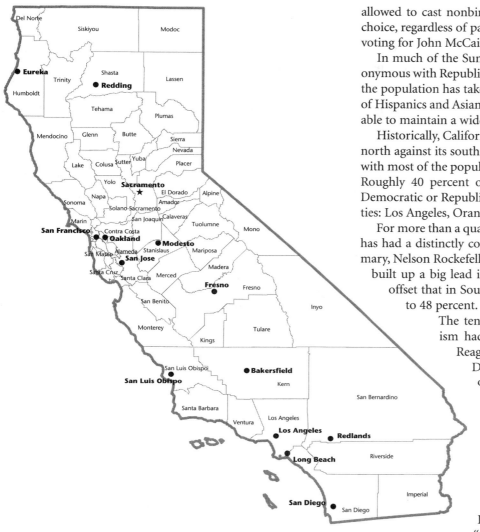

allowed to cast nonbinding ballots for the candidate of their choice, regardless of party. Roughly 2 million did, the plurality voting for John McCain.

In much of the Sun Belt, population growth has been synonymous with Republican growth. But not in California, where the population has taken on a rainbow hue, with a large influx of Hispanics and Asians. Since the 1930s, Democrats have been able to maintain a wide voter registration edge.

Historically, California elections often have pitted the state's north against its south. But that has become an unfair contest, with most of the population growth concentrated in the south. Roughly 40 percent of the vote in any California primary, Democratic or Republican, is cast in just three southern counties: Los Angeles, Orange, and San Diego.

For more than a quarter century, Southern California's GOP has had a distinctly conservative cast. In the pivotal 1964 primary, Nelson Rockefeller swept the San Francisco Bay area and built up a big lead in the north. But Goldwater more than offset that in Southern California to win the primary, 52 to 48 percent.

The tenor of Southern California Republicanism had not changed that much by 1976, as Reagan swept Los Angeles, Orange, and San Diego counties with at least two-thirds of the vote. President Gerald Ford carried just two counties, San Francisco and its affluent suburban neighbor, Marin.

Democratic primary results sometime, follow the same north-south variation. Both McGovern in 1972 and Hart in 1984 fashioned their victories in Northern California, particularly in the Bay area, which includes the high-tech "Silicon Valley." Both lost Los Angeles County, the anchor of Southern California.

Yet in the 1988 Democratic primary between Michael Dukakis and Jesse Jackson, there was evidence of another faultline developing between the coastal counties and those inland. Jackson ran relatively well in many of the coastal counties where most liberal Democrats are found. But Dukakis dominated in the more conservative counties to the east across the coast range and swamped Jackson statewide.

Some of the same dynamics were present in the Democratic primary four years later. Brown carried many of the environmentally conscious coastal counties in the Bay area and north, the usual starting point for any liberal candidate running in California. But Brown fell short statewide, in part because he lost several counties in the Bay area, including Alameda (which includes Oakland, where Brown was subsequently elected mayor).

gan were also outsiders when they launched their presidential campaigns.

Voter interest in the presidential primary declined as its stature diminished. More Republicans voted in the party's 1980 primary than the 1996 contest between Bob Dole and Pat Buchanan, even though the number of registered California Republicans had increased by more than 1.5 million in the meantime. Similarly, the number of ballots cast in each of the Democratic primaries in the 1990s was lower than any since 1964.

But turnout kicked up in California in 2000, in part because of the earlier primary date and the "blanket" nature of the primary that encouraged mass participation. Only the votes of registered Democrats and Republicans counted for delegate-selection purposes, and they overwhelmingly favored Gore and Bush, respectively. But the rest of California's voters were

The California Rules

Long ignored because of its late primary slot, California again is a significant player in the presidential nominating process. As in 2000, it is the 800-pound gorilla of the huge cross-country votefest that anchors the first Tuesday in March. But the Golden State primary is simpler than it was the last time, when candidates from seven different parties were listed on one ballot.

The primary vote in 2000 was counted in two ways—first, in terms of all votes; then, by party for purpose of delegate selection. For the latter, registered Democrats took ballots marked Democratic. Registered Republicans took ballots marked Republican.

In 2004, the presidential primary will be more straightforward, as only the separate party primaries remain. Registered Democrats and independents may cast ballots in the Democratic primary. Only registered Republicans may participate in the GOP primary. As of September 2003, there were 6.7 million registered Democrats in California, 5.4 million Republicans and nearly 2.5 million independents (or in California parlance, "Declined to State").

DEMOCRATS

THE CALENDAR	
Primary Date (polling hours)	March 2 (7 a.m.–8 p.m.)
Filing Deadline	Dec. 30, 2003
Filing Procedure	The secretary of state announces by Dec. 30, 2003, the names of nationally recognized candidates to be placed on the ballot. Other Democratic candidates must submit petitions signed by 1% or 500 registered Democrats, whichever is fewer, in each congressional district and file them in the county in which the signatures were obtained.

THE DELEGATES	
Number (% of national total)	440 (10.2%)
Distribution:	
By congressional district	241 (from 3 to 7 per district)
At-Large	81
Pledged PEOs	48
Superdelegates	70
Method of Allocation	Proportional—15% of vote needed to win a share of statewide or district delegates.

CONNECTICUT

March 2

For years, Connecticut has literally been the home base of the Bush family. George W. Bush was born in New Haven and graduated from Yale University. His father, George Bush, was raised in Greenwich and was also educated at Yale. His father, Prescott Bush, served the state in the U.S. Senate from 1952 to 1963.

George Bush won Connecticut's Republican presidential primary three times and carried the state in the 1988 general election. George W., however, lost Connecticut twice in 2000, failing to win the state in either the primary or the November election. Yet the GOP primary was close, as John McCain prevailed by barely 4,000 votes out of nearly 180,000 cast.

Bush had two big assets in his battle with McCain: the support of the state's Republican governor, John G. Rowland, and primary rules that limited participation to registered Republicans. But New England, with its moderate brand of Republicanism, was McCain's natural base. He carried five of Connecticut's eight counties, including all four that fronted the Atlantic Ocean, and won places such as Greenwich and New Haven that were near and dear to the Bush family.

The Bush-McCain contest was the most hotly contested Republican primary in Connecticut since 1980, when George Bush, Ronald Reagan and John Anderson were all able to find toeholds.

Bush fashioned his 39 percent to 34 percent victory over Reagan in Connecticut's traditional Republican strongholds, the upper-crust suburbs near New York City and the Yankee towns and villages on the north and east sides of the state.

Reagan nearly offset all that by combining the votes of conservative activists and blue-collar workers in industrial cities such as Bridgeport, Norwalk, Waterbury and New Britain. But to Bush's advantage, more Republican primary votes were cast in suburban Greenwich alone than in any of the state's larger urban centers. Meanwhile, Anderson took 22 percent of the primary vote by carrying communities with large academic institutions, such as New Haven (Yale) and Mansfield (the University of Connecticut).

Bush had a much easier time in 1988 and 1992. Dole withdrew from the race on the day of the Connecticut voting in late March 1988, while Pat Robertson could muster just 3 percent of the vote, his weakest showing of the primary season.

Pat Buchanan did better four years later by tapping into Connecticut's sudden economic discomfort. He took more than 35 percent of the vote in Waterbury, a figure that he almost matched in 1996. But in the latter year, Buchanan finished third in the statewide primary vote behind both Dole and Steve Forbes, who ran best in upscale suburbs such as Greenwich and New Canaan.

Recent Connecticut Primary Results

Connecticut held its first presidential primary in 1980.

	DEMOCRATS			REPUBLICANS		
Year	Turnout	Candidates	%	Turnout	Candidates	%
2000 (March 7)	177,301	AL GORE Bill Bradley	55 42	178,985	JOHN McCAIN George W. Bush	49 46
1996 (March 5)	—	NO PRIMARY		130,418	BOB DOLE Steve Forbes Pat Buchanan	54 20 15
1992 (March 24)	173,119	JERRY BROWN Bill Clinton Paul Tsongas	37 36 20	99,473	GEORGE BUSH* Pat Buchanan	67 22
1988 (March 29)	241,395	MICHAEL DUKAKIS Jesse Jackson	58 28	104,171	GEORGE BUSH Bob Dole	71 20
1984 (March 27)	220,842	GARY HART Walter Mondale Jesse Jackson	53 29 12	—	NO PRIMARY	
1980 (March 25)	210,275	EDWARD KENNEDY Jimmy Carter*	47 41	182,284	GEORGE BUSH Ronald Reagan John Anderson	39 34 22

Note: All candidates are listed that drew at least 10 percent of their party's primary vote. The names of winning candidates are capitalized. An asterisk (*) indicates an incumbent president.

Connecticut's closest presidential primary took place on the Democratic side in 1992, when Jerry Brown slowed Bill Clinton's bandwagon just as it had been picking up steam with a sweep of the Super Tuesday South and St. Patrick's Day voting in Illinois and Michigan. Brown won in Connecticut by fewer than 3,000 votes out of 170,000 cast. But the result, at least temporarily, reopened doubts about the strength of Clinton's candidacy.

Several factors worked to Brown's benefit in Connecticut: a one-on-one shot against Clinton (Paul Tsongas had withdrawn from the race less than a week earlier); a geographically compact electorate, much of which Brown could reach with a media blitz on Hartford television; and low turnout, particularly in the cities where Clinton had hoped to tap the sizable minority vote.

The Democratic base in Connecticut is more urban than the Republican. Still, no Connecticut city dominates the political landscape. The largest are Bridgeport, Hartford and New Haven, and none of the three has more than 5 percent of the state population.

Hartford, the state capital, was roughly 40 percent black when Jesse Jackson carried the city in 1984 and 1988. He added victories in Bridgeport and New Haven (both more than 25 percent black) in the latter campaign.

But Jackson was unable to make headway elsewhere in the state, where Gary Hart marched to victory in 1984 and Michael Dukakis did the same four years later. Dukakis benefited from Al Gore's decision to forgo the all-out effort in Connecticut

that might have produced a more competitive three-way contest. (Gore took just 8 percent of the Democratic primary vote in 1988.)

Gore was much more successful in 2000. As the choice of the Democratic Party establishment, he defeated Bill Bradley in Connecticut by more than a dozen percentage points. Bradley carried many of the well-heeled suburbs near New York, including Greenwich and Darien, but little else. The former professional basketball star was even beaten decisively in Bristol, the longtime home of ESPN (the nationwide cable sports network).

The Connecticut Rules

Connecticut has a heritage of close presidential primaries, with two each on the Democratic and Republican side decided by 6 percentage points or less since 1980.

Participation in the March 2 Connecticut primary is limited to registered voters in each party. As of October 2002, there were roughly 630,000 registered Democrats and 430,000 registered Republicans.

DEMOCRATS

THE CALENDAR

Primary Date (polling hours)	March 2 (6 a.m.–8 p.m.)
Filing Deadline	Jan. 16
Filing Procedure	The secretary of state announces by Dec. 19, 2003, the names of nationally recognized candidates that will be placed on the primary ballot. Other candidates must file petitions with town registrars and the Democratic state committee signed by 1% of their party's registered voters statewide, or 1,000 per district, whichever is less.

THE DELEGATES

Number (% of national total)	61 (1.4%)
Distribution:	
By congressional district	32 (6 or 7 per district)
At-Large	11
Pledged PEOs	6
Superdelegates	12
Method of Allocation	Proportional—15% of vote needed to win a share of statewide or district delegates.

GEORGIA

March 2

Through some shrewd scheduling, Georgia has made its presidential primary more significant in recent years than many states that are much larger. The state's primary in 1976 was held in May. In 1980, it was moved to the second Tuesday in March, and in 1992 to the first Tuesday in March. In the process, Georgia became the first Southern state to vote in 1992 and the second in 1996.

But calendar position has not been the whole story in attracting attention. Unlike many Southern states that have a handful of medium-sized cities, Georgia boasts one large metropolitan area, Atlanta, that is one of the nation's leading transportation and communications centers.

The outcome of Georgia's first two presidential primaries was quite predictable. Native-son Jimmy Carter swept the 1976 and 1980 Democratic primaries with more than 80 percent of the vote, while Ronald Reagan won the first two Republican primaries almost as decisively.

Georgia's primary was first of national import in 1984. As much as any state in the country, Georgia scuttled the presi-

dential hopes of Gary Hart and put Walter Mondale back in the driver's seat for the Democratic nomination. After his devastating loss in New Hampshire, Mondale needed to slow Hart's momentum by scoring at least two primary wins in the trio of Southern states that voted then in early March. Mondale barely did that—carrying Alabama easily and Georgia narrowly.

In 1992, Georgia was again on center stage, giving Bill Clinton his first win of the primary season. Touting his Southern roots and support from much of the state party establishment, Clinton swept all parts of Georgia—from black-majority counties to those with a military orientation. Paul Tsongas ran reasonably close to Clinton in the Atlanta area, where voters from all parts of the country are plentiful. But outside metropolitan Atlanta, it was no contest. The only Georgia county that Tsongas won was the academic enclave of Clarke County, home of the University of Georgia at Athens.

Clinton's broad-based victory in 1992 was a sharp contrast to the Democratic primary four years earlier, which featured Jesse Jackson and Clinton's eventual running mate, Al Gore.

Georgia Primary Results

Georgia held its first presidential primary in 1932, but none between then and 1976.

	DEMOCRATS			REPUBLICANS		
Year	Turnout	Candidates	%	Turnout	Candidates	%
2000 (March 7)	284,431	AL GORE	84	643,188	GEORGE W. BUSH	67
		Bill Bradley	16		John McCain	28
1996 (March 5)	95,103	BILL CLINTON*	100	559,067	BOB DOLE	41
					Pat Buchanan	29
					Lamar Alexander	14
					Steve Forbes	13
1992 (March 3)	454,631	BILL CLINTON	57	453,990	GEORGE BUSH*	64
		Paul Tsongas	24		Pat Buchanan	36
1988 (March 8)	622,752	JESSE JACKSON	40	400,928	GEORGE BUSH	54
		Al Gore	32		Bob Dole	24
		Michael Dukakis	16		Pat Robertson	16
1984 (March 13)	684,541	WALTER MONDALE	30	50,793	RONALD REAGAN*	100
		Gary Hart	27			
		Jesse Jackson	21			
		John Glenn	18			
1980 (March 11)	384,780	JIMMY CARTER*	88	200,171	RONALD REAGAN	73
					George Bush	13
1976 (May 4)	502,471	JIMMY CARTER	83	188,472	RONALD REAGAN	68
		George Wallace	11		Gerald Ford*	32

Note: All candidates are listed who drew at least 10 percent of their party's primary vote. The names of winning candidates are capitalized. An asterisk (*) indicates an incumbent president.

Georgia's Republican primary did not draw much national interest until Pat Buchanan mounted his anti-establishment campaigns against President George Bush in 1992 and Bob Dole in 1996.

The contest between Bush and Buchanan was intense, as Georgia provided the first big test for the two after Buchanan had shocked the president in New Hampshire by drawing nearly 40 percent of the vote. Bush took advantage of the trappings of the presidency by flying *Air Force One* to major population centers around the state. Buchanan filled the role of irreverent challenger, barnstorming rural Georgia in a bus dubbed "Asphalt One." Buchanan ended up carrying 15 counties outside the Atlanta area, but Bush won the primary decisively by garnering roughly two-thirds of the vote in metropolitan Atlanta.

Buchanan returned to Georgia in 1996 with high hopes, having beaten Dole in the New Hampshire primary two weeks earlier. But the results were not much better for him than in 1992. Buchanan won more than 70 counties this time, but they were mainly in rural areas of Georgia where turnout was low for the GOP primary. Like Bush four years earlier, Dole ran well in the leading population centers, including metropolitan Atlanta, to win the statewide vote by a comfortable margin.

Both the Democratic and Republican primaries in 2000 were very one-sided, as Al Gore and George W. Bush registered their highest vote shares of the contested phase of the nominating season in Georgia.

More noteworthy was the voter turnout. For the first time in the state's history, a contested Republican primary for president drew more voters than a contested primary on the Democratic side. It proved a precursor of sorts of GOP success in Georgia in the early years of the new millennium.

The northern third of the state, which borders Tennessee, generally preferred Gore. Jackson carried the rural counties of the "black belt" and nearly all of the state's population centers, including Fulton County (Atlanta).

The Georgia Rules

As in 2000, Georgia will anchor the Southern portion of the Super Tuesday vote, guaranteeing the state a distinctive role in the nominating process once again.

Both parties allocate their delegates to reflect the primary results. There is no party registration in Georgia, so the state's nearly 3.8 million registered voters (as of September 2003) can participate in either the Democratic or Republican primaries.

DEMOCRATS

THE CALENDAR

Primary Date (polling hours)	March 2 (7 a.m.–7 p.m.)
Ballot Access	The Presidential Candidate Selection Committee announces in the first week of January the candidates that will be listed on the primary ballot. Other candidates seeking ballot access must file with the secretary of state by Jan. 15 a written request, which is decided by the Presidential Candidate Selection Committee.

THE DELEGATES

Number (% of national total)	102 (2.4%)
Distribution:	
By congressional district	56 (from 3 to 6 per district)
At-Large	19
Pledged PEOs	11
Superdelegates	16
Method of Allocation	Proportional—15% of vote needed to win a share of statewide or district delegates.

MARYLAND

March 2

When H. L. Mencken was penning his bitingly incisive political essays early in the twentieth century, his hometown of Baltimore dominated the state. But that is no longer the case. Fast-growing suburbs have grown to define Maryland politically.

Yet while large tracts of suburbia give Republicans a strong base in many states, that has not been the case in Maryland, where a large complement of federal workers and minority voters, and a heritage closely linked to the South, has long given Democrats the upper hand and meant the Democratic primary is often where the action takes place.

Sometimes, the vote in the Democratic presidential primary has reflected the Southern character of this border state. In 1964, George Wallace collected a surprising 43 percent of the vote against the state's favorite-son candidate, Sen. Daniel Brewster. Embarrassed by that outcome, state officials scrubbed the primary in 1968. But when it was reinstituted in 1972, Wallace was back to win it easily, one day after an assassination attempt in Laurel left him paralyzed from the waist down.

Wallace swept not only the conservative counties of Maryland's Eastern Shore, which have a cultural affinity to Dixie, but most of the suburban counties as well. Among the venues he carried that year was Prince George's County outside Washington, then a predominantly white, blue-collar constituency that has since become primarily black.

Yet since then, with the exception of Jimmy Carter's victory in 1980 over Edward Kennedy, the result of the Democratic primary in Maryland has tended to accent the state's ties to the northern side of the Mason-Dixon line. That was demonstrated in the two presidential campaigns of Tennessee's Al Gore. As vice president in 2000, Gore had strong support from the national Democratic establishment and won the Maryland primary with two-thirds of the vote. As a more Southern-based candidate in 1988, Gore drew only 9 percent of the vote among Maryland Democrats. Bill Clinton did better four years later, but he lost to Paul Tsongas (who scored his lone primary victory outside his native New England).

Tsongas built up his margin of victory among "Volvo Democrats" in the suburban corridor from Baltimore to

Recent Maryland Primary Results

Maryland held its first presidential primary in 1912.

		DEMOCRATS			REPUBLICANS	
Year	Turnout	Candidates	%	Turnout	Candidates	%
2000 (March 7)	507,462	AL GORE	67	376,034	GEORGE W. BUSH	56
		Bill Bradley	28		John McCain	36
1996 (March 5)	293,829	BILL CLINTON*	84	254,246	BOB DOLE	53
		Uncommitted	11		Pat Buchanan	21
					Steve Forbes	13
1992 (March 3)	567,243	PAUL TSONGAS	41	240,021	GEORGE BUSH*	70
		Bill Clinton	33		Pat Buchanan	30
1988 (March 8)	531,335	MICHAEL DUKAKIS	46	200,754	GEORGE BUSH	53
		Jesse Jackson	29		Bob Dole	32
1984 (May 8)	506,886	WALTER MONDALE	42	73,663	RONALD REAGAN*	100
		Jesse Jackson	26			
		Gary Hart	24			
1980 (May 13)	477,090	JIMMY CARTER*	47	167,303	RONALD REAGAN	48
		Edward Kennedy	38		George Bush	41
1976 (May 18)	591,746	JERRY BROWN	48	165,971	GERALD FORD*	58
		Jimmy Carter	37		Ronald Reagan	42
1972 (May 16)	568,131	GEORGE WALLACE	39	115,249	RICHARD NIXON*	86
		Hubert Humphrey	27			
		George McGovern	22			
1968	—	NO PRIMARY		—	NO PRIMARY	

Note: All candidates are listed who drew at least 10 percent of their party's primary vote. The names of winning candidates are capitalized. An asterisk (*) indicates an incumbent president.

Washington, swamping Clinton in Montgomery and Howard counties by margins of more than 2-to-1. Clinton won rural Maryland—the mountainous western panhandle that is part of Appalachia, as well as southern Maryland and the Eastern Shore. And Clinton won the city of Baltimore and Prince George's County, both with black majorities, which had boosted Jesse Jackson to second-place primary finishes in both 1984 and 1988.

None of the Democratic primary winners from 1972 through 1992 was able to attract a majority of the Maryland vote. Winners on the Republican side, though, have often won by lopsided margins, and moderates have fared well. President Gerald Ford easily won Maryland's GOP primary in 1976 by beating Ronald Reagan in Baltimore and all the major suburban counties. Reagan triumphed in May 1980 at a time his campaign was moving into overdrive. Yet George Bush still carried Baltimore and much of the suburban corridor, and might have beaten Reagan if John Anderson had not drained away nearly 10 percent of the primary vote.

Bush dominated the Maryland primary in 1988 and 1992, carrying every county each time. Pat Robertson's 6 percent showing in Maryland in 1988 was his weakest in any state

south of the Mason-Dixon line. Four years later, Bush defeated Pat Buchanan, a native of nearby Washington, D.C., who lived for a time in the Maryland suburb of Chevy Chase.

In 2000, Maryland Republicans opened their primary to independent voters. It helped produce a record turnout for the party of more than 375,000 voters. But it did not appreciably help John McCain, whose success in many other states had been dependent on votes from non-Republicans. George W. Bush defeated him in every county in the state.

The Maryland Rules

Maryland is one of a few early presidential primary states that will also hold their primaries for Congress on the same day, giving voters an extra reason to come to the polls March 2.

Maryland's primary is limited to registered members of each party. As of September 2003, there were more than 1.5 million registered Democrats and 830,000 Republicans.

DEMOCRATS

THE CALENDAR

Primary Date (polling hours)	March 2 (7 a.m.–8 p.m.)
Filing Deadline	Jan. 9
Filing Procedure	The secretary of state places names of generally recognized candidates on the ballot, with a deadline of Jan. 2 for the Democrats. Other candidates must file petitions signed by at least 400 registered voters in each district.

THE DELEGATES

Number (% of national total)	98 (2.3%)
Distribution:	
By congressional district	45 (from 4 to 7 per district)
At-Large	15
Pledged PEOs	9
Superdelegates	29
Method of Allocation	Proportional—15% of vote needed to win a share of statewide or district delegates.

MASSACHUSETTS

March 2

Ever since George McGovern went one for 50 in the presidential election of 1972—carrying Massachusetts but no other—the Bay State has been widely regarded as the premier bastion of Democratic liberalism in the United States. That perception may not be untrue, but it is not as simple as that either. Massachusetts has several faces.

There is Yankee Massachusetts that gave President William Howard Taft his only victory over insurgent Teddy Roosevelt in the 1912 Republican primaries.

There is blue-collar Massachusetts, which gave Henry Jackson his biggest win of the 1976 Democratic primaries.

And there is the liberal Massachusetts of suburbia and academe, which has given long-shot challengers such as George McGovern and John Anderson a base to build from in the state's presidential primary, as well as helping to provide John McCain with his highest share of the vote in the 2000 Republican primary season.

Much of the Democratic electorate lives within 25 miles of Boston; roughly 10 percent lives within the city itself. Boston contains two key elements of the Democratic Party statewide—ethnic neighborhoods and academic institutions—but it adds a third element not found in large numbers elsewhere in Massachusetts—minorities.

The combustible mixture can produce unexpected results. When the Democratic primary occurred during the height of a school busing crisis in 1976, George Wallace carried the city.

The Democrats used to be the party of the cities, but as Massachusetts has made the transformation from a declining manufacturing-based economy to the bustling world of high technology, the party has taken root in the growing suburbs.

That has not left much room for the Republicans. The dominant party in Massachusetts for nearly a century after the Civil War, the GOP was the choice of less than one of every seven

Recent Massachusetts Primary Results

Massachusetts held its first presidential primary in 1912.

| Year | DEMOCRATS | | | REPUBLICANS | | |
	Turnout	Candidates	%	Turnout	Candidates	%
2000 (March 7)	570,074	AL GORE	60	501,951	JOHN McCAIN	65
		Bill Bradley	37		George W. Bush	32
1996 (March 5)	155,470	BILL CLINTON*	87	284,833	BOB DOLE	48
					Pat Buchanan	25
					Steve Forbes	14
1992 (March 10)	792,885	PAUL TSONGAS	66	269,701	GEORGE BUSH*	66
		Jerry Brown	15		Pat Buchanan	28
		Bill Clinton	11			
1988 (March 8)	713,447	MICHAEL DUKAKIS	59	241,181	GEORGE BUSH	59
		Jesse Jackson	19		Bob Dole	26
		Richard Gephardt	10			
1984 (March 13)	630,962	GARY HART	39	65,937	RONALD REAGAN*	89
		Walter Mondale	25			
		George McGovern	21			
1980 (March 4)	907,323	EDWARD KENNEDY	65	400,826	GEORGE BUSH	31
		Jimmy Carter*	29		John Anderson	31
					Ronald Reagan	29
1976 (March 2)	735,821	HENRY JACKSON	22	188,449	GERALD FORD*	61
		Morris Udall	18		Ronald Reagan	34
		George Wallace	17			
		Jimmy Carter	14			
1972 (April 25)	618,516	GEORGE McGOVERN	53	122,139	RICHARD NIXON*	81
		Edmund Muskie	21		Paul McCloskey	13
1968 (April 30)	248,903	EUGENE McCARTHY	49	106,521	NELSON ROCKEFELLER#	30
		Robert Kennedy#	28		John Volpe	30
		Hubert Humphrey#	18		Richard Nixon#	26

Note: All candidates are listed that drew at least 10 percent of their party's primary vote. The names of winning candidates are capitalized. An asterisk (*) indicates an incumbent president. A pound sign (#) indicates a write-in candidate.

registered voters in Massachusetts by the early twenty-first century.

Yet while the Republican Party is small, it is not static. For years, the Massachusetts GOP was dominated by moderate Yankees. President Gerald Ford easily won the Republican primary over Ronald Reagan in 1976; George Bush was a narrow winner four years later.

Bush, who was born in Milton and educated at the Phillips Academy in Andover, ran well in old-line Yankee Republican communities, barely offsetting Anderson's appeal in liberal suburbs and academic centers. Reagan finished a close third by carrying many of the working-class mill towns.

Bush won the Republican primaries again in 1988 and 1992, but his victories were not nail-biters like 1980. He swept virtually every community in Massachusetts each time.

But there is a conservative element within the state GOP, often of the ethnic, lunch-bucket variety, that Pat Buchanan was able to tap in the 1990s with his message of economic protest. Buchanan made his most conspicuous inroads in the 1996 primary by carrying old industrial cities like Lawrence, Lowell and Lynn. Bob Dole, though, still easily won the statewide GOP vote.

A big variable in the Republican equation is turnout, which can vary widely from one primary to another. Unenrolled voters (the Massachusetts parlance for independents) account for nearly half the electorate and have been allowed to vote in either party's primary. They often get swallowed up in large-turnout Democratic contests but can shape the outcome in lower-turnout Republican affairs. That was the case in 2000, when the appeal of McCain helped bring a flood of independents into the GOP primary. George W. Bush drew nearly 20,000 more votes than his father did in 1988, but the turnout grew by 260,000—making the younger Bush a big loser in Massachusetts.

Meanwhile, Massachusetts Democrats have had their largest turnouts when one of their own has been on the presidential primary ballot. There have been three home-state entries in recent years—Sen. Edward Kennedy in 1980, Gov. Michael S. Dukakis in 1988 and former senator Paul Tsongas in 1992. All were easy winners. But somewhat surprisingly, the one that ran best, Tsongas, was the only one who was not an incumbent officeholder at the time.

The Massachusetts Rules

The delegate harvest offered by Massachusetts pales in comparison with California, New York and a few other states that vote March 2. Still, Massachusetts is the centerpiece of the quartet of New England primaries that anchor the northeast corner of the Super Tuesday balloting.

Voting in the primary is open to each party's registered voters, plus unenrolled voters who can take a ballot of either party. Unenrolled voters become members of the party in which they cast their ballot, but can change their registration back to unenrolled as they leave the polling place. As of October 2002, Massachusetts had more than 1.4 million registered Democrats, 530,000 Republicans and nearly 2.0 million unenrolled voters.

DEMOCRATS

THE CALENDAR	
Primary Date (polling hours)	March 2 (7 a.m.–8 p.m.)
Filing Deadline	Dec. 19, 2003
Filing Procedure	The secretary of state and each state party chairman designate names to be placed on the ballot. Other candidates must file petitions signed by 2,500 registered voters with local registrars by Dec. 19, 2003. Petitions must reach the secretary of state by Jan. 2.
THE DELEGATES	
Number (% of national total)	121 (2.8%)
Distribution:	
By congressional district	61 (6 or 7 per district)
At-Large	20
Pledged PEOs	12
Superdelegates	28
Method of Allocation	Proportional—15% of vote needed to win a share of statewide or district delegates.

MINNESOTA

March 2

Every generation or so, a presidential primary appears in Minnesota like Brigadoon. There was one in 1916, a pair in the 1950s, and another in 1992. The rest of the time the residents of Minnesota have been content to elect their delegates through caucuses.

The state's presidential primary, though occasional, has often been memorable. In 1952, Dwight D. Eisenhower showed his vote-getting appeal by generating over 100,000 write-in votes in the Republican primary.

In 1956, Estes Kefauver upset Adlai Stevenson in the state's Democratic balloting.

And Bill Clinton's narrow victory over Jerry Brown in the 1992 Democratic primary was the closest of any presidential primary that year.

Yet the caucus system reigns supreme in Minnesota, in part because it heightens the role of activists in both parties. In the Republican camp, many of those activists are evangelical Christians energized by social issues such as abortion.

The Democrats, too, have an ardent anti-abortion element that sent more than a dozen delegates to the 1984 Democratic convention. On the whole, however, the state party that nursed the presidential aspirations of Hubert Humphrey and Walter Mondale remains one of the most liberal in the country.

Recent Minnesota Primary Results

Minnesota held its first presidential primary in 1916, but only three times since then—1952, 1956 and 1992.

	DEMOCRATS			REPUBLICANS		
Year	Turnout	Candidates	%	Turnout	Candidates	%
2000	—	NO PRIMARY		—	NO PRIMARY	
1996	—	NO PRIMARY		—	NO PRIMARY	
1992 (April 7)	204,170	BILL CLINTON	31	132,756	GEORGE BUSH*	64
		Jerry Brown	31		Pat Buchanan	24
		Paul Tsongas	21			

Note: All candidates are listed that drew at least 10 percent of their party's primary vote. The names of winning candidates are capitalized. An asterisk (*) indicates an incumbent president.

That was evident during the party's nonbinding presidential primary in April 1992. Although Clinton's campaign was rolling into high gear nationally, he prevailed over Brown in Minnesota by a margin of barely 1,000 votes out of more than 200,000 cast. Clinton offset Brown's edge in the Twin Cities area (Minneapolis and St. Paul) with a stronger showing in rural parts of the state.

On the Republican side, George Bush was a big winner. He swept every county and nearly two-thirds of the 130,000 ballots cast. Former Minnesota governor Harold Stassen, who had overcome Eisenhower's write-in campaign to win the state's Republican presidential primary in 1952, drew only 3 percent of the primary vote in 1992 but qualified for a delegate. Stassen wanted to cast his one vote for himself at the national convention, but the state convention refused to elect him as a delegate.

Sandwiched around Bush's primary victory in 1992 were two caucus triumphs by Bob Dole. His successful effort in 1988 capitalized on his farm-state ties and the momentum from his win in Iowa barely two weeks earlier. In 1996, Dole had the backing of Minnesota's moderate Republican governor, Arne Carlson.

But with the strong conservative presence among GOP activists, neither of Dole's caucus victories was a landslide. In 1988, he defeated Pat Robertson, 43 to 28 percent, with Robertson running best in the Twin Cities' suburbs and the hardscrabble Iron Range, a Democratic stronghold in northeast Minnesota.

In 1996, Dole defeated Pat Buchanan, 41 to 33 percent—about a 10 percentage point improvement for Buchanan over his primary showing in 1992.

The Minnesota Rules

Although Minnesota has a place in the March 2 votefest, the state's low-profile precinct caucuses are apt to draw more attention from the Democratic candidates than from the media. But Minnesota's significant delegate harvest ensures its appeal to the former. To compete in the Democratic caucuses, a candidate must file a statement of candidacy with the state party by Feb. 2.

Minnesota does not have party registration. Any of the state's nearly 2.9 million registered voters (as of February 2003) can participate in the Democratic precinct caucuses, although participants must sign a statement indicating they are a Democrat.

DEMOCRATS

THE CALENDAR
Precinct Caucuses	March 2
County Conventions	March 2–April 2
Congressional District Conventions	April 17–May 22
State Convention	May 23

THE DELEGATES
Number (% of national total)	86 (2.0%)
Distribution:	
By congressional district	47 (from 5 to 8 per district)
At-Large	16
Pledged PEOs	9
Superdelegates	14
Method of Allocation	Proportional—15% of vote needed to win a share of statewide or district delegates.

NEW YORK

March 2

For much of the twentieth century, New York's political leaders chose control of their state's nominating process over widespread voter participation. The Empire State held a presidential primary, but it was often a late spring event devoted solely to the election of delegates on a district-by-district basis; it produced a delegation that was readily transferable to the preferred candidate of the party's kingpins. That ballot access was difficult and voter interest often minimal was just fine with party leaders.

It was not until 1980 that New York Democrats held their first presidential primary with voters able to ballot directly for the candidates. But New York GOP leaders have been slow to jettison the old system, and in 2000 lined up early behind George W. Bush.

Roughly 700,000 Republicans participated in the primary, close to double the number that had voted in 1996. John McCain won delegates in eight congressional districts in New York City and the suburbs of Long Island. But the arcane nature of the system prevented McCain from making deeper inroads in this citadel of moderate Republicanism.

Compared with the Republicans, New York's Democratic presidential primary has been open and showy, and in recent years, hotly contested.

The state's ethnically variegated Democratic electorate has been comfortable with traditional New Deal-style politicians. Henry M. Jackson won more delegates than anyone else in New York in 1976; Edward Kennedy won easily in 1980, as did Walter Mondale in 1984 and Michael Dukakis in 1988.

Bill Clinton won the primary in 1992 by piecing together a biracial coalition in New York City and holding his own in the rest of the state. But like many of Clinton's other primary triumphs in 1992, his New York victory was not overwhelming. He took barely 40 percent of the vote against Jerry Brown and Paul Tsongas, who had suspended his campaign more than two weeks before the April balloting, but still placed second. Only in one county, the Bronx, did Clinton win a majority of the vote.

Recent New York Primary Results

New York Democrats instituted a presidential primary with a direct vote for candidates in 1980. New York Republicans have cast their primary ballots for delegates without a direct vote for presidential candidates.

		DEMOCRATS			REPUBLICANS	
Year	Turnout	Candidates	%	Estimated turnout	Candidates	%
2000 (March 7)	974,463	AL GORE Bill Bradley	66 33	720,000#	GEORGE W. BUSH John McCain	51 43
1996 (March 7)	—	NO PRIMARY		360,000#	BOB DOLE Steve Forbes Pat Buchanan	55 30 15
1992 (April 7)	1,007,726	BILL CLINTON Paul Tsongas Jerry Brown	41 29 26		NO PRIMARY	
1988 (April 19)	1,575,186	MICHAEL DUKAKIS Jesse Jackson Al Gore	51 37 10		NO PRIMARY	
1984 (April 3)	1,387,950	WALTER MONDALE Gary Hart Jesse Jackson	45 27 26		NO PRIMARY	
1980 (March 25)	989,062	EDWARD KENNEDY Jimmy Carter*	59 41		NO PRIMARY	

Note: All candidates are listed that drew at least 10 percent of their party's primary vote. The names of winning candidates are capitalized. An asterisk (*) indicates an incumbent president. A pound sign (#) indicates the estimated Republican turnout based on the vote for delegates.

None of the candidates seemed to excite the voters. Turnout for the Democratic primary in 1992 was barely 1 million, the lowest since 1980, and Clinton's winning total was almost 400,000 votes less than Dukakis' four years earlier.

Clinton's winning coalition was also different. In 1988, Dukakis narrowly lost New York City to Jesse Jackson, but swamped Jackson in the more conservative suburbs and upstate. In contrast, Clinton built up a big lead in New York City but barely beat Tsongas in the suburbs and was caught in a close battle with Brown and Tsongas in the small cities and towns of upstate New York. Clinton was strong in the western end of the state, which faces the Midwest. Tsongas and Brown dominated voting in the Hudson River Valley, which is adjacent to New England.

But the prime battleground was New York City, where more than half the Democratic primary ballots are cast, and there Clinton readily prevailed with a significant edge among the city's large component of Jewish and black voters. It enabled him to become the first Southern Democrat to win the New York primary.

Jimmy Carter had lost it twice, denouncing the primary in 1976 as boss-dominated. Al Gore finished a weak third in New York in 1988—despite heavy emphasis on the event—and shortly thereafter suspended his campaign. Gore drew less than 10 percent of the primary vote in the city, less than 15 percent in the suburbs, and could crack 20 percent in only two small upstate counties.

Gore did win the Democratic primary easily in 2000. But as Clinton's vice president, he was able to run as a national Democrat, well connected to the state party establishment and New York's myriad interest groups.

That gave his challenger, Bill Bradley, little running room. Even in New York City, where Bradley was a household name from his days as a professional basketball star with the New York Knicks, Gore won by a margin of roughly 2-to-1. With the Democratic presidential race barely registering a pulse by the time New York voted in early March, turnout for the Democratic primary fell below 1 million for the first time since 1980.

The New York Rules

New York's once arcane presidential primary is now relatively straightforward, as both parties for the first time have adopted a presidential preference vote to govern the allocation of delegates.

For much of its history, the New York primary did not provide for a direct vote for presidential candidates. Instead, the vote was for delegates only, which were elected by congressional district. Democrats went to a direct vote for candidates in 1980. Republicans were to follow suit in 2004, but no GOP primary will be held if President George W. Bush is the only candidate to file.

Only registered Democrats can vote in the Democratic primary and registered Republicans in the GOP primary. As of November 2003, there were 5.1 million registered Democrats and nearly 3.1 million registered Republicans in New York.

DEMOCRATS

THE CALENDAR	
Primary Date (polling hours)	March 2 (6 a.m.–9 p.m. in New York City plus counties of Nassau, Suffolk, Westchester, Rockland, Orange, Putnam, and Erie; noon to 9 p.m. in rest of state.)
Filing Deadline	Jan. 6
Filing Procedure	Candidates must file petitions signed by 5,000 registered Democratic voters with the state board of elections.
THE DELEGATES	
Number (% of national total)	284 (6.6%)
Distribution:	
By congressional district	154 (5 or 6 per district)
At-Large	51
Pledged PEOs	31
Superdelegates	48
Method of allocation	Proportional—15% of vote needed to win a share of the statewide or district delegates.

OHIO

March 2

Ohio likes to portray itself as a bellwether, a microcosm of the national mood. In the 25 presidential elections held in the twentieth century, Ohio voted for the winner 23 times, a success rate exceeded by no other state and matched by just one, Missouri. And like Missouri, it voted for the winner in 2000.

For its part, Ohio's presidential primary has been as much a harbinger as a bellwether, particularly on the Democratic side. Nominees who have struggled in the primary have rarely had much success in winning the pivotal Buckeye State in the general election. Hubert Humphrey edged George McGovern in the 1972 Democratic primary, giving the party an early warning of McGovern's lackluster appeal among blue-collar Democrats. Jimmy Carter scored a big win in Ohio on the final day of the primary season in 1976, offsetting a loss the same day in California and taking the air out of an incipient stop-Carter movement.

As president, Carter won the Ohio primary again in 1980. But with much of the state in the economic doldrums, the vote

was much closer. Edward Kennedy had strong labor backing and ran tough television ads. ("Carter equals Hoover equals Depression," said one.) Kennedy carried much of the state's industrial northern tier from Toledo to Youngstown, traditionally the source of about half the Democratic primary vote. But Kennedy did not have enough strength elsewhere in the state to win the primary.

Four years later, Gary Hart appropriated a similar message, tying Walter Mondale to the Carter administration's economic record. Hart ended up running virtually even with Mondale in northern Ohio's industrial belt. And with his edge in rural Ohio, Hart scored a narrow victory that revitalized his struggling campaign for the final wave of primaries.

The Democratic primaries since then have been more one-sided. Michael Dukakis lost Franklin (Columbus) and Hamilton (Cincinnati) counties to Jesse Jackson in 1988, but still rolled up more than 60 percent of the vote statewide. Bill Clinton also surpassed 60 percent in 1992, with his "weakest" showing in Cuyahoga County (Cleveland), where he was held

Recent Ohio Primary Results

Ohio held its first presidential primary in 1912.

Year	DEMOCRATS			REPUBLICANS		
	Turnout	Candidates	%	Turnout	Candidates	%
2000 (March 7)	978,512	AL GORE	74	1,397,528	GEORGE W. BUSH	58
		Bill Bradley	25		John McCain	37
1996 (March 19)	776,530	BILL CLINTON*	92	963,422	BOB DOLE	67
					Pat Buchanan	22
1992 (June 2)	1,042,335	BILL CLINTON	61	860,453	GEORGE BUSH*	83
		Jerry Brown	19		Pat Buchanan	17
		Paul Tsongas	11			
1988 (May 3)	1,383,572	MICHAEL DUKAKIS	63	794,904	GEORGE BUSH	81
		Jesse Jackson	27		Bob Dole	12
1984 (May 8)	1,447,236	GARY HART	42	658,169	RONALD REAGAN*	100
		Walter Mondale	40			
		Jesse Jackson	16			
1980 (June 3)	1,186,410	JIMMY CARTER*	51	856,773	RONALD REAGAN	81
		Edward Kennedy	44		George Bush	19
1976 (June 8)	1,134,374	JIMMY CARTER	52	935,757	GERALD FORD*	55
		Morris Udall	21		Ronald Reagan	45
		Frank Church	14			
1972 (May 2)	1,212,330	HUBERT HUMPHREY	41	692,828	RICHARD NIXON*	100
		George McGovern	40			
1968 (May 7)	549,140	STEPHEN YOUNG	100	614,492	JAMES RHODES	100

Note: All candidates are listed that drew at least 10 percent of their party's primary vote. The names of winning candidates are capitalized. An asterisk (*) indicates an incumbent president.

to 53 percent. Al Gore took nearly 75 percent of the Democratic primary vote in 2000, sweeping past Bill Bradley in all parts of the state.

The Republican side of the presidential primary ballot in Ohio has not tended to be very competitive. Since Ray Bliss chaired the Ohio GOP in the 1950s and early 1960s, the party has emphasized nuts-and-bolts organization and political pragmatism. It gave President Gerald Ford an early endorsement that discouraged Ronald Reagan from mounting a full-scale effort in Ohio in 1976. Although Ford won the primary with a modest 55 percent of the vote, his tally was remarkably consistent around the state and gave him the delegates he needed to stake his claim to a first-ballot nomination.

For all practical purposes, 1976 was the last year until 2000 that Ohio Republicans had a say in their party's nominating process, because over the next two decades the GOP contest was usually over before the state voted. Ronald Reagan (in 1980 and 1984) and George Bush (in 1988 and 1992) each took more than 80 percent of the Ohio GOP primary vote. Dole won almost as easily in 1996.

Pat Buchanan was a distant second in both the 1992 and 1996 primaries and failed to carry even one of Ohio's 88 counties. The best Buchanan could do was to take slightly more than one-third of the vote in 1996 in a trio of counties in the industrial Youngstown area.

George W. Bush's victory in the 2000 Republican primary was not so one-sided. John McCain carried congressional dis-

tricts that included Akron and the majority-black east side of Cleveland. But Bush carried the rest of Ohio, denying McCain a victory in a major heartland state that might have helped keep his upstart challenge alive.

As it was, the Bush-McCain contest drew nearly 1.4 million voters—a record for a Republican presidential primary in Ohio.

The Ohio Rules

Ohio's presidential primary used to bounce around the calendar from early May to early June, but of late it has joined the march of states to the front of the nominating process. In 1996, the Buckeye State voted on the third Tuesday in March as part of a short-lived regional primary in the industrial Midwest. Since then, Ohio has voted on the first Tuesday in March.

Any registered voter may cast a ballot in either the Democratic or Republican primary, although they are then considered a member of that party. In November 2003, there were more than 7.1 million registered voters in Ohio.

DEMOCRATS

THE CALENDAR
    Primary Date (polling hours)   March 2 (6:30 a.m.–7:30 p.m.)
    Filing Deadline   Jan. 2
    Filing Procedure   Candidates must submit petitions signed by at least 1,000 registered voters of their party to the secretary of state.

THE DELEGATES
    Number (% of national total)   159 (3.7%)
    Distribution:
      By congressional district   91 (from 4 to 8 per district)
      At-Large   31
      Pledged PEOs   18
      Superdelegates   19
    Method of Allocation   Proportional—15% of vote needed to win a share of statewide or district delegates.

RHODE ISLAND

March 2

Rhode Island is heavily Catholic, urban and ethnic, and one of the most Democratic states in the country. But Rhode Island Democrats have often used their presidential primary to rebuke their party's eventual nominee. An uncommitted slate adopted by Jerry Brown beat Jimmy Carter in 1976; Edward Kennedy routed Carter in 1980; Gary Hart defeated Walter Mondale in 1984; and Paul Tsongas overwhelmed Bill Clinton in 1992.

An exception to this trend came in 2000, when Al Gore defeated Bill Bradley. Still, while Gore tended to dominate the vote in the industrial northern half of the state, Bradley carried nearly a dozen communities in the southern half, many around the Narragansett Bay.

These anomalous results were partly attributable to low turnout, which allowed relatively small numbers of voters to tip the results. Even though Rhode Island independents are permitted to vote in either the Democratic or Republican primary, as they are in much of the rest of New England, that allure has failed to produce high turnouts. Since the state's first presidential primary was held in 1972, no more than 75,000 voters have gone to the polls in any year.

Recent Rhode Island Primary Results

Rhode Island held its first presidential primary in 1972.

| Year | DEMOCRATS | | | REPUBLICANS | | |
	Turnout	Candidates	%	Turnout	Candidates	%
2000 (March 7)	47,079	AL GORE	57	36,143	JOHN McCAIN	60
		Bill Bradley	40		George W. Bush	36
1996 (March 5)	8,780	BILL CLINTON*	89	15,009	BOB DOLE	64
					Lamar Alexander	19
1992 (March 10)	50,709	PAUL TSONGAS	53	15,636	GEORGE BUSH*	63
		Bill Clinton	21		Pat Buchanan	32
		Jerry Brown	19			
1988 (March 8)	49,029	MICHAEL DUKAKIS	70	16,035	GEORGE BUSH	65
		Jesse Jackson	15		Bob Dole	23
1984 (March 13)	44,511	GARY HART	45	2,235	RONALD REAGAN*	91
		Walter Mondale	34			
1980 (June 3)	38,327	EDWARD KENNEDY	68	5,335	RONALD REAGAN	72
		Jimmy Carter*	26		George Bush	19
1976 (June 1)	60,348	UNCOMMITTED	32	14,352	GERALD FORD*	65
		Jimmy Carter	30		Ronald Reagan	31
		Frank Church	27			
1972 (May 23)	37,864	GEORGE McGOVERN	41	5,611	RICHARD NIXON*	88
		Edmund Muskie	21			
		Hubert Humphrey	20			
		George Wallace	15			

Note: All candidates are listed that drew at least 10 percent of their party's primary vote. The names of winning candidates are capitalized. An asterisk (*) indicates an incumbent president.

With such a limited turnout, liberal activists have often had the upper hand in Democratic primary voting in spite of Rhode Island's heritage as a heavily unionized state with conservative social values.

But geography also has driven the vote in a number of Democratic primaries. In 1992, Tsongas continued Rhode Island's tradition of supporting candidates from neighboring Massachusetts.

Both Kennedy in 1980 and Michael Dukakis in 1988 took more than two-thirds of the primary ballots in Rhode Island, besting their showings in their home state. Tsongas won Rhode Island easily in 1992 with 53 percent of the vote, his best showing in a primary outside Massachusetts. Clinton finished a distant second statewide.

While Democratic interest in the presidential primary has never been high, the GOP turnout has been downright minuscule, only once surpassing 20,000 (that in 2000). Most Rhode Islanders who cast Republican primary ballots seem satisfied with moderates of the Gerald Ford–George Bush stripe.

Conservative Republicans, even well-known ones, have had trouble reaching one-third of the vote in competitive GOP primaries in Rhode Island. Ronald Reagan drew only 31 percent against Ford in 1976. Pat Buchanan garnered only 32 percent against Bush in 1992. And George W. Bush, brandishing his "compassionate" brand of conservatism, could muster only 36 percent against John McCain in 2000. McCain's victory over the future president was broad based, as he carried all 39 Rhode Island cities and towns.

The Rhode Island Rules

Rhode Island may be located in the midst of New England, but its small size is apt to leave it off the beaten path in the rush of March 2 primaries.

The primary is open to registered voters in each party plus unaffiliated voters, who automatically become members of the party in which they cast a primary ballot (although they can change back as they leave the polling place). In November 2002, there were more than 670,000 registered voters in Rhode Island, although party registration is compiled on a local, rather than a statewide, basis.

DEMOCRATS

THE CALENDAR

Primary Date (polling hours)	March 2 (polls open by 9 a.m. except in New Shoreham (Block Island), which opens at noon; close at 9 p.m.)
Filing Deadline	Dec. 19, 2003
Filing Procedure	Candidates must provide the secretary of state written notification of their intention to run in the primary by Nov. 30, 2003. Thereafter, petitions signed by 1,000 registered voters must be filed with the secretary of state.

THE DELEGATES

Number (% of national total)	32 (0.7%)
Distribution:	
By congressional district	13 (6 or 7 per district)
At-Large	5
Pledged PEOs	3
Superdelegates	11
Method of Allocation	Proportional—15% of the vote needed to win a share of the statewide or district delegates.

VERMONT

March 2

Vermont has undergone a metamorphosis in recent years. Long associated with the flinty Yankee Republicanism of Calvin Coolidge, it is now as apt to be identified in the public mind with its socially conscious ice cream makers, Ben & Jerry.

But voting in the wake of neighboring New Hampshire, its presidential primary has been strongly affected by geography and momentum. Ever since Vermont reinstituted its primary in 1976 after a half-century hiatus, its winners have been the same as in the Granite State. That is, with one exception. In 1996, Pat Buchanan won New Hampshire; Bob Dole won Vermont, as the momentum in the Republican race shifted sharply in the two-week interval between the two contests.

By and large, moderate Republicans tend to run better in Vermont than New Hampshire. In 1980, John Anderson barely got on the radar screen in New Hampshire but nearly won the GOP primary in Vermont. In 1996, Richard Lugar pulled barely 5 percent of the primary vote in New Hampshire but rose to 14 percent in Vermont, where he chose to make his last stand.

On the other hand, conservative Republicans have not run that well in Vermont's presidential primary. Ronald Reagan won it in 1980 with only 30 percent of the vote. Buchanan drew

less than 20 percent in 1996, just two weeks removed from his New Hampshire triumph. George W. Bush lost Vermont by 25 percentage points to John McCain in 2000.

For both parties, the more conservative voters are generally found in the northern part of the state, where there is a large concentration of French Canadians and rural Republicans. Both Reagan and Buchanan ran best in northern Vermont, each posting his highest percentage in Essex County in the farthest reaches of the sparsely populated and long-isolated "Northeast Kingdom."

To the south and west, voters generally tend to be more moderate. Anderson carried four counties in his 1980 primary run, including Vermont's most populous, Chittenden, which features several colleges and some high-tech industry around Burlington. Just to the south is Addison County, the home of Middlebury College, where Lugar made his best showing in 1996 (20 percent of the vote). Anderson also carried Addison, as did Dole in his 1988 primary challenge to George Bush. It was the only Vermont county that Dole won that year.

Meanwhile, Bennington County, in Vermont's southwest corner, was the only county to back Bush in the closely fought

Recent Vermont Primary Results

Vermont held its first presidential primary in 1916, but none between 1920 and 1976.

| Year | DEMOCRATS | | | REPUBLICANS | | |
	Turnout	Candidates	%	Turnout	Candidates	%
2000 (March 7)	49,283	AL GORE	54	81,355	JOHN McCAIN	60
		Bill Bradley	44		George W. Bush	35
1996 (March 5)	30,838	BILL CLINTON*	97	58,113	BOB DOLE	40
					Pat Buchanan	17
					Steve Forbes	16
					Richard Lugar	14
					Lamar Alexander	11
1992	—	NO PRIMARY		—	NO PRIMARY	
1988 (March 1)	50,791	MICHAEL DUKAKIS	56	47,832	GEORGE BUSH	49
		Jesse Jackson	26		Bob Dole	39
1984 (March 6)	74,059	GARY HART	70	33,643	RONALD REAGAN*	99
		Walter Mondale	20			
1980 (March 4)	39,703	JIMMY CARTER*	73	65,611	RONALD REAGAN	30
		Edward Kennedy	26		John Anderson	29
					George Bush	22
					Howard Baker	12
1976 (March 2)	38,714	JIMMY CARTER	42	32,157	GERALD FORD*	84
		Sargent Shriver	28		Ronald Reagan#	15
		Fred Harris	13			

Note: All candidates are listed that drew at least 10 percent of their party's primary vote. The names of winning candidates are capitalized. An asterisk (*) indicates an incumbent president. A pound sign (#) indicates a write-in candidate.

1980 primary. It is an area of settled wealth where Republicans have been described as "moderate but not daring."

With the exception of 2000, when Bill Bradley took 44 percent of the vote in Vermont—his best showing outside New Hampshire—the liberal nature of Vermont's activist Democrats has been less evident in the primary than the separate caucus process. Until 1996 caucuses elected the national convention delegates independent of the primary vote. And for years, the two systems produced different winners, with the comparatively small cadre of caucus voters (around 6,000 in recent years) regularly opting for the more liberal alternative.

In 1980, for instance, President Jimmy Carter easily won the primary, but Edward Kennedy prevailed in the Democratic caucuses. In 1988, Michael Dukakis was the primary winner, while Jesse Jackson won the caucuses. In 1992, Jerry Brown won his highest share of the vote—primary or caucus—in Vermont. By winning nearly half of the state convention delegates, he finished a solid first in the first-round Democratic caucus voting, with uncommitted next. Bill Clinton ran third, even though Clinton boasted an endorsement from Democrat Gov. Howard Dean.

Dean, though, did endorse the Vermont Democratic primary winner in 2000, Al Gore. The latter returned the favor in late 2003, as Dean was gearing up his own campaign for the Democratic presidential nomination.

The Vermont Rules

Vermont holds a presidential primary March 2, but its main claim to fame is as the home base of Democratic presidential aspirant Howard Dean. He should win the March 2 primary easily, although his victory margin will be of interest. He won a bare majority of the vote when he last ran for governor of Vermont in 2000.

Since there is no party registration in Vermont, any of the state's nearly 415,000 registered voters (as of March 2003) may vote in either the Democratic or Republican primary.

DEMOCRATS

THE CALENDAR	
Primary Date (polling hours)	March 2 (open by 10 a.m., close at 7 p.m.)
Filing Deadline	Jan. 19
Filing Procedure	Candidates must pay a $2,000 filing fee and file petitions with the secretary of state signed by at least 1,000 registered voters.
THE DELEGATES	
Number (% of national total)	22 (0.5%)
Distribution:	
By congressional district	10
At-Large	3
Pledged PEOs	2
Superdelegates	7
Method of allocation	Proportional—15% of the vote needed to win a share of the statewide or district delegates.

REST OF THE WAY

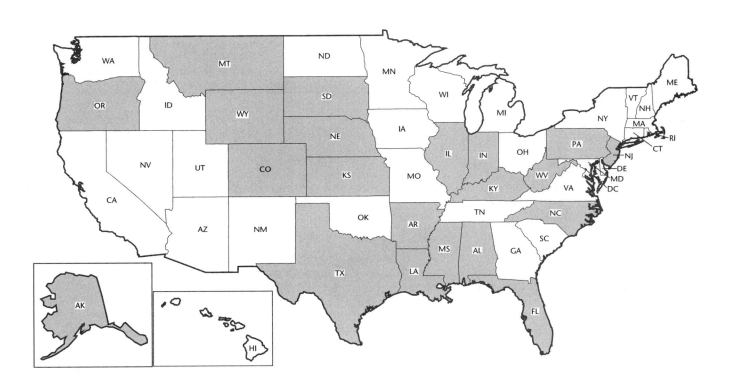

FLORIDA

March 9

In the beginning, there was Florida. The state enacted the nation's first presidential primary law in 1901. But it was not until 1972, when Florida officials began scheduling the primary on the second Tuesday in March that the Sunshine State became an important stop for White House aspirants looking for something other than rest and recreation. In the years that followed, Florida was joined on its early March date by other Southern states that created a regional votefest known as "Super Tuesday." As one of the most populous states in the country, Florida—along with Texas—tended to dominate the event.

In recent years, vote-rich Florida has assumed an increasingly influential part in the November presidential balloting—witness, the 2000 cliffhanger that made Florida the center of the political universe for weeks afterwards. But the

state's early March primary date no longer guarantees it a major role in the nominating process. By the time the Florida primary was held in 2000, the principal challengers to Democrat Al Gore and Republican George W. Bush had already quit the race.

From 1976 through 1988, during the heyday of the Florida primary, the candidates who won the first-in-the-nation primary in New Hampshire also won in Florida. But what had been a one-week interval between the two primaries in the early 1970s had grown to three weeks in the 1990s, a length of time in which the momentum from the New Hampshire primary could largely dissipate. In 1996, Granite State winner Pat Buchanan ran third in Florida's GOP primary with less than one-third the vote of the victorious Bob Dole. Four years

Recent Florida Primary Results

Florida held its first presidential primary in 1928.

	DEMOCRATS				REPUBLICANS		
Year	Turnout	Candidates	%	Turnout	Candidates	%
2000 (March 14)	551,995	AL GORE Bill Bradley	82 18	699,503	GEORGE W. BUSH John McCain	74 20
1996 (March 12)	—	NO PRIMARY		898,516	BOB DOLE Steve Forbes Pat Buchanan	57 20 18
1992 (March 10)	1,123,857	BILL CLINTON Paul Tsongas Jerry Brown	51 35 12	893,463	GEORGE BUSH* Pat Buchanan	68 32
1988 (March 8)	1,273,298	MICHAEL DUKAKIS Jesse Jackson Richard Gephardt Al Gore	41 20 14 13	901,222	GEORGE BUSH Bob Dole Pat Robertson	62 21 11
1984 (March 13)	1,182,190	GARY HART Walter Mondale Jesse Jackson John Glenn	39 33 12 11	344,150	RONALD REAGAN*	100
1980 (March 11)	1,098,003	JIMMY CARTER* Edward Kennedy	61 23	614,995	RONALD REAGAN George Bush	56 30
1976 (March 9)	1,300,330	JIMMY CARTER George Wallace Henry Jackson	35 31 24	609,819	GERALD FORD* Ronald Reagan	53 47
1972 (March 14)	1,264,554	GEORGE WALLACE Hubert Humphrey Henry Jackson	42 19 13	414,207	RICHARD NIXON*	87
1968 (May 28)	512,357	GEORGE SMATHERS Eugene McCarthy Uncommitted	46 29 25	51,509	UNCOMMITTED	100

Note: All candidates are listed that drew at least 10 percent of their party's primary vote. The names of winning candidates are capitalized. An asterisk (*) indicates an incumbent president.

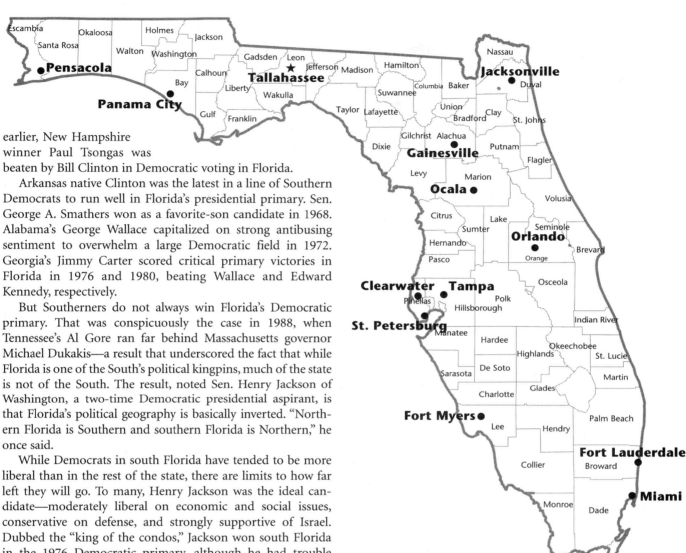

earlier, New Hampshire winner Paul Tsongas was beaten by Bill Clinton in Democratic voting in Florida.

Arkansas native Clinton was the latest in a line of Southern Democrats to run well in Florida's presidential primary. Sen. George A. Smathers won as a favorite-son candidate in 1968. Alabama's George Wallace capitalized on strong antibusing sentiment to overwhelm a large Democratic field in 1972. Georgia's Jimmy Carter scored critical primary victories in Florida in 1976 and 1980, beating Wallace and Edward Kennedy, respectively.

But Southerners do not always win Florida's Democratic primary. That was conspicuously the case in 1988, when Tennessee's Al Gore ran far behind Massachusetts governor Michael Dukakis—a result that underscored the fact that while Florida is one of the South's political kingpins, much of the state is not of the South. The result, noted Sen. Henry Jackson of Washington, a two-time Democratic presidential aspirant, is that Florida's political geography is basically inverted. "Northern Florida is Southern and southern Florida is Northern," he once said.

While Democrats in south Florida have tended to be more liberal than in the rest of the state, there are limits to how far left they will go. To many, Henry Jackson was the ideal candidate—moderately liberal on economic and social issues, conservative on defense, and strongly supportive of Israel. Dubbed the "king of the condos," Jackson won south Florida in the 1976 Democratic primary, although he had trouble establishing a toehold elsewhere in the state. Meanwhile, zealously anti-Castro Cubans have become a major force in Republican politics in south Florida, especially Dade County (Miami).

The other end of Florida is quite different. Northern Florida has long resembled its Southern neighbors in both geography and attitude. For years the area from the panhandle east to Jacksonville was "Wallace country"; it was the backbone of the former Alabama governor's successful 1972 primary campaign and his unsuccessful 1976 effort. Gore ran well across northern Florida in his first try for the Democratic presidential nomination in 1988, carrying more than a dozen counties, including those with Panama City and Pensacola. But Gore finished fourth statewide because he ran poorly in the other, more populous portions of the state.

In between the two ends of the state is central Florida, which includes the GOP's historic base in the retirement communities along the Gulf Coast. It is in central Florida where many

primary battles are decided. That includes the Ford-Reagan contest of 1976, which not only had ideological overtones but was by far the most competitive presidential primary that Florida Republicans have ever had. Reagan won north and south Florida, but still lost because of Ford's strength in central Florida and the Gulf Coast.

Although Florida Republicans are approaching parity with the long-dominant Democrats in voter registration, the burgeoning size of the GOP has not resulted in increased competition in the party's presidential primary. Only the Ford-Reagan contest was decided by a margin of less than 25 percentage points.

The Florida Rules

George W. Bush won the White House in 2000 with a protracted, razor-thin victory in Florida. But he will not have to break a sweat to win the state's Republican presidential primary March 9. In fact, there may not be a GOP primary at all if Bush is the only candidate.

Participation in the Florida primary is limited to registered voters in each party. As of October 2003, there were more than 3.9 million registered Democrats and 3.6 million Republicans.

DEMOCRATS

THE CALENDAR

Primary Date (polling hours)	March 9 (7 a.m.–7 p.m. local time; most of Florida is in the Eastern time zone, although the western part of the panhandle is in the Central time zone.)
Ballot Access	A state selection committee meets Jan. 6 to decide which names to put on the ballot and announces their list the following day. Other candidates can request consideration at a meeting of the committee on Jan. 13. There is no alternative petition route to the ballot.

THE DELEGATES

Number (% of national total)	201 (4.7%)
Distribution:	
By congressional district	115 (from 3 to 7 per district)
At-Large	39
Pledged PEOs	23
Superdelegates	24
Method of Allocation	Proportional—15% of vote needed to win a share of statewide or district delegates.

LOUISIANA

March 9

In the last two elections, Louisiana Republicans were the most ambitious of the players challenging Iowa for the lead-off position on the presidential nominating calendar. They held delegate-selection caucuses in early February 1996, a week before the Iowa caucuses, and had planned before abandoning the idea a similar event in 2000.

But Louisiana's caucuses in 1996 were sparsely attended (less than 25,000 of the roughly 500,000 registered Republicans) and virtually ignored by most of the contenders. Bob Dole led a lobbying effort on Iowa's behalf, and most of the Republican candidates signed a letter urging Louisiana to stick with its Super Tuesday primary.

Ultimately, only Phil Gramm, Pat Buchanan and Alan Keyes competed in Louisiana. Yet while the early event did not make the Bayou State a kingmaker, it did establish which candidate would anchor the right side of the GOP field.

The caucuses severely wounded Gramm, who had appeared to be a prohibitive favorite to win them. But Buchanan closed fast and won 13 of the 21 delegates at stake in the district caucuses. Dole won the remaining Louisiana delegates that were at stake in the Super Tuesday primary.

All and all, the experience was not out of character for Louisiana. While state and local politics are often colorful and absorbing, Louisiana voters have seemed less than enchanted with presidential politics.

Cost-conscious state officials tried to kill the presidential primary in 1984, just four years after it was instituted. When a federal court intervened, then-Gov. Edwin Edwards encouraged voters to stay away from the polls. Many white Democrats took his advice, which helped Jesse Jackson score his only primary win that year outside the District of Columbia.

In 1988, Louisiana Democrats joined the Super Tuesday lineup and doubled their primary turnout to more than 600,000. But the result was the same: Jackson won again. In predominantly black New Orleans, Jackson took nearly two-thirds of the vote. Elsewhere, he and runner-up Al Gore ran about even. Jackson won the large population centers—including Caddo (Shreveport), East Baton Rouge (Baton Rouge) and Calcasieu (Lake Charles) parishes—as well as the largely black parishes on the Mississippi River.

Gore carried Winn Parish, birthplace of the legendary Huey Long, and much of the rest of Protestant northern Louisiana. And he won Lafayette Parish, the heart of Cajun country. But Gore had to share his base. Michael Dukakis carried New Orleans' major suburban parishes—Jefferson, St. Bernard, and St. Tammany.

Recent Louisiana Primary Results

Louisiana held its first presidential primary in 1980.

Year	Turnout	DEMOCRATS Candidates	%	Turnout	REPUBLICANS Candidates	%
2000 (March 14)	157,551	AL GORE Bill Bradley	73 20	102,912	GEORGE W. BUSH	84
1996 (March 12)	154,701	BILL CLINTON* Lyndon LaRouche	81 12	77,789	BOB DOLE Pat Buchanan Steve Forbes	48 33 13
1992 (March 10)	384,397	BILL CLINTON Paul Tsongas	69 11	135,109	GEORGE BUSH* Pat Buchanan	62 27
1988 (March 8)	624,450	JESSE JACKSON Al Gore Michael Dukakis Richard Gephardt	35 28 15 11	144,781	GEORGE BUSH Pat Robertson Bob Dole	58 18 18
1984 (May 5)	318,810	JESSE JACKSON Gary Hart Walter Mondale	43 25 22	16,687	RONALD REAGAN* Uncommitted	90 10
1980 (April 5)	358,741	JIMMY CARTER* Edward Kennedy Uncommitted	56 23 12	41,683	RONALD REAGAN George Bush	75 19

Note: All candidates are listed that drew at least 10 percent of their party's primary vote. The names of winning candidates are capitalized. An asterisk (*) indicates an incumbent president.

The Republican primary in 1988 was not so close. George Bush outpolled runner-up Pat Robertson by a margin of more than 3-to-1. Dole ran second to Bush in the New Orleans area, but Robertson won three small parishes in southwestern Louisiana and finished second most everywhere else.

Bush was an easy winner again four years later. But the big story was the collapse of David Duke as a credible political force. The former Ku Klux Klan leader had frightened Louisiana's political establishment with unexpectedly strong runs for the Senate in 1990 and governor in 1991. But Duke's share in the 1992 GOP presidential primary was just 9 percent.

Pat Buchanan finished a distant second in the 1992 Republican primary, but he did better in 1996. His 33 percent share was his best in any Sun Belt primary that year. Buchanan carried more than two dozen parishes, about evenly divided between Protestant northern Louisiana and the Catholic Cajun country to the south.

In 2000, the state's mid-March presidential primary came after both the Democratic and Republican nominations were settled. Of the two "nominees in waiting," Republican George W. Bush drew a higher percentage of his party's primary vote—a precursor of his victory in Louisiana that fall.

The Louisiana Rules

While Louisiana holds colorful primaries for governor and senator in which candidates and voters of all parties participate, the primaries for president are closed and are rarely very dramatic. Voting in the Democratic primary is limited to the state's nearly 1.6 million registered Democrats. Participation in the GOP primary is limited to Louisiana's nearly 650,000 Republicans. Both registration figures are as of October 2003.

DEMOCRATS

THE CALENDAR	
Primary Date (polling hours)	March 9 (6 a.m.–8 p.m.)
Filing Deadline	Jan. 30
Filing Procedure	Candidates must pay a qualifying fee of $750 to the secretary of state and $375 to the state party in which they are running, or submit petitions signed by 1,000 registered voters of their party from each congressional district.
THE DELEGATES	
Number (% of national total)	72 (1.7%)
Distribution:	
By congressional district	39 (from 4 to 8 per district)
At-Large	13
Pledged PEOs	8
Superdelegates	12
Method of Allocation	Proportional—15% of vote needed to win a share of statewide or district delegates.

MISSISSIPPI

March 9

Mississippi's presidential primary has been distinguished more by who has not done well in it than who has.

Mississippi is in the midst of the Bible Belt and would seem to have been favorable terrain for religious broadcaster Pat Robertson. But Robertson drew only 13 percent of the vote in the 1988 GOP primary.

Mississippi has a reputation for rock-ribbed conservatism. Yet Pat Buchanan never reached 30 percent of the vote there in two tries for the Republican presidential nomination.

Rather, voters in the Mississippi primary have seemed comfortable casting a pragmatic vote for the presidential front-runner, especially in Republican balloting.

In 1988, Mississippi provided George Bush with his highest percentage of the vote in any Southern primary—66 percent, with Robertson and Bob Dole dividing most of the other ballots.

Bush won an even larger share in the 1992 primary, even though Buchanan bought TV ads and paid a well-publicized visit to a Confederate cemetery. Buchanan netted only 17 percent of the vote and had to share the anti-Bush element of the primary electorate with David Duke, who reached his only double-digit percentage of the primary season in Mississippi.

The Magnolia State's only close presidential primary was on the Democratic side four years earlier, when Jesse Jackson defeated Al Gore, 45 to 33 percent. Blacks make up 36 percent

Recent Mississippi Primary Results

Mississippi Republicans held a presidential primary to select delegates in 1980. Both parties held their first primary with a direct vote for candidates in 1988.

		DEMOCRATS			REPUBLICANS	
Year	Turnout	Candidates	%	Turnout	Candidates	%
2000 (March 14)	88,602	AL GORE	90	114,979	GEORGE W. BUSH	88
1996 (March 12)	93,788	BILL CLINTON*	92	151,925	BOB DOLE	60
					Pat Buchanan	26
1992 (March 10)	191,357	BILL CLINTON	73	154,708	GEORGE BUSH*	72
					Pat Buchanan	17
					David Duke	11
1988 (March 8)	359,417	JESSE JACKSON	45	158,526	GEORGE BUSH	66
		Al Gore	33		Bob Dole	17
					Pat Robertson	13
1984	—	NO PRIMARY		—	NO PRIMARY	
1980 (June 3)	—	NO PRIMARY		25,751	RONALD REAGAN	89

Note: All candidates are listed that drew at least 10 percent of their party's primary vote. The names of winning candidates are capitalized. An asterisk (*) indicates an incumbent president. There was no direct vote for candidates in the 1980 Republican primary; results are based on the vote for delegates.

of Mississippi's population (the highest percentage of any state), and exit polls showed nearly half the Democratic ballots were cast by blacks. By all indications, they voted almost unanimously for Jackson. He won in most parts of the state, including virtually all the major population centers.

Gore swept most of the predominantly white Hill Country of northeast Mississippi (which borders Gore's home state of Tennessee), the high-growth suburbs of Jackson and Memphis, Tennessee, and a scattering of majority-white counties in other parts of the state.

Several of those counties that Gore carried were longtime symbols of the white South. Lafayette County (Oxford) includes "Ole Miss," the University of Mississippi, as well as the home of novelist William Faulkner. Lee County (Tupelo) was the birthplace of Elvis Presley. And Neshoba County has been best known for its annual county fair that draws politicians from across the state and sometimes the nation, although Neshoba acquired a more infamous reputation in 1964 when three civil rights workers were slain near the county seat of Philadelphia.

In those days, the state Democratic Party was bitterly divided. The conservative "regular" faction held control of the party machinery at the state and local level, while a "loyalist" faction of blacks and liberal whites controlled the presidential delegate-selection process.

The two factions merged before the 1976 election. And since then, the state party has been in the mainstream of Southern Democratic politics. That biracial spirit was evident in the party's presidential primary in 1992, when Bill Clinton swept all parts of Mississippi and won nearly three-fourths of the vote.

The Mississippi Rules

Mississippi's presidential primary has found a comfortable niche on the second Tuesday in March, a date abandoned by most other southern states.

Mississippi does not have party registration, so any of the state's nearly 1.9 million registered voters (as of December 2002) may participate in the primary of their choice.

DEMOCRATS

THE CALENDAR

Primary Date (polling hours) — March 9 (7 a.m.–7 p.m.)

Filing Deadline — Jan. 9

Filing Procedure — By Dec. 15, 2003, the secretary of state will compile a list of generally recognized candidates to be placed on the primary ballot. Other Democratic candidates must file petitions with their state party signed by 500 registered voters or at least 100 registered voters in each of the four congressional districts.

THE DELEGATES

Number (% of national total) — 41 (0.9%)

Distribution:

By congressional district — 22 (from 5 to 7 per district)

At-Large — 7

Pledged PEOs — 4

Superdelegates — 8

Method of Allocation — Proportional—15% of vote needed to win a share of statewide or district delegates.

TEXAS

March 9

Texas is the most populous state in the South, the second-most populous in the nation, and has been the anchor of the early March Southern voting since 1988. Of late, that has been a dubious honor, as much of the rest of the country has voted earlier and earlier in the election year.

Befitting a state so large, Texas has a variety of racial and ideological divisions. But these are most apparent among the once-dominant Democrats. Within the fast-growing Republican Party, there is little evidence of a moderate wing; rather, there are gradations of conservatism.

That has been plainly visible since the Texas GOP's first presidential primary in 1964 produced 104,137 votes for Barry Goldwater and 6,207 for Nelson Rockefeller. Faced with a choice in 1976 between Ronald Reagan and President Gerald Ford, Texas Republicans spurned Ford and elected their entire complement of 100 delegates for Reagan.

Reagan won again in 1980, but his margin over George Bush in the primary was less than 20,000 votes out of more than 500,000 cast. Reagan swept most of the state, but Bush ran close by winning his home base of Harris County (Houston) with 63 percent of the vote.

In 1988 and 1992, Texas formed the cornerstone of a Bush sweep of the Super Tuesday South. It was not the "kinder, gentler" Bush that dominated the Texas primary both years, but the Bush with the ten-gallon hat and the oilman's swagger.

Both times Bush won his adopted home state with roughly two-thirds of the vote. That left little room for Bob Dole, who finished a poor third in Texas in 1988 behind Pat Robertson. Dole ran a distant second in most of the urban areas, but Robertson ran better in rural Texas, where he won a handful of counties.

Pat Buchanan did not find a much better toehold in the 1992 primary. He taunted the New England-born Bush as an "inauthentic" Texan and conservative. But Buchanan spent little time in the state and carried only two west Texas counties where the total vote was in the dozens. Buchanan carried a few more small counties in 1996, but he ran only slightly closer to Dole in the statewide tally than he had to Bush four years earlier.

The bigger story in 1996 was the turnout in the GOP presidential primary; it exceeded the Democrats for the first time ever. And it was more than just the absence of competition on

Recent Texas Primary Results

Texas Republicans held a presidential primary in 1964. The first year both parties held a presidential primary with a direct vote for candidates was in 1980.

| Year | DEMOCRATS | | | REPUBLICANS | | |
	Turnout	Candidates	%	Turnout	Candidates	%
2000 (March 14)	786,890	AL GORE Bill Bradley	80 16	1,126,757	GEORGE W. BUSH	88
1996 (March 12)	921,256	BILL CLINTON*	86	1,019,803	BOB DOLE Pat Buchanan Steve Forbes	56 21 13
1992 (March 10)	1,482,975	BILL CLINTON Paul Tsongas	66 19	797,146	GEORGE BUSH* Pat Buchanan	70 24
1988 (March 8)	1,767,045	MICHAEL DUKAKIS Jesse Jackson Al Gore Richard Gephardt	33 25 20 14	1,014,956	GEORGE BUSH Pat Robertson Bob Dole	64 15 14
1984 (May 5)	—	NO PRIMARY		319,839	RONALD REAGAN*	97
1980 (May 3)	1,377,354	JIMMY CARTER* Edward Kennedy Uncommitted	56 23 19	526,769	RONALD REAGAN George Bush	51 47

Note: All candidates are listed that drew at least 10 percent of their party's primary vote. The names of winning candidates are capitalized. An asterisk (*) indicates an incumbent president.

the Democratic side that produced it, since the ballots of both parties also featured contests for the Senate and House. But the Republican electorate is still mainly in Texas's metropolitan areas. The Democratic constituency is more disparate—a coalition of south Texas Hispanics, east Texas "Bubbas," urban blacks, and Austin liberals.

The Democratic mosaic was vividly on display in the party's 1988 presidential primary, which Michael Dukakis won with just one-third of the vote. Dukakis, who could speak fluent Spanish, won south Texas and the western panhandle, Bexar (San Antonio) and Travis (Austin) counties, and many of the suburbs around the major population centers.

Jesse Jackson won most of the other big population centers—Harris, Dallas and Tarrant (Fort Worth) counties— all with significant minority populations. Al Gore and Richard Gephardt split much of the heavily white eastern, central, and northern portions of the state.

In the 1992 Democratic primary, Bill Clinton swept everything, but the turnout was down nearly 300,000 from 1988. It was one of many recent signs that the broad base of "yellow dog" Democrats across Texas (those who would vote Democratic even if it meant voting for a yellow dog) was eroding.

The Texas Rules

Texas Democrats employ a unique system of delegate selection. They use the primary results to allocate 127 delegates at the district level, although they also employ a separate caucus process to elect 68 delegates, based on the presidential preferences of delegates to the June state convention.

Texas does not have party registration. As of September 2003, there were 12 million registered voters that could participate in either party's nominating process. But a voter must have cast a vote in the Democratic primary to be eligible to take part in the party's precinct caucuses that are held the evening of March 9. The caucus process continues with county and state Senate district conventions on March 20, and concludes with the state convention June 18–19.

DEMOCRATS

THE CALENDAR

Primary Date (polling hours)	March 9 (7 a.m.–7 p.m.)
Filing Deadline	Jan. 2
Filing Procedure	Candidates must either pay a $2,500 filing fee to the Democratic state chair or submit petitions signed by 5,000 registered voters.

THE DELEGATES

Number (% of national total)	232 (5.4%)
Distribution:	
By district	127 (from 2 to 7 per state Senate district)
At-Large	43
Pledged PEOs	25
Superdelegates	37
Method of Allocation	Proportional—15% of primary vote needed to win delegates in a state Senate district, and 15% of vote at the state convention needed to win a share of statewide delegates.

KANSAS

March 13

Kansas was the birthplace of several candidates who sought the White House in the late twentieth century. Gary Hart grew up in Ottawa in the eastern part of the state. Arlen Specter (who briefly pursued the 1996 Republican nomination) was born in Wichita.

But none made their mark in Kansas politics like Bob Dole, who was born, raised and sunk roots in the small town of Russell. And for nearly two decades, Kansas tried hard to boost Dole's presidential ambitions, although the results were not always as planned.

On Dole's first try for the White House in 1980, Kansas created its first-ever presidential primary. But his candidacy collapsed quickly, and he did not even enter his home-state primary that spring.

On Dole's second presidential run in 1988, Kansas Republicans got their licks in early with a pre–Super Tuesday caucus that Dole dominated. Pat Robertson tried to rally religious conservatives in parts of Kansas but failed to win a single delegate. Yet ultimately, Dole abandoned his candidacy before the convention, and all the Kansas delegates ended up voting for nominee George Bush.

In 1996, Kansas first scheduled a presidential primary, then canceled it, although the change did not threaten Dole's control of the delegation.

Not only were Kansas Republicans loyal to their longtime senator, but they sometimes looked askance at his presidential rivals, even when Dole was not on the ballot. President Bush won a comparatively modest 62 percent of the Kansas GOP primary vote in 1992, his second-lowest share of the primary season behind New Hampshire.

Republicans dominate the political scene in Kansas, but they are not all of a like mind. Voters in small-town Kansas— the party's traditional backbone—do not always vote the same as those in the more affluent suburbs outside Kansas City.

The disparity between the two was noticeable in the 1980 GOP primary. Ronald Reagan won easily, but while he rolled up more than 70 percent of the vote in many rural counties, he was held to a bare majority in suburban Johnson County, where both George Bush and John Anderson established toeholds.

The two Democratic presidential primaries in Kansas have been won by Southerners who were able to appeal to the state's rural nature. President Jimmy Carter trounced Edward Kennedy by 25 percentage points in 1980. Twelve years later, Bill Clinton won a majority of the vote against a crowded Democratic field.

Yet Clinton did not win everywhere in Kansas. Rawlins County, in the far northwest corner of the state, opted for its local entry, Dean Beamgard, a longtime community activist and retired postmaster. The vote in Rawlins County: Beamgard, 174; Clinton, 89.

Recent Kansas Primary Results

Kansas held its first presidential primary in 1980, but only one since then.

| Year | DEMOCRATS | | | REPUBLICANS | | |
	Turnout	Candidates	%	Turnout	Candidates	%
2000	—	NO PRIMARY		—	NO PRIMARY	
1996	—	NO PRIMARY		—	NO PRIMARY	
1992 (April 7)	160,251	BILL CLINTON	51	213,196	GEORGE BUSH*	62
		Paul Tsongas	15		Uncommitted	17
		Uncommitted	14		Pat Buchanan	15
		Jerry Brown	13			
1988	—	NO PRIMARY		—	NO PRIMARY	
1984	—	NO PRIMARY		—	NO PRIMARY	
1980 (April 1)	193,918	JIMMY CARTER*	57	285,398	RONALD REAGAN	63
		Edward Kennedy	32		John Anderson	18
					George Bush	13

Note: All candidates are listed that drew at least 10 percent of their party's primary vote. The names of winning candidates are capitalized. An asterisk (*) indicates an incumbent president.

The Kansas Rules

Over the years, several states in the agricultural Midwest have been major players in the presidential nominating process. But not Kansas. Nor is it likely to be in 2004, as the state's Democratic caucus process does not begin until mid-March.

There will be 50 first-round caucuses around the state that closely follow the state Senate districts. Participation in these gatherings, known as "local unit caucuses," is limited to registered Democrats and those voters willing to change their registration to Democratic at the caucuses. As of October 2002, there were more than 740,000 registered Republicans in Kansas, 440,000 Democrats and 420,000 unaffiliated voters.

DEMOCRATS

THE CALENDAR

Local Unit Caucuses	March 13
Congressional District Conventions	April 3
State Committee	April 24
Filing Deadline	Feb. 27
Filing Procedure	Candidates must pay a $1,000 filing fee to the Democratic state party or submit petitions signed by at least 1,000 registered Democrats.

THE DELEGATES

Number (% of national total)	41 (1.0%)
Distribution:	
By congressional district	22 (5 or 6 per district)
At-Large	7
Pledged PEOs	4
Superdelegates	8
Method of Allocation	Proportional—15% of vote needed to win a share of statewide or district delegates.

ILLINOIS

March 16

For years, the Illinois primary stood alone as a gateway to the later primaries in the industrial Frost Belt. But no more. Once near the beginning of the presidential nominating process, Illinois' mid-March vote is now closer to the end.

Yet Illinois still offers a rich harvest of delegates plus the reputation it has earned as a harbinger of things to come. Every Republican presidential nominee since 1976 and six of the last seven Democratic nominees have first won the Illinois preference primary.

When candidates come to Illinois, there is no guesswork as to where they go. Democrats head to Chicago—fully 35 percent black and 25 percent Hispanic—and the source of more than one-third of the party's statewide primary vote.

Republicans go to the suburban "collar" counties that surround Chicago on the north, south, and west before campaigning in the small cities, towns, and farm country downstate.

The collar counties, paced by Du Page and Lake, are among the most affluent in the country. Loaded with white-collar professionals, they tend to prefer more moderate Republican candidates than do GOP voters in rural Illinois. In 1980, native-son John Anderson won Cook (which includes Chicago) and Lake counties and ran virtually even with Ronald Reagan in Du Page.

Downstate, there is a more conservative brand of Republicanism that Reagan knew intimately. He was born in Tampico in the northwest part of the state and grew up in nearby Dixon.

Reagan's Illinois roots were not much help in his 1976 challenge to President Gerald Ford, as Ford easily swept the state. But in 1980, downstate Republicans found Reagan preferable to Anderson, which pushed Reagan to a comfortable victory statewide and Anderson toward an independent presidential bid.

In 1980, Illinois was still near the beginning of the primary calendar. Not so in 1988. Then, the Republican presidential

Recent Illinois Primary Results

Illinois held its first presidential primary in 1912.

	DEMOCRATS			REPUBLICANS		
Year	Turnout	Candidates	%	Turnout	Candidates	%
2000 (March 21)	809,667	AL GORE Bill Bradley	84 14	736,921	GEORGE W. BUSH John McCain	67 22
1996 (March 19)	800,676	BILL CLINTON*	96	818,364	BOB DOLE Pat Buchanan	65 23
1992 (March 17)	1,504,130	BILL CLINTON Paul Tsongas Jerry Brown	52 26 15	831,140	GEORGE BUSH* Pat Buchanan	76 22
1988 (March 15)	1,500,930	PAUL SIMON Jesse Jackson Michael Dukakis	42 32 16	858,637	GEORGE BUSH Bob Dole	55 36
1984 (March 20)	1,659,425	WALTER MONDALE Gary Hart Jesse Jackson	40 35 21	595,078	RONALD REAGAN*	100
1980 (March 18)	1,201,067	JIMMY CARTER* Edward Kennedy	65 30	1,130,081	RONALD REAGAN John Anderson George Bush	48 37 11
1976 (March 16)	1,311,914	JIMMY CARTER George Wallace Sargent Shriver	48 28 16	775,893	GERALD FORD* Ronald Reagan	59 40
1972 (March 21)	1,225,144	EDMUND MUSKIE Eugene McCarthy	63 36	33,569	RICHARD NIXON* #	97
1968 (June 11)	12,038	EUGENE McCARTHY# Edward Kennedy# Hubert Humphrey#	39 34 17	22,403	RICHARD NIXON#	78

Note: All candidates are listed that drew at least 10 percent of their party's primary vote. The names of winning candidates are capitalized. An asterisk (*) indicates an incumbent president. A pound sign (#) indicates a write-in candidate.

contest essentially ended in Illinois. Bob Dole had considered dropping out of the race after winning zero states on Super Tuesday. But he chose instead to plunge on into Illinois the next week, hoping that support from farm areas would revive his candidacy and raise fresh doubts about George Bush.

It was not to be. Dole carried a few rural counties but did not come close to the breakthrough he needed in the mother lode: Chicago's Republican suburbs.

The Illinois Democratic primary has rarely produced much drama. For years, Democratic presidential politics in Illinois was neat and tidy. Chicago mayor Richard J. Daley controlled the bulk of the delegation and took it to the national convention uncommitted. Since Daley's death in 1976, the party's Democratic nominating process within the state has been less orderly. But the Democratic primary has often provided a big win for the early front-runner at a critical point in the process.

President Jimmy Carter's 1980 demolition of Edward Kennedy (the margin was more than 2-to-1) essentially removed Kennedy as a realistic threat to Carter's renomination. In 1984, Walter Mondale's 5 percentage point victory over Gary Hart brought Mondale back from the verge of elimination and marked Hart's last chance to land a knockout blow. In 1992, Bill Clinton so thoroughly dominated the mid-March primaries in Illinois and Michigan that his major rival, Paul Tsongas, quit the race shortly thereafter.

The Illinois Rules

For better or worse, Illinois has the third Tuesday in March to itself, making the state either a site of high drama or a rest stop in the "mop up" stage of the nominating process.

Illinois does not have party registration, so any registered voter can participate in the primary of their choice. As of November 2002, there were slightly more than 7 million registered voters in Illinois.

DEMOCRATS

THE CALENDAR

Primary Date (polling hours) — March 16 (6 a.m.–7 p.m.)

Filing Deadline — Jan. 14

Filing Procedure — Candidates must submit petitions signed by at least 3,000 registered voters to the state board of elections.

THE DELEGATES

Number (% of national total) — 186 (4.3%)

Distribution:

By congressional districts — 102 (from 4 to 8 per district)

At-Large — 34

Pledged PEOs — 20

Superdelegates — 30

Method of Allocation — Proportional—15% of vote needed to win a share of statewide or district delegates.

ALASKA

March 20

Alaska is one of the few states in the country that has never held a presidential primary, although it dabbled with one during its territorial days in 1956 that produced victories for the eventual nominees, Adlai Stevenson on the Democratic side and President Dwight Eisenhower on the Republican.

While Alaska has not held a presidential primary since then, the state's Republicans have sought ways to offset the state's small delegate prize and remote location. In 1996, the answer was late January precinct caucuses accompanied by a statewide straw poll. The timing made Alaska the first event of the nominating season, ahead of both Iowa and New Hampshire, and it attracted more than 9,000 caucus participants, far more than the usual number.

The two top vote-getters in Alaska, Pat Buchanan, with 33 percent, and Steve Forbes, with 31 percent, both made campaign forays to the nation's frigid northern frontier. Front-runner, Bob Dole, though, did not, and finished third in the straw vote with 17 percent, in spite of endorsements from much of the state Republican hierarchy.

The ability to surprise has always been a part of the Alaska delegate-selection process. In 1988, it was the only state in the country to buck the political mainstream and give first-round caucus victories to the two preachers who were running, Democrat Jesse Jackson and Republican Pat Robertson.

Robertson's success reflected the rise of social conservatives within the Alaska GOP in recent years. But it has not always been that way. In 1964, Alaska Republicans broke with the rest of the West to give most of its delegates to former Pennsylvania governor William Scranton, rather than Arizona's Barry Goldwater. And in 1976, Alaska had one of the few Republican delegations from the West that supported President Gerald Ford, rather than Ronald Reagan.

Meanwhile, Alaska Democrats have a penchant for taking their time in deciding whom to support. In much of the last

quarter century, the winner of the Democratic mass meetings has been "uncommitted."

In 2000, Alaska Republicans were back with another early straw vote, this time held on the same late January night as the Iowa caucuses. George W. Bush emerged the winner over Steve Forbes by just 5 votes out of more than 4,000 cast. Voters on the largely vacant northern and western frontiers of Alaska, as well as in Washington, D.C., were allowed to cast their ballots via the Internet. And 35 did so, giving Bush his margin of victory.

The Alaska Rules

Alaska Republicans attracted a modicum of attention in 1996 and 2000 by holding precinct caucuses in late January, complete with a statewide straw vote.

But Alaska Democrats traditionally launch their caucus process two months later, when interest in the nominating process is often ebbing.

The Democratic precinct caucuses are open to registered voters in that party, as well as any new voters or other registered voters who are willing to change their registration at the caucuses. There were roughly 120,000 registered Republicans, 70,000 Democrats and 275,000 other voters in Alaska, as of November 2003.

DEMOCRATS

THE CALENDAR	
Precinct Caucuses	March 20
Legislative District Caucuses	March 20
State Convention	May 22
Filing Deadline	Jan. 16
Filing Procedure	Candidates must pay a $1,000 filing fee to the state Democratic Party.
THE DELEGATES	
Number (% of national total)	18 (0.4%)
Distribution:	
By congressional district	8
At-Large	3
Pledged PEOs	2
Superdelegates	5
Method of Allocation	Proportional—15% of vote at state convention needed to win a share of statewide or district delegates.

WYOMING

March 20

Although presidential primaries are much in vogue in the rest of the country, they have not caught on in Wyoming. But in a sense, the traditional caucus fits the old-fashioned style of the state's politics. There is no major media market and Wyoming has been likened to one town "spread over miles and miles."

Neither party's caucuses in 2000 drew more than one thousand voters statewide. But while GOP voters in the heavily Republican state can be found all over, Democrats are concentrated in the southern tier. More than a century ago, immigrant laborers came to southern Wyoming to build the Union Pacific rail line; the state's first coal miners fol-

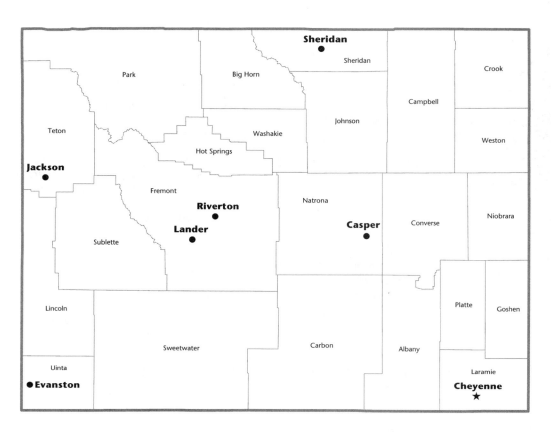

lowed. Like their counterparts in other states, most of these working men were drawn to the Democratic Party.

But the hearty band of Wyoming Democrats is hardly a liberal club. Democratic caucus-goers provided Bill Clinton with his first win outside the South in 1992 and gave Al Gore his initial victory anywhere in 1988. Four years earlier, Wyoming Democrats voted overwhelmingly for regional favorite son, Gary Hart of Colorado.

For a time, Wyoming's Democratic caucuses were held in early March on the eve of Super Tuesday. In 1988, the result was something of a split decision. Michael Dukakis ran ahead in the head count of caucus participants, but in the vote that mattered most—the election of delegates to the state convention—Al Gore won by a narrow margin. Gore thus gained a measure of momentum going into the Super Tuesday events, which would be the high-water mark of his candidacy that year.

In Wyoming two factors worked in Gore's favor. He was seen as a moderate Democrat, and he had the support of popular former Democratic governor Ed Herschler. Gore carried

Natrona County (Casper), the second most populous in the state, as well as much of rural Wyoming.

Republicans in the Cowboy State are as conservative as their GOP brethren in other Rocky Mountain states, but they do not always move in lockstep with them.

In 1952, the Wyoming delegation divided evenly between Dwight Eisenhower and Robert Taft when most other states in the region were overwhelmingly for Taft. In 1976, though a majority of Wyoming's delegation was for Ronald Reagan, President Gerald Ford won more delegates in Wyoming than any other Rocky Mountain state.

Still, one thing has remained constant about Wyoming and that is its bit role in the presidential nominating process. The last time that Wyoming took center stage was at the 1960 Democratic convention. With John Kennedy on the verge of victory, Wyoming's divided delegation regrouped to vote as a bloc and dramatically put Kennedy over the top near the end of the first roll call.

The Wyoming Rules

Wyoming's Dick Cheney found his way onto the Republican national ticket in 2000, but it was not due to the state's "mother lode" of delegates. On the Democratic side, only one state (Alaska) will have fewer delegates to the party's convention in Boston than Wyoming.

The county conventions in March are the critical stage of the delegate-selection process. Democratic meetings elect delegates to the state convention in May, where the party's national convention delegates are chosen.

Participation in the caucuses is limited to registered Democratic voters. As of March 2003, there were roughly 130,000 registered Republicans in Wyoming and 55,000 registered Democrats.

DEMOCRATS

THE CALENDAR	
County Conventions	March 20
State Convention	May 15
THE DELEGATES	
Number (% of national total)	19 (0.4%)
Distribution:	
By congressional district	8
At-Large	3
Pledged PEOs	2
Superdelegates	6
Method of Allocation	Proportional—15% of vote needed at the state convention to win a share of the statewide or district delegates.

COLORADO

April 13

Colorado's decision to hold its first presidential primary in 1992 was due in no small part to the contentious caucus process that Democrats went through four years earlier.

The precinct caucuses in 1988 were held in early April, just as Jesse Jackson's candidacy was peaking. The critical Wisconsin primary was to be held the next day. When Colorado Democratic officials seemed slow in tallying the caucus results, Jackson cried foul. He accused the state party chairman, a supporter of Michael Dukakis, of delaying the count so that Colorado would not influence Wisconsin.

State party officials countered that they were tabulating the votes from the nearly 3,000 precinct caucuses more quickly than they usually did. But they were clearly caught off-guard by the clamor of both Jackson and the national media for quicker returns. When the results were finally in, Dukakis had won (as sample precincts had

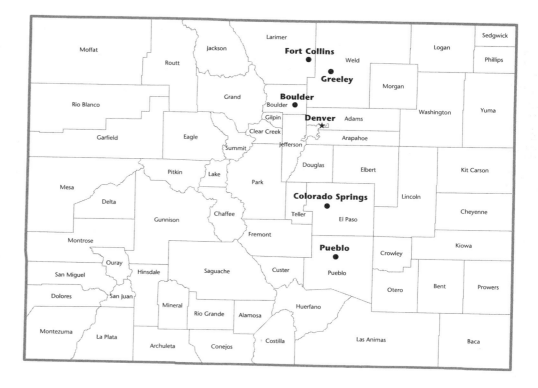

indicated from the beginning), but the whole episode helped fuel momentum for a state-operated presidential primary.

When the first primary was held four years later, Jackson and Dukakis were gone from the scene, but the race on the Demo-

Recent Colorado Primary Results

Colorado held its first presidential primary in 1992.

	DEMOCRATS				REPUBLICANS		
Year	Turnout	Candidates	%	Turnout	Candidates	%
2000 (March 10)	88,735	AL GORE	71	180,655	GEORGE W. BUSH	65
		Bill Bradley	23		John McCain	27
1996 (March 5)	54,527	BILL CLINTON*	89	247,930	BOB DOLE	44
		Lyndon LaRouche	11		Pat Buchanan	22
					Steve Forbes	21
1992 (March 3)	239,643	JERRY BROWN	29	195,690	GEORGE BUSH*	68
		Bill Clinton	27		Pat Buchanan	30
		Paul Tsongas	26			
		Bob Kerrey	12			

Note: All candidates are listed who drew at least 10 percent of their party's primary vote. The names of winning candidates are capitalized. An asterisk (*) indicates an incumbent president.

cratic side was as closely contested as it had been in 1988. The early March date that Colorado voted was at a time when all of the candidates were looking for traction. And when the nearly quarter million votes were cast, less than 8,000 separated the top three finishers. Jerry Brown emerged the winner, one of only two primaries he was to win in 1992; the other was Connecticut.

Brown won with a pro-environment, anti-establishment appeal that swept Colorado's liberal "granola belt," which extends westward from Denver through the college town of Boulder and skiing communities on the Western Slope, such as Aspen (Pitkin County), Vail (Eagle) and Telluride (San Miguel). Denver and Boulder counties, in particular, have a disproportionate influence on Democratic primaries. In 1992, 20 percent of the ballots cast in the party's presidential primary came from Denver, 10 percent from Boulder County.

Bill Clinton finished a close second by winning the farm counties of the High Plains, ranching counties of the Western Slope, Hispanic counties of southern Colorado and blue-collar strongholds such as Pueblo and Adams counties (the latter in the Denver suburbs). Paul Tsongas ran a close third by carrying the more upscale suburban counties of Arapahoe and Douglas, as well as El Paso County (Colorado Springs).

None of the Republican presidential primaries have been nearly as compelling as the inaugural Democratic contest in 1992. Each GOP primary has given a boost to the front-runner.

President George Bush swept all 63 counties in winning the Republican primary in 1992. His lone challenger, Pat Buchanan, reached 40 percent only in tiny Gilpin County, high in the mountains west of Denver.

Bob Dole won Colorado's Republican primary in 1996 almost as convincingly. He garnered more votes than his two nearest rivals combined, Buchanan and Steve Forbes, and carried every county except small, predominantly Hispanic Costilla, along Colorado's southern border. It went for Forbes.

The bulk of both parties' voters, though, can be found in a strip less than 200 miles long along the Front Range of the Rocky Mountains. Democrats tend to be strongest at the two ends—Boulder, Adams and Denver counties on the north and Pueblo on the south. Republicans tend to be stronger in between: in the affluent suburbs of Arapahoe and Jefferson counties near Denver, and just to the south in El Paso County (Colorado Springs), with its large representation of military and Christian conservatives.

No part of Colorado, though, whether the populous Front Range or more rural reaches, played much of a role in either party's presidential nominating process in 2000. Both Democrat Al Gore and Republican George W. Bush were already into a victory lap by the time Colorado voted that March. It proved to be the swan song, at least temporarily, for the state's presidential primary, as both parties return to a caucus process in 2004 to select their delegates.

The Colorado Rules

After trying for a higher profile role in the presidential nominating process in the 1990s with its March presidential primary, Colorado seems content for now to resume the low-profile part it previously held. The state's Democrats will select delegates in 2004 through a caucus process that does not begin until April.

Participation in the precinct caucuses is limited to voters who have been registered as a Democrat for at least two months prior to the caucuses and have lived in their precinct for at least 30 days. As of August 2002, there were roughly 850,000 registered Democrats in Colorado, slightly more than 1 million Republicans and almost 940,000 unaffiliated voters.

DEMOCRATS

THE CALENDAR	
Precinct Caucuses	April 13
County Conventions	April 23–May 13
Congressional District Conventions	May 21
State Convention	May 22
THE DELEGATES	
Number (% of national total)	63 (1.5%)
Distribution:	
By congressional district	34 (4 or 5 per district)
At-Large	12
Pledged PEOs	7
Superdelegates	10
Method of Allocation	Proportional—15% of vote required at all levels of the process.

PENNSYLVANIA

April 27

Pennsylvania held its first presidential primary on April 13, 1912—just one day before the Titanic encountered the iceberg. But the heyday of the Keystone State primary came more than a half century later, when candidates who fashioned themselves as champions of the lunch-bucket crowd first had to prove themselves in Pennsylvania.

Hubert Humphrey in 1972, Edward Kennedy in 1980, and Walter Mondale in 1984 all scored key victories in Democratic primary voting in Pennsylvania that advanced their candidacies. Henry Jackson lost the Pennsylvania primary decisively to Jimmy Carter in 1976 and folded his campaign shortly thereafter.

The state's electorate is less trendy and liberal than some of its Eastern neighbors. Rather, it has earned a reputation as the quintessential Frost Belt industrial state. Long dependent on coal and steel, it has a strong union tradition, a rich variety of ethnic groups, and fairly potent party organizations in the major population centers.

Pennsylvania's blue-collar Democrats have looked with suspicion on some of the party's more liberal presidential aspirants. George McGovern in 1972 and Morris Udall in 1976 both ran a poor third in the primary. Gary Hart fared little better in 1984, running nearly 200,000 votes behind Mondale. Of Pennsylvania's 67 counties, the only one to vote for McGovern, Udall, and Hart was Centre County (which includes Penn State University).

Candidates, though, do not spend much time around Penn State in bucolic central Pennsylvania. The greatest concentration of votes is at opposite ends of the state, which frequently leads to intense regional competition. The Philadelphia area is an integral part of the Eastern megalopolis that spreads from Washington, D.C., to Boston. Western Pennsylvania, anchored by Allegheny County (Pittsburgh), faces the industrial Midwest. It tends to vote more like the adjacent "smokestack" region of Ohio than more cosmopolitan Philadelphia 300 miles away.

Recent Pennsylvania Primary Results

Pennsylvania held its first presidential primary in 1912.

Year	DEMOCRATS			REPUBLICANS		
	Turnout	Candidates	%	Turnout	Candidates	%
2000 (April 4)	707,990	AL GORE	74	651,809	GEORGE W. BUSH	72
		Bill Bradley	21		John McCain	22
1996 (April 23)	724,069	BILL CLINTON*	92	684,204	BOB DOLE	64
					Pat Buchanan	18
1992 (April 28)	1,265,495	BILL CLINTON	57	1,008,777	GEORGE BUSH*	77
		Jerry Brown	26		Pat Buchanan	23
		Paul Tsongas	13			
1988 (April 26)	1,507,690	MICHAEL DUKAKIS	66	870,549	GEORGE BUSH	79
		Jesse Jackson	27		Bob Dole	12
1984 (April 10)	1,656,294	WALTER MONDALE	45	621,206	RONALD REAGAN*	99
		Gary Hart	33			
		Jesse Jackson	16			
1980 (April 22)	1,613,551	EDWARD KENNEDY	46	1,241,411	GEORGE BUSH	50
		Jimmy Carter*	45		Ronald Reagan	43
1976 (April 27)	1,385,042	JIMMY CARTER	37	796,660	GERALD FORD*	92
		Henry Jackson	25			
		Morris Udall	19			
		George Wallace	11			
1972 (April 25)	1,374,839	HUBERT HUMPHREY	35	184,801	RICHARD NIXON*#	83
		George Wallace	21		George Wallace#	11
		George McGovern	20			
		Edmund Muskie	20			
1968 (April 23)	597,089	EUGENE McCARTHY	72	287,573	RICHARD NIXON#	60
		Robert Kennedy#	11		Nelson Rockefeller#	18

Note: All candidates are listed that drew at least 10 percent of their party's primary vote. The names of winning candidates are capitalized. An asterisk (*) indicates an incumbent president. A pound sign (#) indicates a write-in candidate.

The regional rivalry can be quite sharp in Democratic contests. When Kennedy beat President Carter in 1980 by barely 4,000 votes, out of more than 1.6 million cast, Kennedy won decisively in the Philadelphia area and carried several other industrial counties in eastern Pennsylvania. But west of the Susquehanna River, Kennedy could carry just one county.

The Democratic primary was not close at all in 1984, since Mondale was able to win both ends of the state. And it has not been particularly relevant since then, with the April voting coming too late to affect the nominating contests. Jesse Jackson could carry little more than Philadelphia in 1988 against Michael Dukakis. Four years later against Bill Clinton, Jerry Brown won only Luzerne (Wilkes-Barre) and Lackawanna (Scranton) counties, the home base of the state's anti-abortion Democratic governor, Robert P. Casey.

Republican strength in Pennsylvania has long been concentrated in two areas—the Philadelphia suburbs and a part of the state known as the Republican "T." The latter is the predominantly rural central portion of the state that extends northward from the Pennsylvania Dutch country through the Susquehanna River Valley to the forested northern tier of counties along the New York border.

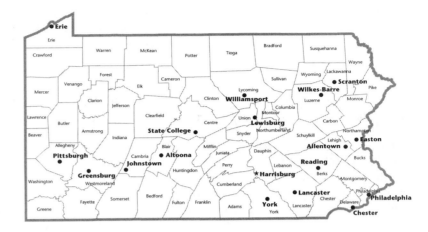

In defeating Ronald Reagan in the 1980 GOP primary, George Bush built up a lead in the Philadelphia suburbs and western Pennsylvania that Reagan could not overcome in the Republican "T" and Philadelphia, where Reagan had the backing of the city's GOP leadership.

Bush's victory in Pennsylvania in 1980, though, came too late to slow Reagan's bid for the GOP nomination. But it did embellish Bush's credentials as a potential running mate for Reagan, an eventuality that came to pass several months later.

The Pennsylvania Rules

Pennsylvania is the most populous state to vote in the spring, giving it a chance to have a huge role in the 2004 Democratic presidential nominating process—or more likely, no role at all.

Participation in the primary is limited to registered voters in each party. As of May 2003, there were 3.6 million registered Democrats in Pennsylvania and nearly 3.2 million Republicans.

DEMOCRATS

THE CALENDAR

Primary Date (polling hours)	April 27 (7 a.m.–8 p.m.)
Filing Deadline	Feb. 17
Filing Procedure	Candidates must pay a $200 filing fee to the secretary of the commonwealth (state) and submit petitions signed by 2,000 registered voters of their party.

THE DELEGATES

Number (% of national total)	178 (4.1%)
Distribution:	
By congressional district	98 (from 4 to 7 per district)
At-Large	33
Pledged PEOs	20
Superdelegates	27
Method of Allocation	Proportional—15% of vote needed to win a share of statewide or district delegates.

INDIANA

May 4

What the West Virginia primary did for John F. Kennedy in 1960, Indiana's did for his brother Robert eight years later, providing a high-profile victory on uncertain political terrain.

Indiana has a more conservative political milieu than many of its larger Midwestern neighbors, which made it a dramatic launching pad for Robert Kennedy's ill-fated, but memorable, presidential campaign. Kennedy crossed and crisscrossed the state, wooing minority voters in the inner cities (where he quoted Aeschylus on the night of the assassination of Martin Luther King) and white voters in the small towns that dot the state. For a time, Kennedy rode on a photogenic campaign train that followed the route of the old Wabash Cannonball.

And on primary day, he rolled to a clear-cut victory over both Eugene McCarthy and Roger Branigin, the state's governor and favorite-son presidential candidate. Kennedy swept most of the major population centers as well as much of rural Indiana, giving the first indication in 1968 of his broad-based voter appeal.

No Indiana primary since then has captured such national attention, although the Hoosier State has an unmistakable history of backing political outsiders that some of its larger Midwestern neighbors would not. George Wallace ran well in the Democratic primary in 1964 and 1972. Ronald Reagan won the 1976 GOP vote, his only primary victory over President Gerald Ford in a Frost Belt state east of the Great Plains. And in the 1984 Democratic contest, Gary Hart edged Walter Mondale, the favorite almost everywhere else in the industrial Frost Belt.

Coupled with his victory the same day in Ohio, Hart's win in Indiana revived his faltering campaign. But it was by the narrowest of margins, barely 6,000 votes out of more than 700,000 Hoosier ballots cast. Basically, Hart won rural Indiana while Mondale had the edge in the urban centers. Jesse Jackson, though, won Marion County (Indianapolis) and sliced away enough of the vote in other major population centers to enable Hart to prevail statewide.

Recent Indiana Primary Results

Indiana held its first presidential primary in 1916.

Year	DEMOCRATS Turnout	Candidates	%	REPUBLICANS Turnout	Candidates	%
2000 (May 2)	293,172	AL GORE / Bill Bradley	75 / 22	406,664	GEORGE W. BUSH / John McCain	81 / 19
1996 (May 7)	329,462	BILL CLINTON*	100	516,514	BOB DOLE / Pat Buchanan	71 / 19
1992 (May 5)	476,849	BILL CLINTON / Jerry Brown / Paul Tsongas	63 / 21 / 12	467,615	GEORGE BUSH* / Pat Buchanan	80 / 20
1988 (May 3)	645,708	MICHAEL DUKAKIS / Jesse Jackson	70 / 22	437,655	GEORGE BUSH	80
1984 (May 8)	716,955	GARY HART / Walter Mondale / Jesse Jackson	42 / 41 / 14	428,559	RONALD REAGAN*	100
1980 (May 6)	589,441	JIMMY CARTER* / Edward Kennedy	68 / 32	568,313	RONALD REAGAN / George Bush	74 / 16
1976 (May 4)	614,389	JIMMY CARTER / George Wallace / Henry Jackson	68 / 15 / 12	631,292	RONALD REAGAN / Gerald Ford*	51 / 49
1972 (May 2)	751,458	HUBERT HUMPHREY / George Wallace / Edmund Muskie	47 / 41 / 12	417,069	RICHARD NIXON*	100
1968 (May 7)	776,513	ROBERT KENNEDY / Roger Branigin / Eugene McCarthy	42 / 31 / 27	508,362	RICHARD NIXON	100

Note: All candidates are listed that drew at least 10 percent of their party's primary vote. The names of winning candidates are capitalized. An asterisk (*) indicates an incumbent president.

The 1976 Republican contest was nearly as close. Ford carried the southwest and northeast portions of Indiana, including traditional industrial counties such as Allen (Fort Wayne) and St. Joseph (South Bend) near his home state of Michigan. Reagan drew much of his strength from vocal and influential conservatives concentrated in the Indianapolis area and several industrial centers nearby.

The Indiana GOP, though, has not been noted for pursuing ideological crusades. And when Pat Buchanan ran in 1992 and 1996, he could not break 20 percent either time.

Still, Indiana has been a reliably Republican state in the fall presidential voting, and Democrat Bill Clinton was unable to carry its electoral votes in either of his presidential victories in the 1990s. But in 1992, Indiana gave him his largest share of the primary vote (63 percent) in any non-Southern state except West Virginia. Clinton won decisively in every Indiana county but Monroe, home of Indiana University in Bloomington, where he edged Jerry Brown by just 2 percentage points.

The Indiana Rules

Indiana has steadfastly refused to join the rush of states to the front of the nominating calendar, holding its primary in May in every election since 1956, the year the event was resurrected after a 28-year hiatus.

Indiana does not have party registration, so its nearly 4.0 million registered voters (the total as of November 2002) may participate in the primary of either party.

DEMOCRATS

THE CALENDAR
Primary Date (polling hours)   May 4 (6 a.m.–6 p.m.)
Filing Deadline   Feb. 10
Filing Procedure   Candidates must submit petitions by Feb. 20 to the secretary of state signed by at least 4,500 registered voters, including at least 500 from each congressional district, certified by the election office in the counties in which they were obtained. Petitions are due at the county level by Feb. 10.

THE DELEGATES
Number (% of national total)   81 (1.9%)
Distribution:
  By congressional district   43 (from 4 to 6 per district)
  At-Large   15
  Pledged PEOs   9
  Superdelegates   14
Method of Allocation   Proportional—15% of vote needed to win a share of statewide or district delegates.

NORTH CAROLINA

May 4

The best known of North Carolina's presidential primaries remains the 1976 duel between Ronald Reagan and President Gerald Ford. Had Reagan not won, his political career probably would have ended there.

Reagan had lost the first five primaries of 1976. But with backing from Sen. Jesse Helms and his potent political organization, Reagan edged Ford in the Tarheel State by about 12,500 votes out of nearly 200,000 cast. It proved a pivotal victory for Reagan that revived his 1976 campaign and helped position him to win the nomination and the White House in 1980.

In besting Ford, Reagan ran well in parts of the state where Helms had demonstrated strength—in the blue-collar, textile-producing centers of the Piedmont, in Helms's home base in the Raleigh area, and in tobacco-growing eastern North Carolina. Ford held his own in populous Mecklenburg County (Charlotte) and beat Reagan in the western mountains, the historic cornerstone of the North Carolina GOP since the Civil War.

At the same time that North Carolina Republicans were resurrecting Reagan's presidential ambitions, the state's Democratic voters were sounding the death knell for those of George Wallace. In the 1972 primary, Wallace had swamped the favorite-son candidacy of former North Carolina governor Terry Sanford by putting together much the same coalition on the Democratic side that Reagan did on the Republican.

But when North Carolina voted in 1976, Wallace was a fading force, both nationally and in the South. Jimmy Carter had gone head-to-head with him in Florida in early March and won by 4 percentage points. Two weeks later in North Carolina, Carter's margin expanded to nearly 20 points, and Wallace was done as a serious presidential contender.

The only other time that the North Carolina primary had a make-or-break quality was in 1988, when Bob Dole suffered a critical loss that enabled George Bush to sweep the Super Tuesday South and essentially wrap up the Republican nomination. North Carolina was one of Dole's best chances for a Super Tuesday victory that year, due in no small part to his wife, Elizabeth, who was born in the textile-producing town of Salisbury and graduated from Duke University in Durham. Dole carried several urban counties, including Mecklenburg and Wake (Raleigh). But Bush won most of the rest of the state and prevailed narrowly.

Recent North Carolina Primary Results

North Carolina held its first presidential primary in 1920, but did not hold another until 1972.

Year	Turnout	DEMOCRATS Candidates	%	Turnout	REPUBLICANS Candidates	%
2000 (May 2)	544,922	AL GORE / Bill Bradley	70 / 18	322,517	GEORGE W. BUSH / John McCain	79 / 11
1996 (May 7)	572,160	BILL CLINTON* / Uncommitted	81 / 12	284,212	BOB DOLE / Pat Buchanan	71 / 13
1992 (May 5)	691,875	BILL CLINTON / Uncommitted / Jerry Brown	64 / 15 / 10	283,571	GEORGE BUSH* / Pat Buchanan	71 / 20
1988 (March 8)	679,958	AL GORE / Jesse Jackson / Michael Dukakis	35 / 33 / 20	273,801	GEORGE BUSH / Bob Dole	45 / 39
1984 (May 8)	960,857	WALTER MONDALE / Gary Hart / Jesse Jackson	36 / 30 / 25		NO PRIMARY	
1980 (May 6)	737,262	JIMMY CARTER* / Edward Kennedy	70 / 18	168,391	RONALD REAGAN / George Bush	68 / 22
1976 (March 23)	604,832	JIMMY CARTER / George Wallace	54 / 35	193,727	RONALD REAGAN / Gerald Ford*	52 / 46
1972 (May 6)	821,410	GEORGE WALLACE / Terry Sanford	50 / 37	167,899	RICHARD NIXON*	95

Note: All candidates are listed that drew at least 10 percent of their party's primary vote. The names of winning candidates are capitalized. An asterisk (*) indicates an incumbent president.

It was a considerably better showing for Bush than his first presidential run against Reagan in 1980. Then, he could carry only the most liberal of North Carolina's 100 counties—Orange, home of the University of North Carolina at Chapel Hill and a cornerstone of the state's Research Triangle.

Pat Buchanan tried to emulate Reagan's success in his 1992 challenge to Bush, highlighting themes tailored to conservative Republicans—from criticism of the Voting Rights Act to putting the Confederate stars and bars on his North Carolina bumper stickers. But Buchanan could not come close to carrying a single county, either in 1992 against Bush or in 1996 against Dole.

Over the course of much of the twentieth century, North Carolina was a model for peace and prosperity in the South. And from 1972 through 2000, every Democratic primary winner except one (Walter Mondale in 1984) was a son of the South. Wallace, Carter (twice), Al Gore (twice), and Bill Clinton (twice) all won North Carolina's Democratic primary.

Gore's 2 percentage point victory over Jesse Jackson in 1988 was the closest of the recent Democratic contests. Gore swept most of the western half of the state, which is adjacent to Tennessee; Jackson won most of the eastern half, which includes the state's largest concentration of black voters. The party's eventual nominee, Michael Dukakis, carried Orange County.

The North Carolina Rules

North Carolina's most meaningful presidential primaries came when the state voted in March (1976 and 1988). But in 2004, the primary will once again be held in May.

As of October 2003, there were roughly 2.4 million registered Democrats in North Carolina and 1.7 million registered Republicans. They may vote only in their party's primary. Nearly 900,000 unaffiliated voters, though, may vote in either party's primary.

DEMOCRATS

THE CALENDAR	
Primary Date (polling hours)	May 4 (6:30 a.m.–7:30 p.m.)
Filing Deadline	Jan. 14
Filing Procedure	Candidates eligible for matching federal funds by Feb. 3 are placed on the ballot by the state board of elections. Other candidates must file petitions with county election boards by Jan. 14 signed by 10,000 registered voters of the candidate's party. Certified petitions must be filed with the state board of elections by Jan. 24.
THE DELEGATES	
Number (% of national total)	107 (2.5%)
Distribution:	
By congressional district	58 (from 4 to 6 per district)
At-Large	20
Pledged PEOs	12
Superdelegates	17
Method of Allocation	Proportional—15% of vote needed to win a share of statewide or district delegates.

NEBRASKA

May 11

Nebraska's presidential primary is not nearly as important as it once was. A generation ago, when there were only a handful of primaries, Nebraska served as a connecting rod between the opening round of contests in states such as New Hampshire and Wisconsin with the climactic round of voting in Oregon and California.

That was true as late as 1968, when Robert Kennedy scored a notable victory over Eugene McCarthy in Nebraska. But as primaries have become more important since then, Nebraska's has become less so. The proliferation of such events, coupled with Nebraska's late date and small delegate yield, robbed the event of much of its significance.

From time to time, though, Nebraska voters still use their primary to send a message. Disenchanted with President Jimmy Carter in 1980 for imposing a grain embargo on the Soviet Union (and canceling the state's grain sales), farmers in many of the crop-growing counties in eastern Nebraska cast their primary ballots for Edward Kennedy.

In 1976, Republican primary voters turned their backs on President Gerald Ford, who was born in Omaha under the name Leslie King Jr. Ford carried Douglas (Omaha) and Lancaster (Lincoln) counties, but was crushed by Ronald Reagan in the state's vast rural sector.

Reagan's victory was in line with the previous voting behavior of Nebraska Republicans, who had tended to prefer the most doctrinaire conservative in the primary field. They chose Robert A. Taft over Dwight Eisenhower in 1952 and Barry Goldwater over several more moderate alternatives in 1964.

Nebraska Democrats have a quite different tradition that goes back to the prairie populism of the state's most famous Democrat, William Jennings Bryan. Given a choice, Democratic voters have preferred "new ideas" Democrats over more traditional "New Dealers." In 1972, George McGovern defeated Hubert Humphrey. Twelve years later, McGovern's former campaign manager, Gary Hart, beat Humphrey's protégé, Walter Mondale.

The McGovern-Humphrey race was fairly close; the Hart-Mondale race was not. While Humphrey carried the Omaha area and a sprinkling of counties elsewhere, Mondale lost all 93 counties. Hart ran particularly well in the western part of the

Recent Nebraska Primary Results

Nebraska held its first presidential primary in 1912.

	DEMOCRATS			REPUBLICANS		
Year	Turnout	Candidates	%	Turnout	Candidates	%
2000 (May 9)	105,271	AL GORE Bill Bradley	70 26	185,758	GEORGE W. BUSH John McCain	78 15
1996 (May 14)	94,176	BILL CLINTON* Lyndon LaRouche	87 11	170,591	BOB DOLE Pat Buchanan	76 10
1992 (May 12)	150,587	BILL CLINTON Jerry Brown Uncommitted	46 21 16	192,098	GEORGE BUSH* Pat Buchanan	81 13
1988 (May 10)	169,008	MICHAEL DUKAKIS Jesse Jackson	63 26	204,049	GEORGE BUSH Bob Dole	68 22
1984 (May 15)	148,855	GARY HART Walter Mondale	58 27	146,648	RONALD REAGAN*	99
1980 (May 13)	153,881	JIMMY CARTER* Edward Kennedy	47 38	205,203	RONALD REAGAN George Bush	76 15
1976 (May 11)	175,013	FRANK CHURCH Jimmy Carter	38 38	208,414	RONALD REAGAN Gerald Ford*	54 45
1972 (May 9)	192,137	GEORGE McGOVERN Hubert Humphrey George Wallace	41 34 12	194,272	RICHARD NIXON*	92
1968 (May 14)	162,611	ROBERT KENNEDY Eugene McCarthy	52 31	200,476	RICHARD NIXON Ronald Reagan	70 21

Note: All candidates are listed that drew at least 10 percent of their party's primary vote. The names of winning candidates are capitalized. An asterisk (*) indicates an incumbent president.

state, where the Corn Belt gives way to wheat growing and ranching.

Democratic candidates from the South, even those with campaigns that arrived in Nebraska in overdrive, have had only mixed success in the state's primary. In 1976, peanut farmer Carter lost narrowly to Frank Church. In 1980, Carter won the Nebraska primary but with less than a majority of the vote. In 1992, Bill Clinton also won the Democratic primary with less than 50 percent. Part of the antipathy to Clinton no doubt was due to his rivalry with the state's popular senator, Bob Kerrey, who had been forced from the Democratic presidential race long before his home state voted. And in 2000, Al Gore's erstwhile opponent, Bill Bradley, drew fully 25 percent of the vote in Nebraska, his best showing in any primary state after he quit the Democratic race in early March. The former professional basketball star even carried a pair of rural Nebraska counties.

The Nebraska Rules

Nebraska's presidential primary was a major part of the American political scene for much of the twentieth century, but it barely made it to the twenty-first. State party and elected officials considered abandoning the primary and electing delegates through a caucus process. But the primary was given a reprieve for 2000 and will still be around in 2004.

Participation in the primary is limited to registered voters in each party. As of November 2002, there were slightly more than 540,000 registered Republicans in Nebraska and 380,000 Democrats.

DEMOCRATS

THE CALENDAR
Primary Date (polling hours) — May 11 (8 a.m.–8 p.m. CST or 7 a.m.–7 p.m. MST)
Filing Deadline — March 31
Filing Procedure — The secretary of state announces in mid-March the names of nationally recognized candidates to be placed on the ballot. Other candidates must submit petitions signed by at least 100 registered Democratic voters from each congressional district.

THE DELEGATES
Number (% of national total) — 31 (0.7%)
Distribution:
By congressional district — 16 (5 or 6 per district)
At-Large — 5
Pledged PEOs — 3
Superdelegates — 7
Method of Allocation — Proportional—15% of vote needed to win a share of statewide or district delegates.

WEST VIRGINIA

May 11

West Virginia's presidential primary assured itself a place in American political lore in 1960, when John F. Kennedy chose it as the place to test whether an urban Catholic could win in a rural Protestant environment. After an expensive and closely watched campaign that has become a part of "Camelot" lore, Kennedy defeated Hubert Humphrey, 61 to 39 percent, knocking Humphrey from the race and moving Kennedy's own candidacy a big step closer to the Democratic nomination.

No presidential primary before or since in West Virginia has had such an impact on the nominating process. In many years, it takes second billing on the May primary ballot to party gubernatorial contests that are decided at the same time.

Presidential candidates that do come to West Virginia find a state that is poor and viscerally Democratic. The backdrop has long made West Virginia fertile ground for Democratic candidates willing to embrace New Deal-style programs that are out of vogue in much of the rest of the country. Humphrey avenged his loss to Kennedy by swamping George Wallace by a margin of better than 2-to-1 in the 1972 primary. Twelve years later,

Recent West Virginia Primary Results

West Virginia held its first presidential primary in 1916.

	DEMOCRATS				REPUBLICANS		
Year	Turnout	Candidates	%	Turnout	Candidates	%
2000 (May 9)	253,310	AL GORE Bill Bradley	72 18	109,404	GEORGE W. BUSH John McCain	80 13
1996 (May 14)	297,121	BILL CLINTON* Lyndon LaRouche	87 13	127,454	BOB DOLE Pat Buchanan	69 16
1992 (May 12)	306,866	BILL CLINTON Jerry Brown	74 12	124,157	GEORGE BUSH* Pat Buchanan	81 15
1988 (May 10)	340,097	MICHAEL DUKAKIS Jesse Jackson	75 13	143,140	GEORGE BUSH Bob Dole	77 11
1984 (June 5)	369,245	WALTER MONDALE Gary Hart	54 37	136,996	RONALD REAGAN*	92
1980 (June 3)	317,934	JIMMY CARTER* Edward Kennedy	62 38	138,016	RONALD REAGAN George Bush	84 14
1976 (May 11)	372,577	ROBERT BYRD George Wallace	89 11	155,692	GERALD FORD* Ronald Reagan	57 43
1972 (May 9)	368,484	HUBERT HUMPHREY George Wallace	67 33	95,813	UNPLEDGED	100
1968 (May 14)	149,282	UNPLEDGED	100	81,039	UNPLEDGED	100

Note: All candidates are listed that drew at least 10 percent of their party's primary vote. The names of winning candidates are capitalized. An asterisk (*) indicates an incumbent president.

Humphrey's protégé, Walter Mondale, took a majority of the Democratic vote. West Virginia was the only primary state that Mondale carried in 1984 with more than 50 percent.

Edward Kennedy sought to duplicate his brother's success in West Virginia in 1980 but fell short. Forced to choose between nostalgia and loyalty, West Virginia Democrats chose to be loyal. The United Mine Workers and much of the state party hierarchy lined up behind President Jimmy Carter, who carried all but one county.

Bill Clinton was an easy winner in the West Virginia primary the two times he ran, although in 1996 he lost 13 percent of the vote to Lyndon LaRouche. It was the largest share of the vote that LaRouche won that year in any primary where he went head-to-head with Clinton.

No recent Republican primaries have been very compelling. The closest was in 1976 between President Gerald Ford and Ronald Reagan. But with the backing of the state's most powerful Republican at the time, Gov. Arch Moore, Ford swept all but three of West Virginia's 55 counties. Wood County (Parkersburg) was the largest that voted for Reagan.

The West Virginia Rules

Competitive presidential primaries may be a thing of the past in West Virginia, but because the event is held in conjunction with primary contests for state and local offices, turnout has remained high. In 2000, the number of ballots cast in the May primary was 56 percent of the statewide total in the November presidential election. That made West Virginia's primary turnout rate the third-highest in the nation—behind only New Hampshire and California.

Voting in the Democratic primary is limited to the state's 640,000 registered Democrats (as of November 2002). Participation in the Republican primary is open to West Virginia's nearly 310,000 registered Republicans and approximately 100,000 registered voters who are not identified with either party.

DEMOCRATS

THE CALENDAR	
Primary Date (polling hours)	May 11 (6:30 a.m.–7:30 p.m.)
Filing Deadline	Jan. 31
Filing Procedure	Candidates must pay a $4,000 filing fee to the secretary of state or submit petitions signed by at least 16,000 registered voters.
THE DELEGATES	
Number (% of national total)	39 (0.9%)
Distribution:	
By congressional district	18 (6 per district)
At-Large	6
Pledged PEOs	4
Superdelegates	11
Method of Allocation	Proportional—15% of vote needed to win a share of statewide or district delegates.

ARKANSAS

May 18

For the third time in the last few elections, Arkansas is represented in the Democratic presidential race. But the backgrounds of the state's White House aspirants have been dramatically different. The current one, Wesley Clark, is a retired Army general making his political debut in 2004. The other, Bill Clinton, may be Arkansas' most famous politician ever. Although he won the presidency in 1992 and 1996, the state's Democrats often gave him little more than a passing grade.

Running for a fifth term as governor in 1990, Clinton was renominated with a lackluster 55 percent of the primary vote. In the state's presidential primary two years later, he took a more impressive 68 percent. Still, his home-state percentage was less than the share of the vote he won in six other primaries in 1992. And in 1996, running essentially unopposed for renomination, his 79 percent share in Arkansas was his third-lowest percentage in any Democratic primary in the country.

To know him may not have been to love him. But Clinton's presidential primary victories in the 1990s reflected the coalition he had put together to dominate the state for more than a decade. He won by large margins in the Little Rock area, the heavily black counties of rural eastern Arkansas, and rural white-majority counties such as Hempstead (Hope), where he was born.

Meanwhile, Republicans have had a slow time constructing a base in Arkansas, and the presidential primary has been of little help. Before 1996, each party conducted its own, with Republicans lacking enough workers in some counties to open more than one polling place. The frequent result: minimal interest in the GOP contest, to the point that in 1992 just one vote was cast in the Republican presidential primary in all of Lee County (it was for Pat Buchanan).

Even with the state operating the primary for the first time in 1996, more than seven times as many ballots were cast in the Democratic primary—the largest ratio of Democratic to Republican ballots in any state in the nation.

The largest concentration of GOP primary voters is in the historically Republican Ozarks in the northwest quadrant of the state. George Bush handily won the region in the party's most competitive primary in 1988. Pat Robertson showed strength in eastern and southern Arkansas, where Republican turnout was light, and his cadre of supporters, though small, was large enough to carry 19 counties.

On the Democratic side that year, Al Gore won in dominating fashion, leaving little more than beachheads for Michael Dukakis, Jesse Jackson, and Richard Gephardt.

Recent Arkansas Primary Results

Arkansas held its first presidential primary in 1976.

	DEMOCRATS			REPUBLICANS		
Year	Turnout	Candidates	%	Turnout	Candidates	%
2000 (May 23)	246,900	AL GORE	78	44,573	GEORGE W. BUSH	80
		Lyndon LaRouche	22		Alan Keyes	20
1996 (May 21)	300,389	BILL CLINTON*	79	42,814	BOB DOLE	76
		Uncommitted	10		Pat Buchanan	24
1992 (May 26)	502,617	BILL CLINTON	68	52,141	GEORGE BUSH*	87
		Uncommitted	18		Pat Buchanan	13
		Jerry Brown	11			
1988 (March 8)	497,544	AL GORE	37	68,305	GEORGE BUSH	47
		Michael Dukakis	19		Bob Dole	26
		Jesse Jackson	17		Pat Robertson	19
		Richard Gephardt	12			
1984	—	NO PRIMARY		—	NO PRIMARY	
1980 (May 27)	448,290	JIMMY CARTER*	60	—	NO PRIMARY	
		Uncommitted	18			
		Edward Kennedy	18			
1976 (May 25)	501,800	JIMMY CARTER	63	32,541	RONALD REAGAN	63
		George Wallace	17		Gerald Ford*	35
		Uncommitted	11			

Note: All candidates are listed that drew at least 10 percent of their party's primary vote. The names of winning candidates are capitalized. An asterisk (*) indicates an incumbent president.

Gephardt and Dukakis each won a handful of counties in northern Arkansas near the Missouri border, an area loaded with retirees. Jackson carried a cluster of counties with a significant black population, most of them hugging the west bank of the Mississippi River. Gore won the rest of the state.

No presidential primaries before or since then have been so compelling for either party. Ronald Reagan swamped President Gerald Ford in Republican voting in 1976, as Reagan did in many other parts of the South. But in 1980, Arkansas Republicans did not conduct a presidential primary at all. Instead, they positioned themselves on the calendar between Iowa and New Hampshire with a controversial caucus process that was open only to local party officials. GOP candidates that year were encouraged to fill vacant party positions with their supporters.

Former Texas governor John Connally made the most lavish effort, at one point hosting likely caucus participants at an Ozarks resort. But his effort did not pay off. Connally took only one delegate, a conspicuous failure in his expensive, but short-lived, presidential campaign.

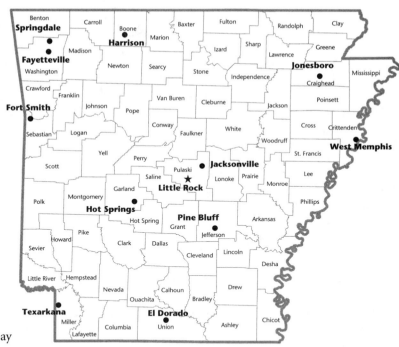

The Arkansas Rules

Bill Clinton put Arkansas on the national political map. But even with native son Wesley Clark running for the Democratic presidential nomination in 2004, the state has neither the advantageous primary date or compelling delegate count to stay there.

With no party registration in Arkansas, voters can participate in either party's primary. As of July 2003, there were nearly 1.6 million registered voters in Arkansas.

DEMOCRATS

THE CALENDAR	
Primary Date (polling hours)	May 18 (7:30 a.m.–7:30 p.m.)
Filing Deadline	March 30
Filing Procedure	Democratic candidates must either pay a $2,500 filing fee to the state party or file petitions signed by a number of voters equal to 3% of the total vote cast in the 2000 Democratic presidential primary.

THE DELEGATES	
Number	47 (1.1%)
Distribution:	
By congressional district	23 (5 or 6 per district)
At-Large	8
Pledged PEOs	5
Superdelegates	11
Method of Allocation	Proportional—15% of vote needed to win a share of statewide or district delegates.

114

KENTUCKY

May 18

Basketball and politics are two of the leading spectator sports in Kentucky, but the state's presidential primary has rarely drawn more than a collective yawn. That has been due in no small part to the fact that it has generally been held in late May, a time when recent nominating contests have been in the mop-up stage.

Since Kentucky held its first presidential primary in 1976, its only vote of significance came in the GOP contest that year between President Gerald Ford and Ronald Reagan. Out of nearly 135,000 votes cast, Ford won by barely 5,000—a narrow victory, but an important one in slowing the momentum that Reagan had built up earlier that month with a series of primary victories.

Reagan carried one stronghold of Kentucky Republicanism—the relatively affluent Louisville suburbs. Ford carried the other—the state's mountainous southeastern corner. Many of the mountaineers are "New Deal Republicans"—joined in poverty with Democrats in nearby hills and hollows but separated from them politically by partisan divisions dating to the Civil War.

The Democratic eastern end of Kentucky is similar to neighboring West Virginia. The region has a long union tradition and the voters have looked favorably on New Deal-style Democrats. It was the only part of Kentucky where Edward Kennedy ran reasonably close to President Jimmy Carter in Kennedy's landslide 1980 primary loss.

Across the state in the western panhandle is a different breed of Democrat. That area resembles the Deep South in its voting habits and contains the only Kentucky counties that supported George Wallace's 1968 third-party presidential bid.

The winner of the Democratic primary has often been the candidate that the Democratic governor supported. (Kentucky has elected only two Republican governors since the end of World War II—in 1967 and 2003.)

In 1988, Gov. Wallace G. Wilkinson backed Al Gore, who won easily. In 1992, Gov. Brereton Jones backed Bill Clinton, who carried the Kentucky primary by an even larger vote.

As it was, Gore's winning 46 percent share in Kentucky was his highest percentage in any 1988 primary outside his home state of Tennessee. Gore had trouble shaking his two closest rivals, Michael Dukakis and Jesse Jackson, in Kentucky's two leading population centers, Jefferson (Louisville) and Fayette (Lexington) counties.

But moving south across the state toward the Tennessee border, Gore's vote share increased dramatically. In Monroe

Recent Kentucky Primary Results

Kentucky held its first presidential primary in 1976.

| Year | DEMOCRATS | | | REPUBLICANS | | |
	Turnout	Candidates	%	Turnout	Candidates	%
2000 (May 23)	220,279	AL GORE Bill Bradley Uncommitted	71 15 12	91,323	GEORGE W. BUSH	83
1996 (May 28)	276,019	BILL CLINTON* Uncommitted	77 16	103,839	BOB DOLE	74
1992 (May 26)	370,578	BILL CLINTON Uncommitted	56 28	101,119	GEORGE BUSH* Uncommitted	75 25
1988 (March 8)	318,721	AL GORE Michael Dukakis Jesse Jackson	46 19 16	121,402	GEORGE BUSH Bob Dole Pat Robertson	59 23 11
1984	—	NO PRIMARY		—	NO PRIMARY	
1980 (May 27)	240,331	JIMMY CARTER* Edward Kennedy	67 23	94,795	RONALD REAGAN	82
1976 (May 25)	306,006	JIMMY CARTER George Wallace Morris Udall	59 17 11	133,528	GERALD FORD* Ronald Reagan	51 47

Note: All candidates are listed that drew at least 10 percent of their party's primary vote. The names of winning candidates are capitalized. An asterisk (*) indicates an incumbent president.

County, which lies about 30 miles north of his hometown of Carthage, Tenn., Gore won 95 percent of the votes cast.

As in much of the rest of the South, George Bush's victory in the 1988 Republican primary in Kentucky was notable for its completeness. He lost only one county, Ballard, a rural Democratic enclave bordering Illinois and Missouri that was carried by Bob Dole.

In 1992 and 1996, neither of the Republican primary winners, Bush and Dole, respectively, lost a single county.

The Kentucky Rules

Kentucky is something of a bellwether on election night in November, as it is one of the first states to report its results. But for years, Kentucky's May primary date has made it an afterthought in the presidential nominating process.

Participation in the primary is limited to registered voters in each party. As of November 2003, there were nearly 1.6 million registered Democrats in Kentucky and 950,000 Republicans.

DEMOCRATS

THE CALENDAR	
Primary Date (polling hours)	May 18 (6 a.m.–6 p.m.)
Filing Deadline	Jan. 27
Filing Procedure	The state board of elections Jan. 13 places on the primary ballot all candidates who have qualified for federal matching funds. Other candidates must show evidence of being on the ballot in at least 20 states or by submitting petitions signed by 5,000 registered Democratic voters with the secretary of state. All candidates must also pay a $1,000 filing fee to the secretary of state by Jan. 27 and file a statement of candidacy with the Democratic state party by Jan. 31.
THE DELEGATES	
Number (% of national total)	56 (1.3%)
Distribution:	
By congressional district	32 (from 4 to 8 per district)
At-Large	11
Pledged PEOs	6
Superdelegates	7
Method of Allocation	Proportional—15% of vote needed to win a share of statewide or district delegates.

OREGON

May 18

Oregon made history in 1996 by being the first state to hold its presidential primary by mail. It was hoped that the innovation would decrease election costs and increase voter participation, and the experiment proved successful enough to make balloting by mail a permanent fixture on the Oregon political scene.

That Oregon would be the first to try a ballot-by-mail primary (beating Nevada to that distinction, as it turns out, by two weeks) is not surprising. Oregon has been in the forefront of creative election procedures, from the establishment of one of the first presidential primaries early this century to widespread use of absentee ballots in recent years.

Oregon's primary voters have often supported the presidential candidate who "cares enough to come" to this part of the Pacific Northwest. Nelson Rockefeller used that slogan in upsetting Barry Goldwater in the 1964 Republican primary.

Four years later, Eugene McCarthy gave the Kennedy family its first electoral defeat in a quarter century, defeating Robert Kennedy in the Democratic balloting.

On the whole, Oregon voters have tended to support moderate Republicans and fairly liberal Democrats in its presidential primary. Twice before he won the Republican nomination in 1980, Ronald Reagan was on the Oregon GOP primary ballot—in 1968 and 1976—and lost both times. Democratic primary winners have included George McGovern, Frank Church, and Gary Hart. In 1988, Jesse Jackson drew 38 percent of the Democratic vote, his best showing that year in any of the 16 primary states that voted after Super Tuesday—including New York, Illinois, and California.

Jackson's performance was built around victories in the two academic-oriented counties, Lane (Eugene) and Benton (Corvallis), the homes of the University of Oregon and Oregon

Recent Oregon Primary Results

Oregon held its first presidential primary in 1912.

Year	DEMOCRATS			REPUBLICANS		
	Turnout	Candidates	%	Turnout	Candidates	%
2000 (May 16)	354,594	AL GORE	85	349,831	GEORGE W. BUSH	84
		Lyndon LaRouche	11		Alan Keyes	13
1996 (March 12)	369,178	BILL CLINTON*	95	407,514	BOB DOLE	51
					Pat Buchanan	21
					Steve Forbes	13
1992 (May 19)	354,332	BILL CLINTON	45	304,159	GEORGE BUSH*	67
		Jerry Brown	31		Pat Buchanan	19
		Paul Tsongas	10			
1988 (May 17)	388,932	MICHAEL DUKAKIS	57	274,486	GEORGE BUSH	73
		Jesse Jackson	38		Bob Dole	18
1984 (May 15)	399,679	GARY HART	58	243,346	RONALD REAGAN*	98
		Walter Mondale	28			
1980 (May 20)	368,322	JIMMY CARTER*	57	315,366	RONALD REAGAN	54
		Edward Kennedy	31		George Bush	35
					John Anderson	10
1976 (May 25)	432,632	FRANK CHURCH	34	298,535	GERALD FORD*	50
		Jimmy Carter	27		Ronald Reagan	46
		Jerry Brown#	25			
1972 (May 23)	408,644	GEORGE McGOVERN	50	282,010	RICHARD NIXON*	82
		George Wallace	20		Paul McCloskey	10
		Hubert Humphrey	13			
1968 (May 28)	373,070	EUGENE McCARTHY	44	312,159	RICHARD NIXON	65
		Robert Kennedy	38		Ronald Reagan	20
		Lyndon Johnson*	12		Nelson Rockefeller#	12

Note: All candidates are listed that drew at least 10 percent of their party's primary vote. The names of winning candidates are capitalized. An asterisk (*) indicates an incumbent president. A pound sign (#) indicates a write-in candidate.

State, respectively, as well as a decent showing in the trio of counties that make up metropolitan Portland. About 40 percent of both parties' primary vote comes from the Portland area.

The Oregon GOP has grown more conservative of late. But in the most memorable of the state's Republican primaries, the more moderate entries ran quite well. A dozen years after Rockefeller's victory, President Gerald Ford narrowly beat Reagan in Oregon, Reagan's only loss that year in a primary west of the Mississippi. In 1980, George Bush and John Anderson together collected nearly half the primary vote, even as Reagan was moving at full gallop toward the Republican nomination.

A generation ago, Oregon held the penultimate primary, with its May contest setting up the make-or-break vote in early June in California. But none of the recent contests have drawn much attention.

Oregon moved its primary to the second Tuesday in March in 1996 in an attempt to return the state to the front ranks of presidential primaries. With both the ease and novelty of balloting by mail, combined turnout in the Democratic and

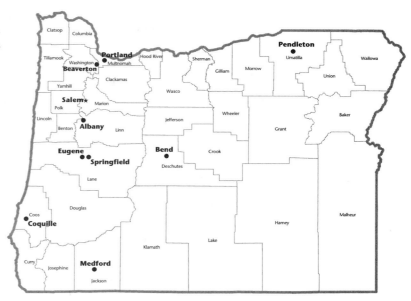

Republican presidential primaries was up by more than 100,000 from 1992. But the vote was still held too late to have much impact on the nominating contest.

The Oregon Rules

Oregon held its first ballot-by-mail presidential primary in 1996 on the second Tuesday in March and sought to do so again in 2000. But with ballots going out to voters weeks before the actual primary date, Oregon ran afoul of national Democratic Party rules that at the time prohibited states from holding their vote before the first Tuesday in March. As a result, Oregon moved its presidential primary back to its traditional May date.

Oregon allows the Democratic and Republican parties to open their primaries to unaffiliated voters, but as of early December neither party had done so. As of November 2003, there were 720,000 registered Democrats in Oregon, nearly 680,000 Republicans and 340,000 unaffiliated voters.

DEMOCRATS

THE CALENDAR	
Primary Date (polling hours)	May 18 (ballot due by 8 p.m.)
Filing Deadline	March 9
Filing Procedure	The secretary of state announces about six weeks before the filing deadline the names of nationally recognized candidates to be placed on the ballot. Other candidates must file petitions signed by 5,000 registered Democratic voters with 1,000 from each congressional district, including Democrats registered in at least one-tenth of the counties in each congressional district.

THE DELEGATES	
Number (% of national total)	58 (1.3%)
Distribution:	
By congressional district	30 (5 to 7 per district)
At-Large	10
Pledged PEOs	6
Superdelegates	12
Method of Allocation	Proportional—15% of vote needed to win a share of the statewide or district delegates.

ALABAMA

June 1

By joining with Florida and Georgia to hold a presidential primary in early March 1980, Alabama helped form the embryo of the Southern regional vote that had developed by 1988 into "Super Tuesday." But Alabama voters never turned out in large numbers for the March primary, certainly when compared to the state's midterm gubernatorial primary. In the 1990s, the presidential primary was returned to June, when party nominations for Congress are also settled.

Those that did vote in Alabama's Democratic presidential primaries in the 1980s disproportionately represented the liberal wing of the party. They handed Walter Mondale a critical victory in 1984 and gave Jesse Jackson a clear-cut primary win in 1988.

Mondale, rocked in early 1984 by an upset loss to Gary Hart in New Hampshire, regained his footing with a narrow victory in Georgia and a decisive triumph the same day in Alabama. With support from organized labor, Mondale rode to a large lead in Alabama's major industrial centers—Birmingham, Gadsden, Anniston, and the Quad Cities of the Tennessee River Valley.

But Mondale also relied on the support of blacks. Exit polls showed him splitting the white vote almost evenly with Hart

and John Glenn. But with help from Birmingham mayor Richard Arrington Jr. and other black leaders, Mondale picked off an estimated one-third to one-half of the black vote. Jackson won virtually all the rest.

The Democratic primary vote was even more racially polarized in 1988. Blacks cast about one-third of the ballots, and Jackson won nearly all of them. Sen. Al Gore of neighboring Tennessee took a majority of the white vote.

The pattern was visible on the map. Except for a pocket of white-majority counties near the Florida panhandle, Jackson swept every county in the southern half of the state. In the rural black-majority counties, his margins were huge. He won by nearly 40-to-1 in Macon County (Tuskegee), which had a population 86 percent black in the 1990 census.

Meanwhile, Gore swept virtually every county in Alabama's hilly and overwhelmingly white northern half. Jackson won statewide by 25,000 votes by virtue of his urban strength. Of the state's five most populous counties, he carried four, losing only Madison (Huntsville), along the Tennessee border, to Gore.

Although Republicans currently hold the governorship, both of Alabama's Senate seats, and a majority of the House

Recent Alabama Primary Results

Alabama held its first presidential primary in 1928 to select delegates, but did not include a direct vote for presidential candidates until 1980.

| Year | DEMOCRATS | | | REPUBLICANS | | |
	Turnout	Candidates	%	Turnout	Candidates	%
2000 (June 6)	278,527	AL GORE	77	203,079	GEORGE W. BUSH	84
		Uncommitted	17		Alan Keyes	12
1996 (June 4)	302,038	BILL CLINTON*	81	211,933	BOB DOLE	76
		Uncommitted	15		Pat Buchanan	16
1992 (June 2)	450,899	BILL CLINTON	68	165,121	GEORGE BUSH*	74
		Uncommitted	20		Uncommitted	18
1988 (March 8)	405,642	JESSE JACKSON	44	213,561	GEORGE BUSH	65
		Al Gore	37		Bob Dole	16
					Pat Robertson	14
1984 (March 13)	428,283	WALTER MONDALE	35		NO PRIMARY	
		John Glenn	21			
		Gary Hart	21			
		Jesse Jackson	20			
1980 (March 11)	237,464	JIMMY CARTER*	82	211,353	RONALD REAGAN	70
		Edward Kennedy	13		George Bush	26

Note: All candidates are listed that drew at least 10 percent of their party's primary vote. The names of winning candidates are capitalized. An asterisk (*) indicates an incumbent president.

delegation, the GOP's primary electorate has been comparatively small and centered on the state's major metropolitan areas. More than half the vote in the 1996 GOP presidential primary was cast in four counties—Jefferson (Birmingham), Madison, Mobile, and Shelby (a fast-growing suburban county outside Birmingham).

Whether balloting in March or June, Republican primary voters have overwhelmingly endorsed the front-runner: Ronald Reagan in 1980, George Bush in 1988 and 1992, Bob Dole in 1996, and George W. Bush in 2000. Conservative Christian activists have had only modest success in spite of Alabama's location in the midst of the Bible Belt. Evangelist Pat Robertson drew just 14 percent of the vote in the 1988 GOP primary.

Yet sometimes it takes an election or two for even establishment candidates to make good in Alabama. Dole was beaten badly by Bush in the 1988 primary. Bush was swamped by Reagan in 1980. Bush's loss that time was not from lack of effort. His TV ads featured an endorsement from former Vietnam prisoner of war Jeremiah Denton (who was on his way to election to the Senate that fall). And Bush's state campaign manager, who was also the national president of the Bass Anglers Sportsman Society, sought to organize Alabama fishermen for Bush. The effort, though, did not land many voters.

The Alabama Rules

Alabama is one of several states that has concluded that an early spot on the presidential primary calendar is not worth the effort. After dabbling with a March primary date in the 1980s, Alabama in 2004 will be holding its fourth straight presidential primary in June.

Alabama does not have party registration, so the state's more than 2.3 million registered voters (as of November 2002) can participate in the primary of their choice.

DEMOCRATS

THE CALENDAR
Primary Date (polling hours) — June 1 (7 a.m.–7 p.m.)
Filing Deadline — April 2
Filing Procedure — Candidates must submit petitions to the Democratic state chair signed by at least 500 registered voters statewide or at least 50 registered voters from each congressional district. In either case, candidates must pay the Democratic state chair a $2,000 filing fee.

THE DELEGATES
Number (% of national total) — 62 (1.4%)
Distribution:
By congressional district — 35 (varies from 4 to 7 per district)
At-Large — 12
Pledged PEOs — 7
Superdelegates — 8
Method of Allocation — Proportional—15% of vote needed to win a share of statewide or district delegates.

SOUTH DAKOTA

June 1

South Dakota is a small state with a long presidential primary tradition that dates back to 1912. But unlike New Hampshire, it has struggled to find a niche on the primary calendar—bouncing back and forth in recent years between dates in February and June.

Candidates that have made it to South Dakota find a state that straddles two regions. On the east side of the Missouri River is the relatively sedate farm land of the agrarian Midwest; on the other side is the wide-open ranch land of the West.

Most voters live in the eastern half, which adjoins the Corn Belt territory of Iowa and Minnesota. Democrats have a registration advantage in more than a dozen of the counties in eastern South Dakota.

The western side of the state is strongly Republican, with plenty of frontier individualists eager for government to let them alone. The Democratic presence west of the Missouri does not extend much beyond the scattered Native American reservations.

The east-west variation was illustrated in the 1976 Republican primary between President Gerald Ford and Ronald Reagan. Ford carried seven of the eight counties on the eastern border, including the state's leading population and trade center, Minnehaha County (Sioux Falls). Reagan swept all six counties on the western border, including South Dakota's second-most populous county, Pennington (Rapid City). Reagan won the primary by also carrying nearly all the counties between Rapid City and Sioux Falls.

The effects of geography can sometimes be felt in the Democratic primary as well. South Dakota provided a farm-state showdown in 1992 between Sens. Bob Kerrey of Nebraska and Tom Harkin of Iowa. Harkin won nearly a dozen counties in the eastern part of the state. But Kerrey won the primary handily by

Recent South Dakota Primary Results

South Dakota held its first presidential primary in 1912.

Year	DEMOCRATS			REPUBLICANS		
	Turnout	Candidates	%	Turnout	Candidates	%
2000 (June 6)	—	NO PRIMARY		45,279	GEORGE W. BUSH John McCain	78 14
1996 (Feb. 27)	—	NO PRIMARY		69,170	BOB DOLE Pat Buchanan Steve Forbes	45 29 13
1992 (Feb. 25)	59,503	BOB KERREY Tom Harkin Bill Clinton	40 25 19	44,671	GEORGE BUSH* Uncommitted	69 31
1988 (Feb. 23)	71,606	RICHARD GEPHARDT Michael Dukakis	44 31	93,405	BOB DOLE Pat Robertson George Bush	55 20 19
1984 (June 5)	52,561	GARY HART Walter Mondale	51 39	—	NO PRIMARY	
1980 (June 3)	68,763	EDWARD KENNEDY Jimmy Carter*	49 45	82,905	RONALD REAGAN	82
1976 (June 1)	58,671	JIMMY CARTER Morris Udall "None"	41 33 13	84,077	RONALD REAGAN Gerald Ford*	51 44
1972 (June 6)	28,017	GEORGE McGOVERN	100	52,820	RICHARD NIXON*	100
1968 (June 4)	64,287	ROBERT KENNEDY Lyndon Johnson* Eugene McCarthy	50 30 20	68,113	RICHARD NIXON	100

Note: All candidates are listed that drew at least 10 percent of their party's primary vote. The names of winning candidates are capitalized. An asterisk (*) indicates an incumbent president.

sweeping the western half, rolling up some of his largest margins in the state's two most heavily Indian counties, Shannon and Todd, where Kerrey was the only one of the major Democratic candidates to spend much time campaigning.

Good times or bad, there has always been a strong strain of agrarian populism among South Dakota Democrats. They cast their primary ballots for Robert Kennedy in 1968 and for his brother, Edward, in 1980. But the party's presidential primary has rarely been very predictive. It was last won by the eventual Democratic nominee in 1976, when Jimmy Carter defeated Morris Udall.

Nor has the primary always been that predictive on the Republican side. In 1988, it was the only primary that George Bush lost (or for that matter, Bob Dole won). South Dakota had never seemed to offer much of a payday for Bush, who as vice president was at a disadvantage defending the Reagan administration's farm policy. After his loss in neighboring Iowa, Bush pulled out of South Dakota to focus on New Hampshire and other, more promising, terrain.

Dole won the South Dakota primary again in 1996, in a contest that was closer but far more helpful to his nomination chances than eight years earlier. His winning percentage was down 10 points from 1988, and after sweeping every county his first try, he lost four counties to Pat Buchanan in 1996. But Dole's South Dakota victory, along with one the same late February day in North Dakota, stabilized his campaign after a rough start and set the stage for a whirlwind of primary victories in March.

The South Dakota Rules

With Senate Minority Leader Tom Daschle up for reelection in 2004 and beleaguered Republican Rep. Bill Janklow stepping down in January, the emphasis in South Dakota's June primary is almost certain to be on the congressional races rather than the nominations for president.

Participation in the primary is limited to registered voters in each party. As of October 2003, there were roughly 220,000 registered Republicans in South Dakota and 180,000 Democrats.

DEMOCRATS

THE CALENDAR
Primary Date (polling hours) June 1 (7 a.m.–7 p.m.)
Filing Deadline April 6
Filing Procedure Candidates must file a letter of intent with the secretary of state and must be certified by their state party chairman.

THE DELEGATES
Number (% of national total) 21 (0.5%)
Distribution:
By congressional district 9
At-Large 3
Pledged PEOs 2
Superdelegates 7
Method of Allocation Proportional—15% of the statewide vote is needed to qualify for a share of the delegates.

MONTANA

June 8

Since its inception, Montana's presidential primary has been an afterthought to an afterthought. It has often been the least populous state to vote on the last big day of the primary season.

The only presidential candidate in recent times to make a significant effort in Montana was Frank Church of neighboring Idaho. His 10 visits in 1976 earned him nearly 60 percent of the Democratic primary vote and victory over Jimmy Carter. Carter followed the norm of most candidates: he did not visit the state at all.

The last time a Republican presidential contest seriously involved Montana was that same year, when Ronald Reagan and President Gerald Ford were nearing the end of their long-running battle for the nomination. Reagan won the Montana primary with 63 percent of the vote, then swept all the delegates (traditionally chosen separately at the GOP state convention).

Generally, a libertarian rather than moralistic strain of Republicanism is dominant in Montana. President George Bush won the primary easily in 1992, with Pat Buchanan running a distant third behind the "no preference" line. Buchanan managed to beat the "no preference" line in 1996, but still trailed Bob Dole by a wide margin.

The last Democratic presidential primary in Montana with much significance came in 1980, when President Carter defeated Edward Kennedy, 51 to 37 percent. While Carter carried most of the state, including its leading population centers, Kennedy took the Native American counties of Big Horn and Glacier and a number of politically volatile wheat-growing counties in northeast Montana, where farmers were unhappy with the Carter administration's grain embargo.

Conspicuously, though, Kennedy failed to win in the Democratic counties of western Montana, such as Deer Lodge (Anaconda) and Silver Bow (Butte), where there is a large ethnic population and a strong union tradition built around the copper mines. Silver Bow is often one of the largest source of votes in a Democratic primary, even though it is not one of Montana's more populous counties.

Bill Clinton scored a lackluster win in Democratic voting in 1992, the party's last presidential primary that was even vaguely competitive. Even though Clinton was already the apparent nominee, he drew less than a majority of the primary vote. To make matters worse, Clinton was ambushed by the "no preference" forces in rural Treasure County, which is in the vicinity of the Little Bighorn battlefield.

Recent Montana Primary Results

Montana held its first presidential primary in 1916, but only one between 1924 and 1976, that in 1956.

Year	DEMOCRATS			REPUBLICANS		
	Turnout	Candidates	%	Turnout	Candidates	%
2000 (June 6)	87,867	AL GORE No Preference	78 22	113,673	GEORGE W. BUSH Alan Keyes	78 18
1996 (June 4)	91,725	BILL CLINTON* No Preference	90 10	117,746	BOB DOLE Pat Buchanan	61 24
1992 (June 2)	117,471	BILL CLINTON No Preference Jerry Brown Paul Tsongas	47 24 18 11	90,975	GEORGE BUSH* No Preference Pat Buchanan	72 17 12
1988 (June 7)	121,871	MICHAEL DUKAKIS Jesse Jackson	69 22	86,380	GEORGE BUSH Bob Dole	73 19
1984 (June 5)	34,214	NO PREFERENCE	83	71,887	RONALD REAGAN*	92
1980 (June 3)	130,059	JIMMY CARTER* Edward Kennedy No Preference	51 37 12	79,423	RONALD REAGAN	87
1976 (June 1)	106,841	FRANK CHURCH Jimmy Carter	59 25	89,779	RONALD REAGAN Gerald Ford*	63 35

Note: All candidates are listed that drew at least 10 percent of their party's primary vote. The names of winning candidates are capitalized. An asterisk (*) indicates an incumbent president.

The Montana Rules

New Jersey in the East and Montana in the West anchor the final day of the 2004 presidential primary season.

There is no party registration in Montana, so the state's 625,000 registered voters (as of November 2002) can participate in the primary of their choice. For delegate-selection purposes, Democrats divide the state into two districts.

DEMOCRATS

THE PRIMARY CALENDAR

Primary Date (polling hours)   June 8 (7 a.m.–8 p.m.)

Filing Deadline   March 18

Filing Procedure   Candidates that have qualified for matching federal funds can get a place on the primary ballot by submitting a filing form to the secretary of state by March 25. Other candidates must submit petitions signed by at least 500 registered voters by March 18 with county election officials in the county in which they were gathered. Petitions must be verified and submitted to the secretary of state by March 25.

THE DELEGATES

Number (% of national total)   21 (0.5%)

Distribution:

  By congressional district   10 (5 per district)

  At-Large   3

  Pledged PEOs   2

  Superdelegates   6

Method of Allocation   Proportional—15% of vote needed to win a share of statewide or district delegates.

NEW JERSEY

June 8

For decades, New Jersey joined with California to provide bicoastal bookends for the final big day of the primary season. But starting in 1996, New Jersey has been the only megastate voting in early June, as California has moved its primary to March in a bid to regain its status as a major player in the nominating process.

Occasionally, New Jersey's role has been noteworthy even on its late date. In 1984, Walter Mondale essentially nailed down the Democratic nomination with a victory in the Garden State over Gary Hart. And in 1980, Edward Kennedy scored a last hurrah of sorts with Democratic primary wins over the front-running Jimmy Carter in both New Jersey and California.

More typically, the exercise has been a yawn, as primary voters often were asked merely to ratify delegate slates put together by their parties' leadership. New Jersey Republicans have not had a competitive primary since 1952, when Dwight Eisenhower swamped Robert Taft by a margin of nearly 2-to-

1. And the moderate tone of the state GOP has not seemed to change a lot since then.

Ronald Reagan did not even enter the 1976 preference primary, and President Gerald Ford took all but four of the state's delegates. In 1980, Reagan entered the primary, but his competition evaporated before the June vote. It has been a similar story since then; the eventual nominees have been acceptable to the state party establishment and have won the New Jersey primary with little or no opposition.

Democratic contests in recent years have been a bit closer and a bit more consequential. In 1980, Kennedy swept New Jersey by a margin of 3-to-2, helping keep alive his challenge for the Democratic nomination—at least in spirit.

In 1984, New Jersey gave Mondale a desperately needed win that offset a loss the same day to Gary Hart in California. Mondale beat Hart by a decisive 15 percentage points in New Jersey, winning virtually all the major suburban counties of

Recent New Jersey Primary Results

New Jersey held its first presidential primary in 1912.

	DEMOCRATS			REPUBLICANS		
Year	Turnout	Candidates	%	Turnout	Candidates	%
2000 (June 6)	378,272	AL GORE	95	240,810	GEORGE W. BUSH Alan Keyes	84 16
1996 (June 4)	266,740	BILL CLINTON*	95	218,812	BOB DOLE Pat Buchanan	82 11
1992 (June 2)	392,626	BILL CLINTON Jerry Brown Paul Tsongas	62 20 12	310,270	GEORGE BUSH* Pat Buchanan	78 15
1988 (June 7)	654,302	MICHAEL DUKAKIS Jesse Jackson	63 33	241,033	GEORGE BUSH	100
1984 (June 5)	676,561	WALTER MONDALE Gary Hart Jesse Jackson	45 30 24	240,054	RONALD REAGAN*	100
1980 (June 3)	560,908	EDWARD KENNEDY Jimmy Carter*	56 38	277,977	RONALD REAGAN George Bush	81 17
1976 (June 8)	360,839	JIMMY CARTER Frank Church	58 14	242,122	GERALD FORD*	100
1972 (June 6)	76,834	SHIRLEY CHISHOLM Terry Sanford	67 33	215,719	UNPLEDGED	100
1968 (June 4)	27,446	EUGENE McCARTHY# Robert Kennedy# Hubert Humphrey#	36 31 20	88,592	RICHARD NIXON# Nelson Rockefeller#	81 13

Note: All candidates are listed that drew at least 10 percent of their party's primary vote. The names of winning candidates are capitalized. An asterisk (*) indicates an incumbent president. A pound sign (#) indicates a write-in candidate.

northern New Jersey, as well as Camden and Mercer (Trenton) to the south. Mondale's New Jersey win ensured that he would have enough delegates at the convention to secure a first-ballot nomination.

Winning margins in the Democratic primary have grown wider since then, with New Jersey giving Bill Clinton one of his more convincing primary victories in 1992 outside the South. Clinton won more than 60 percent of the vote, running best in Essex County (Newark) with its large minority population; Jesse Jackson had carried the county in Democratic primary voting in 1984 and 1988.

Now that it is the last major stop on the campaign trail, New Jersey is finding it hard to match the glitz and glitter that California once offered at the end of the primary season. But at least New Jersey will be spared the comparisons between the two. (Hart got himself in trouble in 1984 with a joke about the state's reputation for toxic-waste dumps.)

And occasionally, New Jersey is able to offer some glamour of its own. Among its Democratic delegates in 1988 was Academy Award-winning actress Olympia Dukakis, a cousin of the New Jersey primary winner that year and the party's eventual nominee, Michael Dukakis.

The New Jersey Rules

By keeping its presidential primary in early June, New Jersey runs the considerable risk of it being of no importance at all. But if there is a race to be decided, New Jersey will be the largest state to vote in the last month of the primary season.

Participation in the primary is open to registered voters in each party as well as unaffiliated voters who have not participated in a primary before. As of October 2003, there were more than 1.1 million registered Democrats, nearly 880,000 Republicans and 2.5 million unaffiliated voters.

DEMOCRATS

THE CALENDAR	
Primary Date (polling hours)	June 8 (6 a.m.–8 p.m.)
Filing Deadline	April 15
Filing Procedure	Candidates must submit to the secretary of state petitions signed by at least 1,000 registered Democratic or unaffiliated voters.
THE DELEGATES	
Number (% of national total)	128 (3.0%)
Distribution:	
By congressional district	70 (3 or 4 per legislative district)
At-Large	23
Pledged PEOs	14
Superdelegates	21
Method of Allocation	Proportional—15% of vote needed to win a share of statewide or district delegates.

PUERTO RICO AND THE U. S. TERRITORIES

Other than Puerto Rico, America's far-flung territories have tiny delegations that are noted more for their exotic locales and the colorful attire of their delegates than for any impact they have on the nominating process.

Democrats, however, award Puerto Rico 58 delegates, as much as a state of comparable size (a population of 3.8 million) that gives the Caribbean island a larger delegate harvest than roughly half the states, including either Iowa or New Hampshire.

The island's presidential primary has occasionally become embroiled in the ongoing controversy over statehood. In 1980, pro-statehood Democrats supported President Jimmy Carter, while their pro-commonwealth colleagues (favoring the status quo) lined up with his challenger, Edward M. Kennedy—even though both men had declared themselves impartial on the issue. Carter's narrow victory—barely 30,000 votes out of more than 850,000 cast—was generally attributed to the close division over the statehood issue.

That February on the GOP side, Puerto Rico Republicans held the first presidential primary of the year. The front-runner, Ronald Reagan, skipped it, but other candidates competed and made distinctive pitches. Howard Baker proposed moving the 1980 summer Olympics from Moscow to Puerto Rico; John Connally campaigned in small towns on horseback; George Bush sent his son, Jeb (now the governor of Florida), to woo voters in fluent Spanish.

Bush had the best local connections, drawing tacit backing from the mayor of San Juan, the island's capital and largest city, and he had momentum from his upset victory in the Iowa caucuses (his loss to Reagan in New Hampshire came nine days later). Bush swept Puerto Rico by nearly 45,000 votes out of roughly 200,000 cast.

More often than not since then, the overwhelming winner of the Puerto Rico primary has been the party's favorite on the mainland. In 2000, for instance, George W. Bush swept the island's GOP primary with 94 percent of the vote.

America's other far-flung territories have long anchored the end of the presidential roll call at the national conventions, usually adding their votes to the nominee's winning total.

American Samoa and Guam in the Pacific and the Virgin Islands in the Caribbean, plus a group called "Democrats Abroad," will have a total of 25 delegates at the Democratic convention in 2004.

Each territory generally elects its delegates through a caucus process, although Democratic voting is scattered across the calendar, with Democrats Abroad from Feb. 6 to 9, American Samoa on March 8, the Virgin Islands on April 17, and Puerto Rico on June 6. (As of early December, Guam had yet to schedule their delegate-selection event.)

Yet while they are little more than an afterthought in the nominating process, territories have been a part of convention lore for more than a century. Arizona was given convention delegates by the Republicans as early as 1872, 40 years before it became a state. Alaska was awarded delegates before the end of the century, as was a designation called "Indian Territory."

America's flirtation with empire brought a host of new overseas territories to the conventions of one or both parties in the early twentieth century. Hawaii first elected convention delegates in 1900, Puerto Rico and the Philippine Islands in 1904, and the Panama Canal Zone in 1920.

The Philippines' participation in American politics ended altogether when the country gained independence after World War II. The Canal Zone disappeared as a delegation to the Democratic convention after passage of the Panama Canal treaties in 1978. It was first folded into a category called "Latin American Democrats," then into Democrats Abroad.

NATIONAL PRIMARY MAPS AND VOTE SUMMARIES, 1968–2000

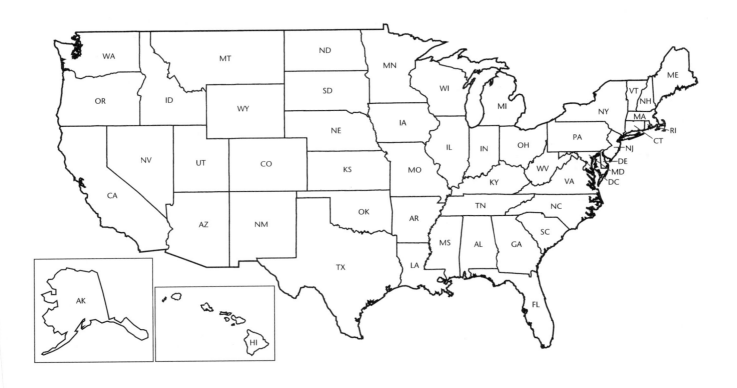

1968	Democratic Primaries	128	1988	Democratic Primaries	138
	Republican Primaries	129		Republican Primaries	139
1972	Democratic Primaries	130	1992	Democratic Primaries	140
	Republican Primaries	131		Republican Primaries	141
1976	Democratic Primaries	132	1996	Democratic Primaries	142
	Republican Primaries	133		Republican Primaries	143
1980	Democratic Primaries	134	2000	Democratic Primaries	144
	Republican Primaries	135		Republican Primaries	145
1984	Democratic Primaries	136			
	Republican Primaries	137			

128

1968 DEMOCRATIC PRIMARIES

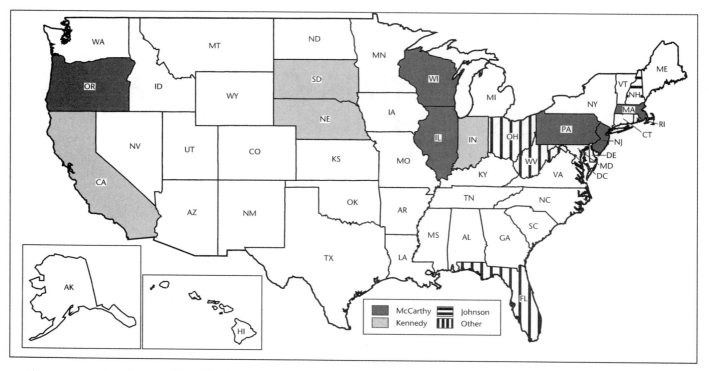

McCarthy
Kennedy
Johnson
Other

There were only a few presidential primaries in 1968. But nearly every one of them had significance, with the first-in-the-nation primary in New Hampshire March 12 setting the tone.

President Lyndon Johnson won on an organized write-in vote, but with less than a majority, while Minnesota Sen. Eugene McCarthy's grass-roots effort, focused around opposition to the Vietnam War, exceeded all expectations.

On March 16, New York Sen. Robert Kennedy entered the race. On March 31, the embattled president left it. Beginning in Wisconsin April 2, McCarthy registered a series of primary

victories before he and Kennedy went head-to-head for the first time May 7 in Indiana.

Kennedy won Indiana, and beat McCarthy in three of four other primaries down the stretch, culminating with a victory in California June 4. But after claiming victory that night in Los Angeles, Kennedy was shot and died less than two days later.

Vice President Hubert Humphrey, who had not run in the primaries, was subsequently nominated that August at a tumultuous Democratic convention in Chicago. He was the last nominee of either major party to win its nomination without having first competed in the primaries.

	Total Vote	Percentage	Primary States Won
Eugene McCarthy (Minn.)	2,914,933	38.7	6
Robert Kennedy (N.Y.)	2,304,542	30.6	4
Lyndon Johnson (Texas)*	383,048	5.1	1
Others	1,932,546	25.6	3
TOTAL	7,535,069		

Note: In this chart and those that follow, all candidates are listed that drew at least 5 percent of their party's nationwide primary vote and were on the ballot in more than one state. The vote for "Others" includes other candidates, miscellaneous write-ins, and any derivation of "Uncommitted" that appeared on the primary ballots. An asterisk (*) indicates an incumbent president. Each candidate's home state is in parentheses. The source for vote data is Congressional Quarterly's *America at the Polls 1960–1996* and *Guide to U.S. Elections.* Results from the primary in the District of Columbia are included in the vote totals, but not territories such as Puerto Rico. The primary winners are shaded on the maps.

1968 REPUBLICAN PRIMARIES

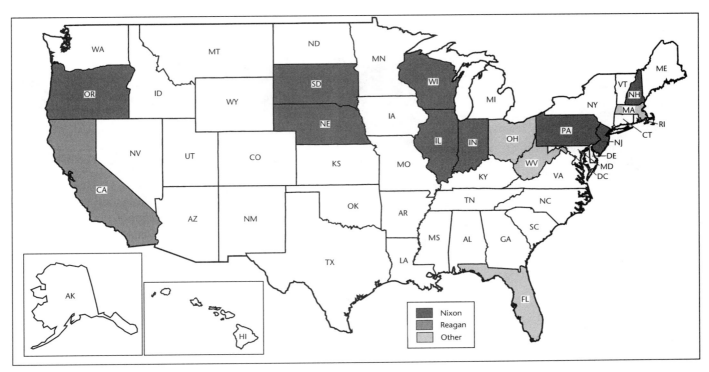

Unlike the Democrats, the Republican primaries in 1968 were like marking time before the August convention. Michigan Gov. George Romney dropped out of the race before the primaries began. New York Gov. Nelson Rockefeller entered too late to compete. And California Gov. Ronald Reagan did not formally announce his candidacy until the eve of the convention, although he was on several primary ballots in the spring, including California, where he ran as an unopposed favorite son.

Elsewhere, former Vice President Richard Nixon was virtually unopposed during the primary season. The only primaries he did not win were those he was not on the ballot. Still, Nixon did not have the nomination locked up when the convention in Miami Beach began. But the ideological gulf between the more liberal Rockefeller and the more conservative Reagan made it difficult for them to agree on a common strategy to stop Nixon, who ultimately prevailed on the first ballot.

	Total Vote	Percentage	Primary States Won
Ronald Reagan (Calif.)	1,696,270	37.9	1
Richard Nixon (N.Y.)	1,679,443	37.5	9
Others	1,097,838	24.5	4
TOTAL	4,473,551		

Note: Richard Nixon lived in New York during the 1968 campaign, although his political career is more associated with California.

1972 DEMOCRATIC PRIMARIES

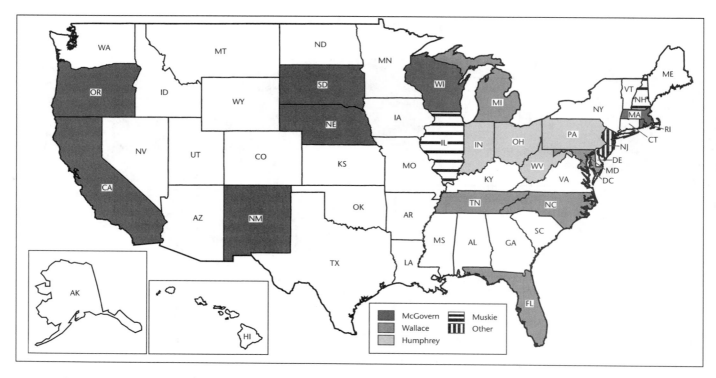

The presidential campaign of 1972 began a new era of nominating politics, where there were more primaries and candidates had to compete in them. Sen. George McGovern of South Dakota was the immediate beneficiary of the new system, mounting a long-shot candidacy that ultimately won the Democratic nomination.

McGovern had some of the same advantages that Eugene McCarthy had in 1968—an issue (opposition to the Vietnam War) and an army of volunteers. And McGovern burst onto the scene in much the same way that McCarthy had, with a stronger-than-expected showing in New Hampshire against a front-runner (Sen. Edmund Muskie from neighboring Maine) who did not do as well as expected.

McGovern carefully picked his way from there to the Democratic nomination, gaining momentum by winning high-profile primary states with progressive traditions, such as Wisconsin, Nebraska, Oregon and California. But he fared poorly in several regions that augured poorly for his chances that fall. He lost all the major industrial states—Pennsylvania and Ohio to former Vice President Hubert Humphrey, and Michigan to Alabama Gov. George Wallace. And he was a nonfactor in the Southern primaries, where Wallace dominated.

Altogether, McGovern received fewer primary votes than Humphrey, and not many more than Wallace. Since McGovern, every major-party nominee has first emerged from the primaries as his party's top vote-getter.

	Total Vote	Percentage	Primary States Won
Hubert Humphrey (Minn.)	4,121,372	25.8	4
George McGovern (S.D.)	4,053,451	25.3	8
George Wallace (Ala.)	3,755,424	23.5	5
Edmund Muskie (Maine)	1,840,217	11.5	2
Others	2,223,501	13.9	1
TOTAL	15,993,965		

1972 REPUBLICAN PRIMARIES

One point that has become clear during the modern era of presidential primaries is that sitting presidents that face little or no opposition for renomination are in great shape to win another term in the fall. On the other hand, every recent president that has struggled through his party's primaries has lost in November.

The first example of the upside of this dynamic was Richard Nixon. He faced minimal opposition for renomination in 1972 from a pair of little-known congressmen—Paul McCloskey of California, who mounted an anti-war challenge, and John Ashbrook of Ohio, who claimed that Nixon was too liberal for the GOP.

The contest was over quickly, as Nixon beat both easily in New Hampshire. Late in the spring, McCloskey did win a delegate in the New Mexico primary; it was the only vote cast against Nixon's renomination at the Republican convention that August.

	Total Vote	Percentage	Primary States Won
Richard Nixon (Calif.)*	5,378,704	86.9	18
John Ashbrook (Ohio)	311,543	5.0	0
Others	498,034	8.0	2
TOTAL	6,188,281		

1976 DEMOCRATIC PRIMARIES

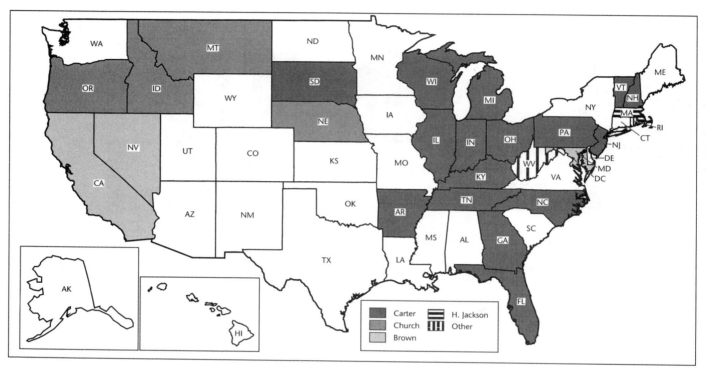

For the second straight election, a dark-horse candidate won the Democratic nomination. But unlike George McGovern four years earlier, former Georgia Gov. Jimmy Carter broke fast from the gate.

Carter established himself as a national candidate with victory in the New Hampshire primary, dispatched George Wallace in their home region with primary triumphs in Florida and North Carolina, eliminated Washington Sen.

Henry Jackson in a key industrial state contest in Pennsylvania, and outpolled Rep. Morris Udall of Arizona at every turn, to the point that Udall became known as "Second Place Mo."

Carter lost some late primaries to two late entries from the West—California Gov. Jerry Brown and Sen. Frank Church of Idaho. But by then, Carter was comfortably ahead in the delegate count.

	Total Vote	Percentage	Primary States Won
Jimmy Carter (Ga.)	6,235,609	38.8	16
Jerry Brown (Calif.)	2,449,374	15.3	3
George Wallace (Ala.)	1,995,388	12.4	0
Morris Udall (Ariz.)	1,611,754	10.0	0
Henry Jackson (Wash.)	1,134,375	7.1	1
Frank Church (Idaho)	830,818	5.2	4
Others	1,795,334	11.2	2
TOTAL	16,052,652		

1976 REPUBLICAN PRIMARIES

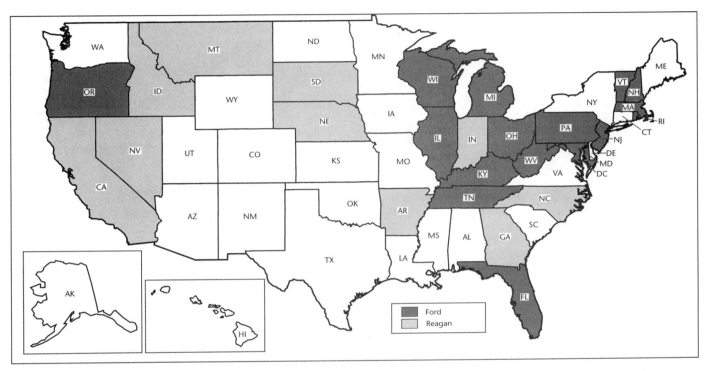

Since presidential primaries were instituted in the early twentieth century, no president who wanted another term has been denied his party's nomination. But in 1976, Gerald Ford found himself more closely challenged in the Republican primaries than any sitting president since William Howard Taft in 1912.

In former California Gov. Ronald Reagan, Ford had a challenger with both strong appeal to the burgeoning conservative wing of the Republican Party and a base in the nation's largest state. The closeness of the challenge was evident from the start, as Ford defeated Reagan by just 1 percentage point in New Hampshire. Ford followed with a string of primary victories that nearly knocked Reagan out of the race. But Reagan steadied himself with a late March victory in North Carolina.

As the primaries unfolded, Ford dominated in the Northeast and major states of the industrial Frost Belt. Reagan had the upper hand in much of the South and West. The only primary state that Ford was able to carry west of the Mississippi River was Oregon.

But Ford prevailed, in large part because he able to pick off some states in the South, including Florida, while Reagan was unable to deeply penetrate Ford's base in the major states of the Frost Belt.

	Total Vote	Percentage	Primary States Won
Gerald Ford (Mich.)*	5,529,899	53.3	16
Ronald Reagan (Calif.)	4,758,325	45.9	10
Others	85,901	0.8	0
TOTAL	10,374,125		

134

1980 DEMOCRATIC PRIMARIES

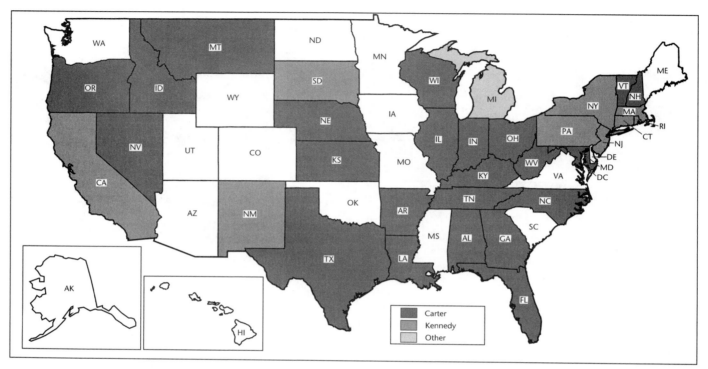

The Democrats had an intra-party brawl of their own in 1980 between an incumbent president (Jimmy Carter) and a well-regarded challenger (Sen. Edward Kennedy of Massachusetts) from the liberal wing of the party. Some polls taken in 1979 showed Kennedy ahead. But a series of events, including the Iranian hostage crisis, shifted sentiment to Carter before the primaries even began.

Carter got off to a fast start, with victories in New Hampshire, Illinois and across the South that removed any suspense about who would win the nomination. But as the primaries

proceeded, Kennedy was able to fashion a bicoastal coalition that gave strong hints of Carter's vulnerability in the general election to come. Kennedy won primaries in New York, Pennsylvania and New Jersey on the East Coast and California on the West.

Yet there was also clear evidence that many Democratic voters would have preferred another choice beyond Carter and Kennedy, as more than 1 million votes were cast in the Democratic primaries for ballot lines that indicated "No preference."

	Total Vote	Percentage	Primary States Won
Jimmy Carter (Ga.)*	9,593,335	51.2	23
Edward Kennedy (Mass.)	6,963,625	37.1	9
Others	2,190,865	11.7	1
TOTAL	18,747,825		

1980 REPUBLICAN PRIMARIES

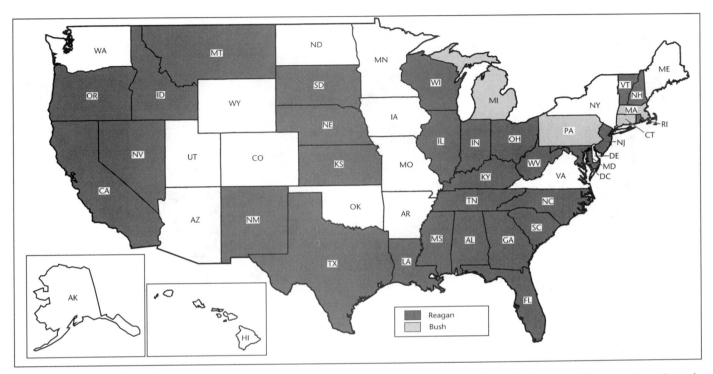

Ronald Reagan's strong showing in the 1976 Republican primaries made him the front-runner for the GOP nomination in 1980. But he got off to a stumbling start, losing the Iowa caucuses to dark-horse challenger, George Bush, who courted the state in a way that Reagan had not.

Bush claimed that he had "Big Mo" after the Iowa vote, but Reagan quickly reestablished his hegemony with a decisive victory in New Hampshire. Bush managed several primary wins in his native New England, and Rep. John Anderson of Illinois briefly was a factor in the race with near-misses in early March voting in Massachusetts and Vermont.

But after losing to Reagan in Illinois and Wisconsin, Anderson quit the Republican race in April in favor of an independent presidential bid. Meanwhile, Bush had fallen far behind after a string of Reagan primary victories in the South and Midwest. But Bush hung around, winning late primaries in Pennsylvania and Michigan that ultimately led to his choice as Reagan's running mate.

	Total Vote	Percentage	Primary States Won
Ronald Reagan (Calif.)	7,709,793	60.8	29
George Bush (Texas)	2,958,093	23.3	4
John Anderson (Ill.)	1,572,174	12.4	0
Others	450,391	3.5	0
TOTAL	12,690,451		

1984 DEMOCRATIC PRIMARIES

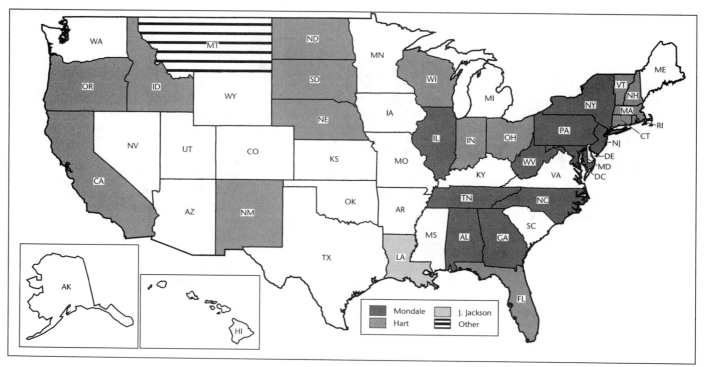

Former Vice President Walter Mondale entered the 1984 Democratic primaries with an array of endorsements from Democratic-related interest groups, including the AFL-CIO. But while the early support tended to serve Mondale well in his head-to-head maneuvering against Ohio Sen. John Glenn, it left Mondale open to an anti-establishment challenge from Sen. Gary Hart.

Hart, who had been campaign manager of George McGovern's 1972 presidential campaign, broke fast from the gate. His second-place finish in the Iowa caucuses put him in contention in New Hampshire, where an upset victory produced two weeks worth of momentum that left Mondale on the ropes. Only by winning Georgia and Alabama on Super Tuesday

(March 13) was Mondale able to stabilize his campaign.

Mondale victories in the industrial states of Illinois, New York and Pennsylvania followed. But he could not shake Hart, as the senator from Colorado posted a succession of primary triumphs in the Midwest and West. On the final big day of primary voting in early June, Hart won California while Mondale took New Jersey, giving the former vice president just enough delegates to claim the nomination.

Although the Rev. Jesse Jackson won primaries only in Louisiana (and the District of Columbia), he was a factor throughout the primary season. Jackson ran well across the South and in urban centers of the Frost Belt by tapping the minority vote.

	Total Vote	Percentage	Primary States Won
Walter Mondale (Minn.)	6,811,214	37.8	10
Gary Hart (Colo.)	6,503,968	36.1	16
Jesse Jackson (Ill.)	3,282,380	18.2	1
Others	1,411,630	7.8	1
TOTAL	18,009,192		

1984 REPUBLICAN PRIMARIES

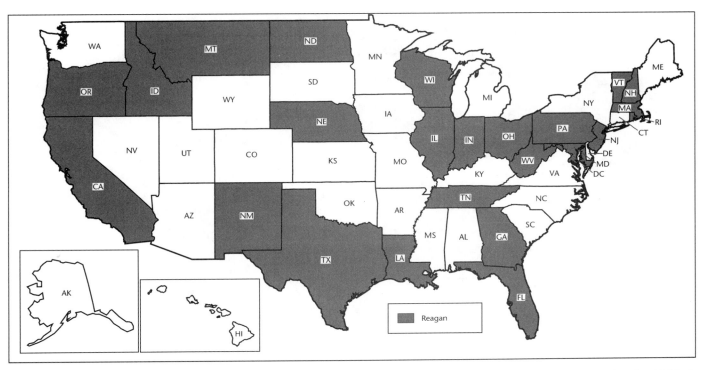

The 1984 GOP nominating process was more notable for what did not happen than what did. After two straight elections in which incumbent presidents faced serious primary challenges within their own party, President Ronald Reagan cruised to renomination over token opposition in 1984. It proved to be the precursor of an easy reelection victory for Reagan that fall.

	Total Vote	Percentage	Primary States Won
Ronald Reagan (Calif.)*	6,484,987	98.6	24
Others	90,664	1.4	0
TOTAL	6,575,651		

138

1988 DEMOCRATIC PRIMARIES

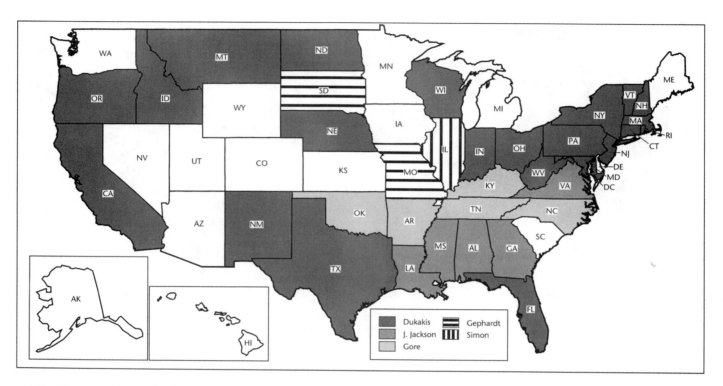

The Democratic nominating process was slow to take shape in 1988. Rep. Richard Gephardt of Missouri won the lead-off caucuses in neighboring Iowa. Gov. Michael Dukakis of Massachusetts won the first-in-the-nation primary in neighboring New Hampshire.

The huge Super Tuesday vote across Dixie in early March was a wash. Dukakis won the two big states on the fringes, Texas and Florida. Jesse Jackson swept five states from the Deep South to Virginia. Sen. Al Gore of Tennessee won five states across the middle of the South from North Carolina to Oklahoma. And Gephardt won his home state of Missouri. The

Democratic race got even more convoluted the following week when Sen. Paul Simon won the primary in his home state of Illinois.

But as fast as one could say "brokered convention," the situation began to clear. Gephardt dropped out, and Dukakis began to win decisively across the industrial Frost Belt, with April victories in Wisconsin and New York sending Simon and Gore to the sidelines and relegating Jackson to also-ran status. In the three months of primary voting after Super Tuesday, Jackson could win only in Puerto Rico and the District of Columbia.

	Total Vote	Percentage	Primary States Won
Michael Dukakis (Mass.)	9,817,185	42.8	22
Jesse Jackson (Ill.)	6,685,699	29.1	5
Al Gore (Tenn.)	3,134,516	13.7	5
Richard Gephardt (Mo.)	1,388,356	6.0	2
Others	1,936,180	8.4	1
TOTAL	22,961,936		

1988 REPUBLICAN PRIMARIES

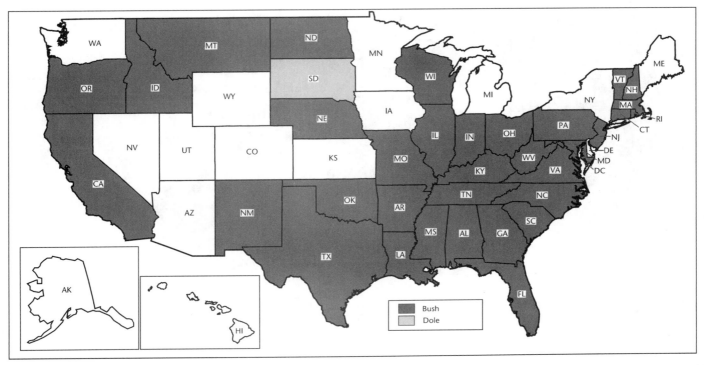

Like the Democrats in 1988, the Republicans began the year with a crowded field. But unlike the Democrats, the Republican picture cleared quickly.

Vice President George Bush could muster only a third-place finish in the first big event of the year, the Iowa precinct caucuses, where he trailed both Kansas Sen. Bob Dole and religious broadcaster Pat Robertson. But Bush rebounded quickly, beating Dole by nearly 10 percentage points in New Hampshire.

From there, Bush's momentum snowballed. A pivotal victory in the early March primary in South Carolina opened the door to a Bush sweep of the Super Tuesday GOP voting three days later, in which all of the remaining Southern states participated.

The results sent New York Rep. Jack Kemp to the sidelines. A week later, Bush's decisive win in Illinois drove Dole out of the race as well. Robertson lingered on, but was a factor only in a handful of caucus states where his small, but dedicated, cadre of supporters had gained a toehold.

In the end, Bush won every Republican primary but one, that a February event in South Dakota that he had essentially conceded to Dole.

	Total Vote	Percentage	Primary States Won
George Bush (Texas)	8,254,654	67.9	34
Bob Dole (Kan.)	2,333,268	19.2	1
Pat Robertson (Va.)	1,097,442	9.0	0
Others	479,751	3.9	0
TOTAL	12,165,115		

1992 DEMOCRATIC PRIMARIES

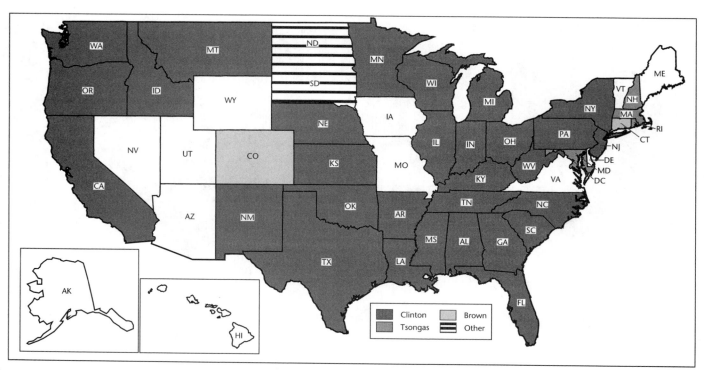

The 1992 Democratic presidential nominating contest had two phases. The first, pre-primary phase, focused on whether New York Gov. Mario Cuomo would run. He decided not to.

With Cuomo out of the race, Arkansas Gov. Bill Clinton was well positioned for the second phase, the primaries themselves. But it began for Clinton on a tenuous note. Hit with charges of womanizing and draft evasion (during the Vietnam War), Clinton did well to survive with a second-place finish in the New Hampshire primary behind former Sen. Paul Tsongas of neighboring Massachusetts.

But survival was enough. Clinton's home region, the South, was the first region to vote en masse and Clinton dominated the early March primaries there. Big victories followed for Clinton in mid-March in Illinois and Michigan that drove Tsongas from the race. Former California Gov. Jerry Brown briefly established himself as a challenger to Clinton with a late March victory in Connecticut. But Clinton swept all the primaries that followed, including a pivotal early April primary in New York that left his route clear to the nomination.

Clinton ended up with 52 percent of the vote in the primaries, the highest vote share for any Democratic nominee since 1956.

	Total Vote	Percentage	Primary States Won
Bill Clinton (Ark.)	10,482,411	51.8	30
Jerry Brown (Calif.)	4,071,232	20.1	2
Paul Tsongas (Mass.)	3,656,010	18.1	4
Others	2,029,732	10.0	2
TOTAL	20,239,385		

1992 REPUBLICAN PRIMARIES

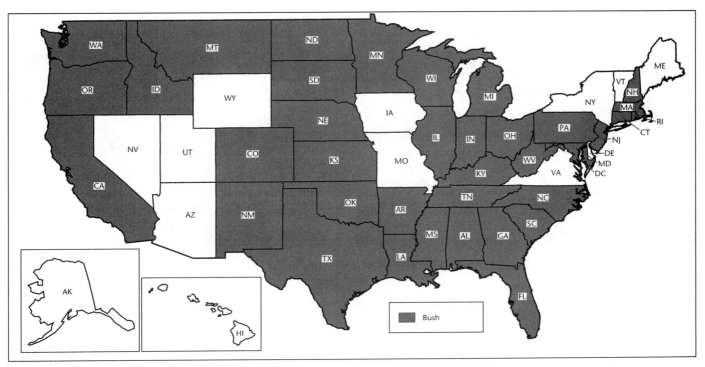

For the third time since 1976, an incumbent president struggled through his party's primaries and ended up a loser at the ballot box in the fall.

In reality, President George Bush was not as closely contested during the Republican primaries in 1992 as Gerald Ford had been in 1976 or Jimmy Carter in the Democratic primaries of 1980. But both Ford and Carter faced more serious challengers than Bush, who was opposed by television commentator Pat Buchanan.

Buchanan came no closer to beating Bush than his 37 percent share of the primary vote in the first-in-the-nation primary in New Hampshire. But Buchanan hung around, sounding a vocal challenge to Bush administration foreign and economic policy and serving as an outlet for anti-Bush protest votes throughout the primary season. Louisiana's David Duke briefly vied with Buchanan for that mantle, but failed to win more than 10 percent of the vote in any Republican primary except Mississippi.

	Total Vote	Percentage	Primary States Won
George Bush (Texas)*	9,199,463	72.5	37
Pat Buchanan (Va.)	2,899,488	22.8	0
Others	597,596	4.7	0
TOTAL	12,696,547		

142

1996 DEMOCRATIC PRIMARIES

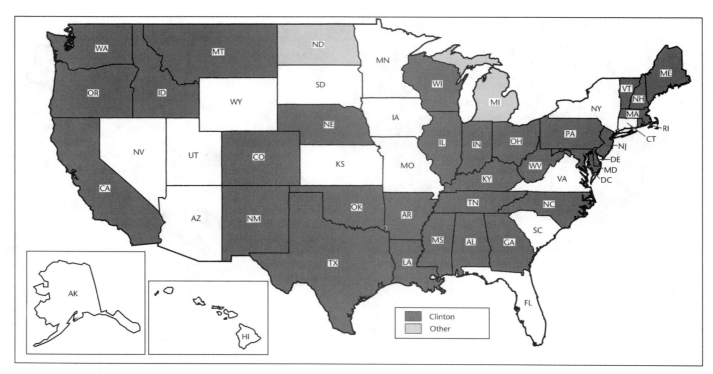

By the time the 1996 Democratic presidential primaries were to begin, President Bill Clinton had already won, as no more than token opposition filed against him. Clinton's most persistent challenge came from perennial presidential aspirant Lyndon LaRouche, but it was opposition the incumbent could safely ignore.

Clinton won easily in every primary that he was on the ballot. And when all the votes were tallied, he had made the best primary showing of any Democratic president since Franklin D. Roosevelt in 1936. That year, FDR took 93 percent of the Democratic primary ballots.

	Total Vote	Percentage	Primary States Won
Bill Clinton (Ark.)*	9,694,499	88.6	32
Lyndon LaRouche (Va.)	596,422	5.4	0
Others	656,443	6.0	2
TOTAL	10,947,364		

1996 REPUBLICAN PRIMARIES

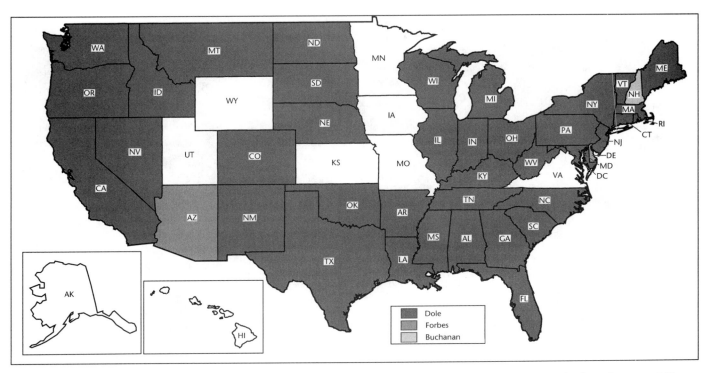

Once former Gen. Colin Powell decided not to seek the Republican nomination in 1996, Bob Dole was the clear front-runner. But he had to survive a turbulent month of February before establishing his hegemony in the myriad primaries that filled the month of March.

Dole basically played ".500 ball" in the opening round of events in February. He won the Iowa caucuses by a small margin, narrowly lost New Hampshire to Pat Buchanan, lost primaries in Delaware and Arizona to Steve Forbes, and won primaries in North and South Dakota.

But once the calendar flipped to March and there was a staccato of primaries on multiple fronts, Dole's considerable assets paid off—a hefty campaign chest, support from much of the Republican establishment and a broad acceptability to GOP voters.

Starting with his pivotal victory in South Carolina March 2, Dole did not lose another primary. He swept all eight primaries on March 5 (including all of New England outside New Hampshire), a New York delegate-selection event on March 7, all seven primaries on March 12 (most in the South), four contests in the industrial Midwest on March 19, and three Western primaries, anchored by California, on March 26. By the end of the month, Dole had won all the delegates he needed to assure himself the Republican nomination.

It marked a reversal of fortune for Dole, who had not won a primary *after* February when he ran in 1988.

	Total Vote	Percentage	Primary States Won
Bob Dole (Kan.)	8,191,239	58.5	38
Pat Buchanan (Va.)	3,020,746	21.6	1
Steve Forbes (N.J.)	1,424,898	10.2	2
Others	1,354,766	9.7	0
TOTAL	13,991,649		

144

2000 DEMOCRATIC PRIMARIES

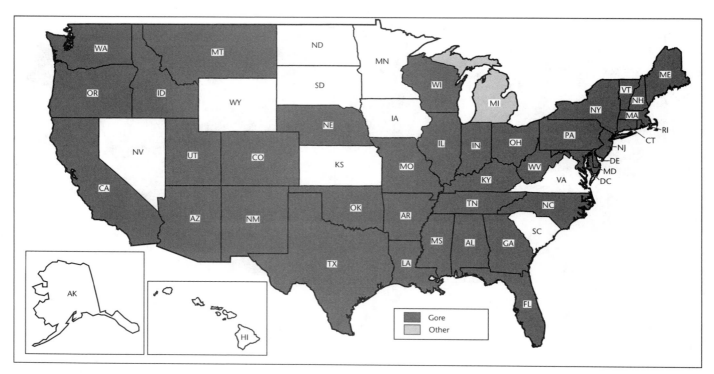

Vice President Al Gore won every Democratic presidential primary he contested. But the shift of barely 3,000 votes in New Hampshire from Gore to Bill Bradley would have given the former New Jersey senator victory in the first-in-the-nation primary and altered the dynamic of the race that followed.

As it was, New Hampshire was Bradley's last best opportunity to make the Democratic race competitive following a decisive loss to Gore the previous week in the Iowa caucuses. But with the lively GOP race between George W. Bush and John McCain drawing the lion's share of attention, Bradley was unable to make a successful late appeal for the votes of New Hampshire's independent voters. They could vote in either party's primary in the Granite State but went in droves for McCain.

Democratic rules at the time prevented any other delegate-selection events from being held before the first Tuesday in March, when a plethora of primaries and caucuses were held from Maine to Hawaii. Brandishing momentum as well as support from the party establishment and key interest groups, Gore won them all.

Bradley was beaten badly in the major battleground states that day, garnering only one-third of the Democratic primary vote in New York, one-quarter of the vote in Ohio, and less than 20 percent in California. He reached even 40 percent of the vote in only a handful of New England primaries. Shortly thereafter, he quit the race, conceding the Democratic nomination to Gore.

	Total Vote	Percentage	Primary States Won
Al Gore (Tenn.)	10,626,645	75.7	38
Bill Bradley (N.J.)	2,798,302	19.9	0
Others	620,798	4.4	1
TOTAL	14,045,745		

2000 REPUBLICAN PRIMARIES

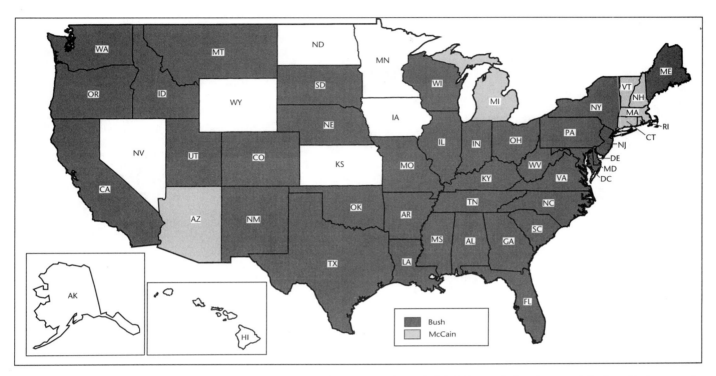

From the beginning, Texas Gov. George W. Bush was the odds-on favorite to win the Republican presidential nomination. The son of the nation's 41st president, he had the support of much of the party establishment—including virtually all of his fellow GOP governors—as well as a campaign chest that reached upwards of $100 million. It was far larger than any of his rivals and a record for any presidential nominating campaign up to that time.

But any thoughts of a quick coronation were dashed by the maverick challenge of Sen. John McCain of Arizona, who boasted an intriguing resume (as a former prisoner-of-war in Vietnam) and an issue, campaign finance reform, that made his candidacy particularly appealing to moderate Republicans and independent voters.

McCain skipped the Iowa caucuses to focus on campaigning in New Hampshire, where he stunned Bush with an 18 percentage point victory. Through the month of February,

Bush and McCain traded primary victories. Bush won in Delaware and South Carolina. McCain followed with wins in Michigan and his home state of Arizona. Bush responded with triumphs in Virginia and Washington. At the end of the month, the two were neck and neck in the overall primary vote count, with Bush amassing less than 3,000 votes more than McCain of the nearly 3.6 million cast to that point.

Republican primaries had unfolded at the rate of one or two per week through February. But once the calendar flipped to March, Bush's superior organization and funding placed him in position to dominate the vast cross-country action scheduled on the first Tuesday of the month. McCain continued to run well in New England that day, but Bush won everywhere else—including California, New York and Ohio. Without a major victory to point to and Bush's home region, the South, coming up, McCain quit the race.

	Total Vote	Percentage	Primary States Won
George W. Bush (Texas)	10,844,129	63.2	35
John McCain (Ariz.)	5,118,187	29.8	7
Alan Keyes (Md.)	914,548	5.3	0
Others	279,253	1.6	0
TOTAL	17,156,117		